ALSO BY TIMOTHY J. HENDERSON

A Glorious Defeat:
Mexico and Its War with the United States

THE MEXICAN WARS FOR INDEPENDENCE

THE
MEXICAN WARS
FOR
INDEPENDENCE

TIMOTHY J. HENDERSON

HILL AND WANG

A DIVISION OF FARRAR, STRAUS AND GIROUX

NEW YORK

Hill and Wang
A division of Farrar, Straus and Giroux
18 West 18th Street, New York 10011

Copyright © 2009 by Timothy J. Henderson
All rights reserved

Printed in the United States of America
Published in 2009 by Hill and Wang
First paperback edition, 2010

The Library of Congress has cataloged the hardcover edition as follows:
Henderson, Timothy J.
The Mexican Wars for Independence / Timothy J. Henderson. — 1st ed.
     p.   cm.
Includes bibliographical references and index.
ISBN: 978-0-8090-9509-4 (hardcover : alk. paper)
1. Mexico—History—Wars of Independence, 1810–1821.   I. Title.

F1232.H45 2009
972'.03—dc22

                                                      2008048141

Paperback ISBN: 978-0-8090-6923-1

Designed by Jonathan D. Lippincott
Map by Jeffrey L. Ward

www.fsgbooks.com

Hereby it is manifest, that during the time men live without a common Power to keep them all in awe, they are in that condition which is called Warre; and such a warre, as is of every man, against every man.   —Thomas Hobbes, *Leviathan*

It is very easy to put a country into combustion, when it possesses the elements of discord; but the difficulties of its re-organization are infinite.   —Lorenzo de Zavala

CONTENTS

COLONIAL MEXICO

ZACATECAS

SAN LUIS POTOSÍ

0 Miles   100   200

0 Kilometers   200

Gulf of Mexico

VERACRUZ

GUANAJUATO

Calderón
Guadalajara

Guanajuato • Dolores
San Miguel el
Grande • Querétaro

GUADALAJARA

MEXICO

✕ Aculco

Valladolid

Mexico City ★

TLAXCALA

Veracruz

Apatzingán
VALLADOLID

Zitácuaro •

Las Cruces ✕

• Puebla

Cuautla ✕

Pacific Ocean

Chilpancingo •

PUEBLA

Oaxaca •

OAXACA

Acapulco •

© 2009 Jeffrey L. Ward

San Antonio •

Area of detail

MEXICO

Gulf of Mexico

Mexico City •

Pacific Ocean

0 Miles   500

0 Kilometers   500

KINGDOM OF
GUATEMALA

CHRONOLOGY

1700 Philip V, of the royal house of Bourbon, becomes king of Spain, initiating a change of dynasty in Spain and sparking the War of the Spanish Succession, which is ended by treaty in 1714.

1753 Miguel Hidalgo y Costilla born near Pénjamo, Guanajuato.

1759 Accession of Charles III to the throne of Spain, beginning a period of intensive reform of the Spanish empire.

1761 Spain signs "Bourbon Family Compact," involving it in the Seven Years' War and later wars in which Spanish rulers back their French kinsmen.

1765 José María Morelos y Pavón born in Valladolid.

1765–1771 *Visita* to Mexico of José de Gálvez, who carries out dramatic reforms in taxation, distribution of political offices, and silver mining.

1767 King Charles III orders expulsion of all Jesuits from the Spanish empire.

1769 Ignacio Allende born in San Miguel el Grande.

1783 Agustín de Iturbide born in Valladolid.

1785–1786 "Year of hunger." Drought and famine in central Mexico kill some 85,000 people.

1788 Charles III dies, is replaced on throne by his son, Charles IV.

1789 Spanish decree of "free trade" in its empire; more famine in central Mexico; start of the French Revolution; Félix María Calleja arrives in Mexico from Spain.

1792 Charles IV appoints Manuel Godoy as his secretary of state;
      Miguel Hidalgo resigns post as rector of College of San
      Nicolás Obispo and takes position as parish priest of Colima.
1793 King Louis XVI and Queen Marie Antoinette executed
      by French revolutionaries, inspiring heated protests from
      Spain.
1795 A badly weakened Spain negotiates alliance with revolution-
      ary France, thus entering the wars of the French Revolution.
1800 Miguel Hidalgo investigated on charges of heresy and even-
      tually cleared by the Inquisition.
1803 Hidalgo becomes parish priest of Dolores. José de Iturri-
      garay becomes viceroy of Mexico.
1804 Law of Consolidation attempts to appropriate wealth of the
      Roman Catholic Church in the American colonies, leading
      to widespread protests.
1805 Spanish fleet wiped out at the Battle of Trafalgar.
1808 Prince Ferdinand of Asturias forces the abdication of his
      father, Charles IV, and claims the Spanish throne as
      Ferdinand VII; Napoleon Bonaparte occupies Spain with
      100,000 troops, forces Ferdinand VII to abdicate, replaces
      him with his brother, Joseph Bonaparte; Peninsular War be-
      gins; Law of Consolidation suspended.
      September 15—Mexico's viceroy José de Iturrigaray deposed
      by conservative Spaniards and replaced by General Pedro
      de Garibay.
1809 Garibay replaced as viceroy by Archbishop Francisco Javier
      de Lizana y Beaumont; Valladolid conspiracy discovered
      and disrupted; another year of hunger hits central Mexico.
1810 Lizana removed as viceroy, power assumed by *audiencia*.
      February—Spanish regency issues call for the American
      colonists to elect deputies to the revived Spanish Cortes.
      September 13—Querétaro conspiracy uncovered.
      September 14—The new viceroy, Francisco Javier Venegas,
      arrives in Mexico City.

September 15—Allende and Juan Aldama go to Dolores to warn Hidalgo of betrayal of their plot.

September 16—Hidalgo's Grito de Dolores begins rebellion in the name of King Ferdinand VII.

September 21—Rebels take town of Celaya without a fight.

September 24—Intendant of Guanajuato, José Antonio Riaño, orders Spaniards of Guanajuato to take refuge in the Alhóndiga de Granaditas.

September 24—First meeting of the Spanish Cortes.

September 28—Hidalgo's army attacks and takes Guanajuato in first military victory of rebellion; Intendant Riaño is killed along with other Spaniards; serious looting and mayhem follow.

October 17—Hidalgo's rebels take Valladolid unopposed.

October 30—Battle of Las Cruces, a very costly victory for the rebels, opens the way to an assault on Mexico City.

November 1—Rebels demand surrender of Mexico City and are rebuffed; Hidalgo orders forces to withdraw shortly after.

November 7—Battle of Aculco, a defeat for the rebels.

November 24—Royalists retake Guanajuato, carry out reprisals.

November 27—Hidalgo arrives in Guadalajara, begins organization of rebel government, decrees end to slavery and Indian tribute, and institutes other reforms; later orders massacres of surrendered Spaniards.

1811 *January 17*—Battle of Calderón Bridge, a devastating defeat for the rebels; Hidalgo removed as leader of rebellion by his officers soon after.

January 21—Royalists take Guadalajara.

March 21—Rebel leaders, including Hidalgo and Allende, captured at Baján.

June 26—Execution of Allende and several other top rebel leaders at Chihuahua.

July 30—Hidalgo executed at Chihuahua.

August—Ignacio López Rayón claims leadership of rebellion, establishes governing junta at Zitácuaro.

1812 *January*—Rayón junta at Zitácuaro dispersed, Zitácuaro demolished.

February 19—Royalist siege of Cuautla begins.

March 12—Liberal Constitution of 1812 proclaimed law of the Spanish empire.

May 2–3—Morelos's forces attempt escape from Cuautla, are massacred by royalists. Morelos escapes.

August—Gutiérrez-Magee expedition invades Texas.

November—Morelos takes Oaxaca.

November 29—First elections held in Mexico for deputies to Cortes, provincial deputations, and constitutional city councils result in major win for creole autonomists. Viceroy Venegas suspends results, charging irregularities.

1813 *March*—General Félix Calleja replaces Venegas as viceroy.

April—Gutiérrez-Magee filibusters take San Antonio.

April 6—Morelos begins assault on Acapulco.

June 28—Morelos issues decree convoking a congress at Chilpancingo.

August—Gutiérrez-Magee filibusters defeated by royalist forces in San Antonio.

August 19—Acapulco falls to rebels.

September 8—Congress of Anáhuac, meeting at Chilpancingo, begins deliberations.

November 6—Rebels' declaration of independence issued.

December 22—Morelos begins attempt to take Valladolid.

December 25—Rebels defeated at Valladolid by Colonel Agustín de Iturbide.

1814 *January 5*—Morelos defeated at Puruarán. Shortly after, Morelos is relieved of supreme command of rebel forces.

February 24—Royalists attack rebel congress at Tlacotepec, seizing archives and disrupting urban support network.

March—Ferdinand VII returns to throne of Spain, suspends

Constitution of 1812, and launches campaign of persecution against liberals.

October 22—Rebel congress promulgates Constitution of Apatzingán.

1815 *Summer*—Rebel chieftains in Veracruz revolt against leadership of Juan Nepomuceno Rosáins.

September 29—Rebel congress begins effort to relocate from Uruapán in the west to Tehuacán in the east.

October—Rebel leader José María Cos accepts amnesty, abandons rebellion.

November 5—Morelos captured at Temalac.

December 15—Manuel de Mier y Terán dissolves rebel congress.

December 22—Morelos executed at Ecatepec.

1816 Agustín de Iturbide relieved of his military command after many complaints are lodged against him.

September 16—Félix Calleja replaced as viceroy by Juan Ruiz de Apodaca.

1817 *March*—Expedition of Spaniard Francisco Xavier Mina sets out to invade Mexico.

October 27—Mina defeated and captured at Venadito.

November 11—Mina and many of his officers executed at Mexico City.

1820 *January 1*—Rebellion begins in Spain demanding restoration of the Constitution of 1812.

March—Rebellion in Spain succeeds in reestablishing the Constitution of 1812 and restoring constitutional monarchy.

1821 *February 10*—Vicente Guerrero joins his forces with those of Agustín de Iturbide in the so-called Abrazo de Acatempan.

February 24—Iturbide issues his Plan of Iguala, also known as the Plan of the Three Guarantees.

May 9—The Spanish Cortes authorizes the creation of provincial deputations in the colonies.

July 5—In Mexico City, hard-line military officers overthrow Viceroy Apodaca, replacing him with Field Marshal Francisco Novella.

July 21—Juan O'Donojú, the newly appointed superior political chief (that title having replaced the title of viceroy), arrives in Mexico.

August 2—Iturbide's rebels take Puebla, Mexico's second-largest city.

August 24—Iturbide and O'Donojú sign the Treaty of Córdoba, wherein O'Donojú, without authorization from his home government, acknowledges Mexico's independence on behalf of Spain.

September 13—Novella capitulates.

September 27—Iturbide's army marches triumphantly into Mexico City. Soon after, he appoints a Sovereign Provisional Governing Junta.

October 8—O'Donojú dies.

December—Elections held for newly created congress.

1822 *February 24*—New congress opens.

March—Mexicans learn that the Spanish king and Cortes have disavowed the Treaty of Córdoba and will not send a Bourbon family member to take the throne of Mexico.

May 19—Popular demonstrations in Mexico City in favor of Iturbide's election as emperor.

May 21—Iturbide's election as emperor declared by congress.

July 21—Iturbide's coronation as emperor.

September 26—Abortive rebellion against Iturbide headed by Felipe de la Garza from the northeastern province of Nuevo Santander.

October 31—Iturbide dissolves the congress by force.

November 2—Iturbide installs National Instituent Junta to replace the dissolved congress.

December 2—Antonio López de Santa Anna begins rebellion against Iturbide in Veracruz.

December 6—Santa Anna issues Plan of Veracruz.

1823 *Early January*—Vicente Guerrero and Nicolás Bravo second Santa Anna's rebellion.

January 4—National Instituent Junta promulgates plan to colonize northern provinces.

February 1—General José Antonio Echávarri, theretofore a close ally of Iturbide, issues Plan of Casa Mata, demanding election of a new congress.

March 4—Iturbide calls on the dissolved congress to reassemble.

March 19—Iturbide abdicates throne.

March 27—Echávarri's Army of Liberation marches into Mexico City.

April 8—Congress formally abolishes the Mexican empire.

April 17—French forces invade Spain with the intention of restoring royal absolutism to that country.

May 11—Iturbide leaves for exile in Italy.

August 31—With their victory in the Battle of Trocadero, the French restore Ferdinand VII as an absolutist monarch. Ferdinand carries out vicious reprisals against his enemies.

November 28—Iturbide leaves Livorno, Italy, in violation of the terms of his exile.

1824 *April 28*—Mexican congress passes law declaring Iturbide a traitor and ordering that he be immediately executed should he return to Mexico.

July 19—Iturbide executed in the town of Padilla, Tamaulipas.

October 4—New federalist constitution adopted for Mexico.

PREFACE

The past is a heavy presence in Mexico. In the nation's capital one sees buildings made from stones taken from demolished Aztec pyramids, some with carved ancient deities serving as humble cornerstones. Without warning, vast excavated sites of black volcanic rock, the remnants of a once mighty civilization, open up amid the teeming city streets and plazas. Ponderous baroque cathedrals with macabre icons and intricate gold and silver ornamentation hark back to the days when Mexico was the jewel in the crown of the Spanish empire. Extraordinary numbers of statues and monuments, patriotic holidays, and streets and parks are named in honor of a crowded cast of national heroes who march and gallop through two centuries of history.

Revolutionary painters did their bit, creating enormous murals on the walls of public buildings, invoking history as the story of the slow, painful process of a people's redemption. Those artists tended to depict the past in the darkest tones, though such depictions were often leavened with the promise of brighter days in the offing. Take, for instance, Diego Rivera's mural on the walls of the National Palace: spanning three large walls, it depicts Indians slaughtered by conquistadors or worked like beasts in the cane fields under the harsh gaze of whip- and gun-toting overseers; slaves branded on the face with hot irons and tethered to heavy ropes and chains; heretics garroted by the Holy Inquisition; striking workers clubbed by police. At the culmination of the mural's left wall, which imagines "Mexico of Today and Tomorrow," appears the startling image of Karl Marx—for Rivera, the bright light of truth—explaining to a group of workers and soldiers, through the words of his *Communist Manifesto*, that it is no use trying to reform the existing society, an entirely new society must be created. In Mexico, the mural seems to suggest, history is about redemption, and redemption is bought with blood.

Mexico's wars for independence, which were fought from 1810 to 1821, were among the bloodiest episodes in the country's history, but in this case blood brought no final redemption. A successful outcome of the wars was frustrated by the many severe divisions within Mexican society. Those divisions had been created quite deliberately during the three centuries when Mexico— or New Spain, as it was then known—was a part of the Spanish empire. Spain's rulers tended to see social inequality as something ordained by God, something mortal folk had no right to question. In accordance with what they considered the Almighty's grand design, those rulers constructed a fairly elaborate racial pyramid. Spaniards and American-born whites (known as creoles) sat at the apex of that pyramid, together accounting for roughly 18 percent of the population. Beneath them, making up about 22 percent of the population, were people of mixed race—white, black, and Indian—known as castes. And occupying the pyramid's ample base were the Indians, comprising about 60 percent of the population. This was no melting pot, but rather a rigid caste system. The races were legally unequal, and it was unlikely that those who occupied society's lower depths might rise very far. In fact, it seemed self-evident to the country's rulers that dark-skinned people were put on earth for the purpose of labor. The castes faced harsh discrimination, while most of Mexico's Indians were marginalized, illiterate, desperately poor, and culturally and linguistically separate from the country's elite.

Yet despite the oppressive realities endured by the majority of

Mexico's people, the colonial centuries were for the most part remarkably peaceful, thanks largely to what the great Prussian natu-
ralist Alexander von Humboldt, who spent most of 1803 traveling
in Mexico, called "the equilibrium established between the hostile
forces."[1] The Roman Catholic Church and the Spanish monarchy—the two most revered institutions in the empire—were key
elements in that equilibrium, for the church taught the poor to
bear their sufferings gracefully, and the king was seen as a remote
but endlessly compassionate figure. Also helping to maintain peace
were the illiteracy and stubborn parochialism of Mexico's rural
society, which ensured that no coordinated mass movement could
arise, and that violence seldom reached beyond the boundaries of
a given village.

Creoles tended to see themselves as the natural and rightful
rulers of the country, yet they too suffered discrimination in the
imperial system. In Humboldt's words, "The most miserable European, without education, and without intellectual cultivation,
thinks himself superior to whites born in the new continent."[2] The
creoles were systematically deprived of political power and economic liberty, and they had ample cause for complaint. Even so,
the idea of rebelling against the mother country was unthinkable.
Most creoles had fully absorbed the colonial ethos: they embraced
inequality with gusto, they revered church and king, they benefited
from the labor of castes and Indians, and they were loath to tam-
per with a system that—a few irritations aside—afforded them an
easy and comfortable life.

It may seem odd that I refer to "wars," for in the broadest sense
there was but one war spanning the decade. In a more profound
sense, however, Mexico witnessed many wars during the independence era. Best known was the war fought by the leaders of the rebellion, most of them creoles, against the Spanish armies and
militias. Those leaders aimed to achieve autonomy or independence from Spain and a few social, political, and economic reforms. Unfortunately for the movement's leaders, most of their

fellow creoles quickly came to be horrified by the savagery of the struggle, and they were hardly eager to share their privileged existence with the dark-skinned masses who made up the rebel armies. They threw their support to the royalist regime, thus recasting the war for independence as a civil war. Along with that civil war came many small wars fought by the rank and file of the movement, mostly impoverished Indians and castes. These wars were fought for a wide variety of reasons, most of which responded to very local and even personal concerns—a desire for vengeance against exploiters, a wish to maintain a village's cultural integrity, a lust for adventure, the will to defend the Spanish king from his heretical tormentors—and those reasons had little to do with any large-scale political project. Few Indians or castes fought to forge a new nation called Mexico; such a scheme would have made little sense, and held little interest, for them. They fought in the hope that their lot in life might in some way improve.

The wars, with all their ambiguity and cross-purposes, only deepened the divisions and antagonisms that plagued Mexico. Predictably, independence was followed by a prolonged period of penury, political paralysis, and ongoing bloodshed, as elites fought one another to advance their notions of what Mexico should become. What Mexico *did* become was a kind of work in progress, a vast conglomeration of people groping toward some sense of common identity and nationhood. The wars for independence, seen in the broad sweep of Mexico's history, may not have resolved the country's dire problems, but they nevertheless played a pivotal part in the story by providing the nation with heroes and myths, even if those heroes and myths were variously interpreted. Many conservatives came to see the wars merely as a cautionary tale revealing the horrors that ensue when the unwashed masses are released from their restraints. Those of a more liberal turn of mind tended to simplify and romanticize the wars' brutal realities, retelling history as one of martyrs who gave their blood and lives to free a nation from tyranny. And even those at the very bottom of the pyramid could find some inspiration in the drama of independence. A hundred years after the war, peasant villagers in the state of Morelos—a state named in honor of one of the rebellion's greatest leaders—still spoke proudly of how local boys—their grandfathers—had smuggled food, gunpowder, and liquor to rebels besieged by Spanish forces in the town of Cuautla, and of how a succeeding generation had battled French invaders with equal valor.[3] As suggested by Rivera's muralistic rendering of Mexican history, perhaps the generation that suffered the cruel shocks of Mexico's independence wars did not suffer in vain. Perhaps that epoch was merely the first act in a slowly unfolding tale of redemption.

THE MEXICAN WARS FOR INDEPENDENCE

ONE

THE COLONY

In the year 1623, so the story goes, a man in the dusty village of San Juan de los Lagos in western Mexico was teaching his young daughters to do acrobatic tricks on the trapeze. To make the show more compelling, he had the girls perform the tricks above several swords affixed in the earth and pointing menacingly toward the heavens. One of the girls fell, was impaled on the swords, and died instantly. The small corpse was taken to a nearby temple, where an old woman named Ana Lucia, renowned for her piety, was caretaker. Ana Lucia took a moth-eaten statue of the Virgin of the Immaculate Conception out of a closet, where the parish priest had hidden it, for he was embarrassed by its sorry condition. When Ana Lucia placed the statue on the child's chest, the girl was at once restored to full life and vigor. Soon after, a mysterious boy appeared by night and transformed the decaying statue into a beautiful and flawless image of the Virgin, then disappeared without asking for payment. The townsfolk assumed he was an angel.

The miracle transformed the rude village of San Juan de los Lagos into one of Mexico's most popular religious sites. Each year thereafter, between December 1 and 9, thousands of pilgrims would descend on the small town to pay their respects to the miraculous figure. In 1810, a hundred thousand souls were expected to attend, most of them desperately poor Indians. Those Indians, it could safely be assumed, would have little to lose, and they would loathe Spaniards. The thought of so many Indians gathered in one place, all of them seething with hatred for Spaniards, in the grip of religious fervor and quite possibly drunk, was irresistible to a small group of American-born whites conspiring to overthrow the government.

This, they reckoned, was the perfect time and place to start a revolution.

Indians and Castes

Although the conspiracy to launch the revolution from the festival of San Juan de los Lagos was ultimately foiled, the very fact that such a plan was laid raises several key questions. Why did Indians bear such ill will toward Spaniards? Was there a natural link between popular religious fervor and violence? What reason did whites have to imagine the Indians would be willing to fight their revolution for them? Would Indians and whites fight with the same goals in mind?

Relations between Europeans and Indians began with violence, race prejudice, and exploitation, and the pattern of those relations did not change in their fundamentals over the three hundred years of the Spanish colony. The Spaniards who conquered the indigenous civilizations of Mexico were not professional soldiers, but rather armed entrepreneurs out for wealth and glory. There was not enough gold in the new colony to satisfy those conquerors, and when Tenochtitlán, the opulent capital of the vast Aztec empire, fell to the invaders in 1521, the discovery of Mexico's rich silver mines was still more than two decades away. The only rewards available, then, were Indians and land. For the Spaniards land had no value without Indians to work it, so royal authorities parceled out the Indians to the conquistadors in the form of grants known as encomiendas. A grant of encomienda allowed the grantee—known as an encomendero—to demand tribute and labor from a specified number of Indian villagers. The demands made on the Indians were often extraordinary, helping to accelerate the appalling decline in their numbers. Waves of epidemic disease swept through the Americas, killing, in some areas, nine out of every ten people. The decline in the native population deprived the Spaniards of labor, but it also freed up quite a bit of land, which the Spaniards hastened to claim. The Spanish American hacienda—an infamous and durable institution that produced crops principally for the Spanish cities and mining camps—was thus born.

The encomienda—the first mechanism the Spaniards used to exploit Indians—was largely ended by the late 1500s, but new forms of exploitation, such as labor drafts and peonage, supplanted it. The essential feature of the system was fixed: Indians worked; whites enjoyed the benefits of their labor.

Catholic missionaries who arrived in New Spain to convert the Indians to Spain's rigid version of Catholic Christianity tended, at least in the early years of the colonization, to see the natives as God's providential compensation for the tragedy of the Protestant heresy, a vast multitude of souls ripe for salvation. The harvest of so many souls would surely, in their view, be the harbinger of the millennium, that thousand-year period foretold in the Book of Revelation during which Satan languishes in prison while Christ rules the world, preparing for the fearsome battles of the world's final days.

Given the high stakes, the missionaries were understandably zealous in their efforts. About sixty Franciscan missionaries claimed to have converted five million Indians to Christianity after only twelve years in Mexico; one friar boasted of having baptized 1,500 in a single day. Obviously, these "conversions" left the Indians with an extremely imperfect understanding of orthodox Christianity.

As late as 1792, one village priest estimated that among his flock of five thousand, fewer than a hundred could mutter even the simplest of prayers. Priests visited remote villages infrequently, so villagers seldom heard mass, took communion, or confessed their sins. Babies went unbaptized, couples lived in sin, and the dead were buried without the proper Christian rites. Secular education was likewise deficient. Village schools were fairly common throughout Mexico by the late colonial period, but their impact was minimal, undone by poverty and Indian resistance. Most Indians in Mexico were never assimilated into the world of the whites.

This is not to say that the Indians were irreligious. In fact, religion penetrated every facet of life. It was a lively, naive folk Catholicism full of spirits in the earth, saints in the heavens, witchcraft, magic, and miracles. From time to time, prophets and messiahs would appear claiming to work miracles and promising an earthly paradise in the offing. One common object of veneration, surprisingly, was none other than the king of Spain. The Indians may have despised Spaniards in general, but they revered the distant king, a figure no less abstract or perennially popular than God himself. When the conspirators of 1810 planned their revolution, they decided to rally the people not to revolution, but rather in defense of the king—"The Indians," explained one of the movement's leaders, "are indifferent to the word liberty."[1] During the rebellion rumors ran among the Indians that the Spanish king was in Mexico, that he wore a silver mask, or rode in a black coach, or was invisible, or was in many places at once.

The Spanish regime's failure to integrate the Indians into their world was ultimately unfortunate, but entirely deliberate. The early missionaries were convinced that the Indians were perpetual children in need of extraordinary protection and guidance lest they die out or succumb to the corrupting influences of white society, and they worked tirelessly to sway the Spanish king to their belief. The sage advice of Mexico's first viceroy, Antonio de Mendoza—"Treat the Indians like any other people, and do not make special rules and regulations for them"[2]—accordingly went unheeded. The society that the friars helped bring into existence was formally segregated into two orders, or "republics": the republic of Spaniards and the republic of Indians. The republic of Indians consisted of villages, many of them created by the missionaries to provide refuge from the ravages of plagues. Those newly created villages were designed to facilitate supervision and conversion, with priests acting as father figures and crucial intermediaries between Indian and white societies.

Starting in the 1530s, the crown of Spain decreed that Indians should have permanent and inalienable possession of croplands, pasturelands, and woodlands, which they were to use mostly to provide for their own needs; they also were exempted from some Spanish laws and taxes, and were granted more lenient treatment by the courts on the grounds that, as irrational creatures, they could not be expected to understand and obey the conventions of polite society. Indians were not to dress in European clothing, ride horses, or bear arms. Apart from priestly supervision and white demands for labor, the Indian village was largely self-governing, with traditional native authorities overseeing the distribution of land and water and defending village interests in law courts set up specifically to hear Indian complaints. Indians were required to pay tribute, a burden from which whites—who became the de facto nobility of the New World—were exempt. The system was intended to perpetuate inequality, in accordance with the Spanish conviction that God designed human society along hierarchical lines. Whites, in this conception, were *gente de casta limpia*, people of pure lineage; Indians were *gente sin razón*, people incapable of reason; and blacks, who were brought in increasing numbers to the colonies to labor in mines, plantations, and workshops, were *infames por derecho*, legally debased.

This neat separation of the races was soon rendered little more than an ideal, or a fantasy of social engineering. The pristine system imagined by the missionaries could not withstand the trend toward race mixing that began early in the colonial period, when European women were scarce and white men saw Indian women as, by definition, sexually available. The mixing of the races—Indian, African, and European—continued throughout the colonial period and beyond. By the late 1700s, nearly a quarter of the population of the viceroyalty of New Spain consisted of "castes," or people of mixed race, whose legal and social status was maddeningly ambiguous. In the official conception of things, the castes were simply not supposed to exist, so it is not altogether surprising that policy toward them was incoherent. At times they were barred from public office, the clergy, and the honorable trades, while at other times they were admitted; some were required to pay tribute, but others were not. Most became artisans or laborers, but some aspired to high status. Late in the colonial period, a fortunate few were able to purchase certificates declaring them white for most legal purposes. Ambiguous though their condition was, they were the most dynamic and fastest-growing segment of an increasingly complex, multiracial, multicultural society. During the eighteenth century, whites, jealous of their "purity" and the privileges it entailed, took to devising a new and bizarre taxonomy of races in hopes of preserving a rigid, if complicated, racial hierarchy. Some such taxonomies claimed to recognize as many as twenty distinct, identifiable "races." One's status declined as one moved further from the ideal of "pure" whiteness.

Indians and castes did not necessarily inhabit the same world, and they did not necessarily get along well with one another; but they tended to share a deep and abiding resentment of the whites who discriminated against them. They resented Spaniards in particular.

Creoles and Spaniards

The Indians and castes were not alone in resenting Spaniards. White society was itself divided between those who had been born in Spain (*peninsulares* or, less politely, *gachupines*) and those who had been born in America (*criollos*, or creoles). Although that division was often smoothed over by intersecting interests, it could also be deep and bitter. The division was not necessarily a matter of simple bigotry: the notion of "hierarchies and classes" was an essential ingredient of the worldview that underlay Spain and its empire, a set of cherished ideas that, in the era of independence, would clash violently with the radical notion that all men are created equal. Hierarchies and classes, in the words of an official statement made in 1806 by the Council of the Indies—the supreme governing organ for the Spanish American colonies—were "of the greatest importance to the existence and stability of a monarchical state, since a graduated system of dependence and subordination sustains and insures the obedience and respect of the last vassal to the authority of the sovereign." Such a system was especially necessary in America because it was far from Spain, and filled with people of "vicious origin and nature, [who were] not comparable to the commoners of Spain and constitute a very inferior species."[3]

Creoles, who considered themselves a kind of New World nobility, chafed at being dumped into a category with their dark-complexioned countrymen. Spaniards discriminated against creoles from the beginning of the colony, resenting their pretensions to equality, and seeing them as inherently dim-witted, lazy, unreliable, and obnoxious. The upper ranks of the bureaucracy and clergy were closed to them, even though some creole families gained considerable wealth and, at least in the eyes of creole society itself, status. The wealthiest creoles, many claiming descent from conquistadors and encomenderos, held impressive titles of nobility and vast entailed estates, and they married into the most exalted Spanish families. Roughly fifty such families lived in Mexico by the late eighteenth century. Beneath them were creole merchants, lawyers, priests, craftsmen, farmers, and ranchers, all of them demanding respectability within the colonial system. But the Spanish government did its best to limit the creoles' opportunities and to rig the system against them. During the sixteenth century, the best creoles could do politically was to dominate the *cabildos*, or town councils, but they managed to use these lowly positions to maximize their own advantages, often in defiance of royal commands. It was during this time that creoles developed their resentment toward Spaniards. Thomas Gage, an English monk who traveled to Mexico in the early seventeenth century, wrote of creoles "who do hate the Spanish government, and all such as come from Spain; and reason they have for it, for by them they are much oppressed, and are always watching any opportunity to free themselves from the Spanish yoke."[4]

Despite the tensions between them, there was one area where creoles and Spaniards were able to agree: they both lived in mortal fear of the Indians and castes, and believed that Spain's conservative traditions—respect for hierarchy and authority, strict adherence to orthodox religion, a king with unhindered and unquestioned power—must be maintained if the masses were to be kept under control. During what whites—creole and Spaniard alike—thought of as normal times, the traits that they esteemed most highly in the masses were docility, obsequiousness, and deference, though they seem to have understood, perhaps at some submerged level, that the mood of the masses could quickly turn ugly, and that the whites might well become victims of centuries of repressed anger. In normal times, whites—Spaniards and creoles together—enjoyed a near monopoly on weapons, riches, prestige, and power, but they were at the apex of a squat pyramid, surrounded by bitterly oppressed people who inhabited a world they did not understand. In the words of one historian, in Mexico "there were Indians, castes, nobles, soldiers, priests, merchants and lawyers, but there were no citizens."[5]

A Golden Age of Sorts: The Seventeenth Century
During the 1600s, the creoles experienced an agreeable reprieve from the elaborate pecking order upon which the imperial system

was theoretically based. In theory, the power of the monarchy was absolute, the king sitting near the apex—together with the pope, but one remove from God himself—of a pyramid, his royal wishes passed down along a smooth chain of command involving royal councilors and colonial officials and ultimately shaping the lives of the humblest of the king's subjects. But even during the heyday of the empire, the mechanisms of royal control were far from perfect. As one viceroy put it, "God is on high, the king in Madrid, and I am in Mexico." In practice, governing the American colonies was always a complex and often corrupt process of negotiation, compromise, and accommodation. The real business of the colonies got done not through well-oiled bureaucratic machinery, but in backroom deals and bribes, disputes and agreements among interest groups, claims and counterclaims among the functionaries of overlapping jurisdictions, and favors granted to cronies and kinsmen. Laws, it seemed, were made to be ignored or evaded—obeyed only as a last resort. It was, in the words of one historian, "a workable compromise between what the central authorities ideally wanted and what local conditions and pressures would realistically tolerate."[6]

The extent of effective royal control grew more attenuated with time. That had much to do with the colony's principal reason for existence, at least as far as the crown of Spain was concerned. During the 1540s, rich veins of silver were discovered in the provinces of Zacatecas and Guanajuato, several hundred miles north of Mexico City. From that point onward, the obsessive focus of the Spanish government was on getting silver out of American ground and into Spanish coffers, while losing as little as possible along the way. To that end, the Spanish regime devised an oppressively rigid system of trade, only to squander much of its windfall defending the Catholic Church during the religious wars over the next century and a half. Meanwhile, Spain's elites stubbornly adhered to the medieval notions that God was the source of all truth, that science was pernicious, that war was the only fitting occupation for a gentleman, and that productive labor was for rubes. Spain's ruling class was, by most measures, the most parasitic, intellectually bankrupt, and resolutely mediocre in Europe, helping to ensure that Spain fell further and further behind the rest of Europe in developing its productive capacities. During the seventeenth century, while England was laying the groundwork for the industrial revolution, Spain seemed to be moving backward. Although Spain jealously guarded its absolute monopoly on trade with its American colonies, it could not begin to supply the sorts of goods that colonists needed, wanted, or demanded. In exchange for American silver, the Spaniards were able to ship a handful of agricultural products—wine and olive oil, raw wool—along with some iron implements and crude textiles. The bulk of what they sent—products that the colonists, a captive market, had to purchase at often scandalously inflated prices—was in fact produced in the countries of northern Europe and reexported from Spain. By 1680, fully two-thirds of Spain's silver was being sent directly to foreigners to pay for these products, and foreigners exercised nearly complete, albeit indirect, control over Spain's colonial commerce.

By the mid-1600s, Spain seemed to have entered into a mortal decrepitude. It had been defeated in war; lost portions of its vast empire to the English, French, and Dutch; had primitive agriculture and little industry, a shaky currency, and a demoralized population ravaged by wars and plagues. Nothing symbolized Spain's decline more poignantly than the king himself. Charles II, who inherited the throne in 1665, suffered from mental retardation and bone disease, and was so feeble that he had to be breast-fed for his first six years. In later life, he was subject to convulsive seizures that experts reckoned to be the result of demonic possession, the province not of doctors but of exorcists, wizards, and visionary nuns. His sad, elongated face; his jutting lower jaw (a common characteristic of the Spanish Habsburgs, of whom Charles was the last); his oversized tongue, which made it hard for him to speak and caused him to drool; his legendary lethargy and ignorance; and his inability to produce an heir all made him the perfect symbol of the decaying empire.

Spain's decrepitude was good news for the creoles. It meant that those Spanish fleets that took American silver to Spain and brought overpriced goods to the colonies did not sail regularly, and some years did not sail at all, creating wonderful opportunities for smugglers who sold goods at a fraction of the price charged by the Spanish monopoly merchants. Silver continued to be mined in significant, if declining, quantities, and more and more of that silver stayed in the colony. Creole merchants found it relatively easy to avoid paying many taxes and duties, and to evade the byzantine restrictions Spain placed on its trade. Likewise, Spain's inability to supply its colonies with necessary goods meant that colonists were able to step into that void, manufacturing substantial quantities of textiles and other goods. Spain, always jealous of its commercial monopoly, had impeded trade among the colonies themselves, but during the seventeenth century colonists were able to develop a lively intercolonial trade in livestock products, sugar, cacao, and textiles. The colonists now found themselves with greater economic opportunity than ever before.

Spain's decline also brought political benefits. Increasingly desperate for funds, the Spanish government placed one political office after another up for sale. The process began with lowly notarial offices in the mid-1500s, but by the time of Charles II creoles were buying their way into practically every office in the colony. While creoles generally found themselves outbid for the middling but highly profitable position of *alcalde mayor*—a local official who was able to enrich himself from his near monopoly on financial dealings with Indian villages—they were eventually able to dominate the powerful *audiencias*, high-level governing bodies whose authority in the colonies was second only to that of the viceroy. By 1770, creoles held six of the eight judgeships on the Mexico City *audiencia*. Creoles also happily purchased whatever the Spanish regime was willing to sell: titles of nobility, certificates legitimizing patently illegal land titles, extensions of encomienda grants, pardons for crimes, legitimacy for illegitimate children, the right to contract forbidden marriages, and bonds to prop up the government. Such transactions were ultimately damaging to the royal treasury—many of the political offices that were sold carried salaries that continued to be paid long after the purchase price had been redeemed—and they further weakened Spain's grip on its faraway colonies and convinced the colonists that they had the right and the ability to govern themselves. They also led to an unfortunate conviction that political influence and social status were commodities to be bought and sold.

The 1600s saw a few welcome developments for the lower ranks of Mexican society as well, though their lives remained hard. The terrible decrease in the Indian population in the decades after the conquest, tragic though it was, reduced competition for land and water and other resources, allowing Indian communities to live relatively unmolested, and their dwindling numbers gave them some real power. The encomiendas and forced labor drafts disappeared in most areas by the first quarter of the seventeenth century. In place of coercion, some landowners and mine operators found themselves obliged to offer relatively high wages and other perks to attract workers. Indians generally needed cash to make their tribute payments, so many gravitated toward the larger Spanish cities and mines, and to the farms that surrounded them, receiving cash, credit, and land in exchange for their labor. Mine workers were allowed to keep quantities of silver ore known as *partidos*. The Spanish and Indian races remained, of course, profoundly unequal. But the Indians' increased bargaining power and the steady increase in the mixed-race population tended gradually to soften the lines between the all-powerful and the utterly powerless.

Some modest blurring of Indian and creole identities occurred as some Mexicans, eager to differentiate themselves from Spaniards and to claim a proud lineage, took to celebrating the glories of the Aztec empire, so cruelly destroyed by the Spanish conquistadors. Some, such as the mestizo historian Fernando de Alva Ixtlilxochitl and the creole intellectual Carlos de Sigüenza y Góngora, elaborated theories that freed them, symbolically at least, from Spanish tutelage. Loath to credit the Spaniards with transmitting the true faith to the New World—the one great gift that none could possibly gainsay—Ixtlilxochitl and Sigüenza insisted that St. Thomas the Apostle had in fact traveled throughout the Americas preaching the gospel. In Mexico, according to one theory, he had gone by the name of Quetzalcoatl, a Mesoamerican deity generally associated with wisdom and benevolence. Over time, in this view, the Indians had drifted from the faith, but the Spaniards could at best take credit only for reminding the Indians of what, at some submerged level, they already knew, rather than for pointing them in a new direction entirely. Mexicans who believed such fantasies were reassured that the Spaniards had in fact given them nothing but centuries of oppression, and that the true natives of their land were not unworthy.

Rich or poor, Indian or creole, Mexicans of every race and class enjoyed the taste of independence, dignity, and self-rule they got during the seventeenth century, and they were therefore all the more disgruntled when the Spaniards began systematically to revive and perfect the despotism of the empire. Their resentments would eventually lead to the chaotic and bloody revolution for independence.

TWO

SHOCKS TO THE SYSTEM

While the exorcists performed their futile rituals on the hapless King Charles II, and Charles's mother ineptly held the reins of power, vultures gathered. Charles left no heir, but a pro-French faction at court managed to persuade him to designate as his successor, in preference to his own Austrian kin, one Philip of Anjou, grandson of the opulent French monarch Louis XIV, the Sun King. That set the stage for the War of the Spanish Succession, a Spanish civil war in which all of the great powers of Europe took part. After twelve years of bloodshed, the war ended in favor of the French claimant, who became King Philip V, the first of the Spanish Bourbon line. Suddenly, Frenchmen and their protégés, with their powdered wigs and elegant new notions about the rational way to run an empire, took charge.

The first two Spanish Bourbon kings, Philip V and Ferdinand VI, concentrated on reforming Spain itself, leaving the colonies to their customary arrangements. The first Bourbon king to focus his attention resolutely on the Americas was Charles III, who succeeded to the throne in 1759. A large man with a beaklike nose, a kindly grin, and a passion for shooting driven game, Charles III was easily the most enlightened and best of the Bourbon kings, though his reputation clearly benefited by comparison with those who preceded and followed him on the throne. Charles III was in many ways a typical Spanish king: he was untroubled by the severe inequalities of the society he ruled and, as a pious Catholic, considered his kingly powers as absolute and divinely ordained. To him the American colonies were distant appendages of Spain, their sole purpose to buy Spain's products, supply it with certain plantation crops, and fill its coffers with silver. He summed up his priority for the colonies with admirable simplicity: "To bring my royal revenues to their proper level."[1]

As Charles III was brainstorming ways to raise revenues and quicken all economic activity, progressive intellectuals throughout the rest of Europe were coming to the conclusion that reason, not divine revelation and hidebound tradition, was the surest route to truth, and that individual freedom was the key to happiness for the greatest number of people. To these Enlightenment thinkers, people who claimed unearned rights and privileges, laws that told people what they must think and believe, governments that intruded upon people's private property and interests, and kings who claimed to rule in God's name all obstructed society's progress toward happiness. In Spain, where rigid Catholic orthodoxy and inherited privilege had become ingrained habits of mind to a far greater degree than in other European countries, such ideas encountered a good deal of skepticism and outright hostility.

Something of a rude awakening came about in the early 1760s, when Charles III, seeing Great Britain as a rival for dominance in the Americas, unwisely entered the Seven Years' War on the side of France. In 1762, as part of that war, Britain seized the Spanish port of Havana, Cuba, and held it for ten months. The British opened the previously closed port to trade with Britain and its North American colonies, allowing in a flood of consumer and capital goods—including modern machinery for the processing of sugarcane—as well as foodstuffs and African slaves. The transformation of the island was quick and impressive, demonstrating to Spain just how badly it had been underutilizing its assets and suggesting what the country might hope for if it were to implement dramatic reforms to its highly restrictive trading system. At the same time, Britain's capture of Havana made it apparent that Spain's American possessions were vulnerable to foreign encroachments. The lesson was clear: Spain must either reform and secure its domination of the colonies or risk losing its empire. New freedoms for merchants, new tax structures, new incentives, new crops, new administration—therein, Charles III and his ministers came to believe, lay the seeds of Spain's rebirth as a great world power. The Spaniards could embrace Enlightenment ideas to this extent; those trending toward freedom of conscience and popular sovereignty were, of course, dismissed.

José de Gálvez and the Bourbon Reforms

The first step in this transformation was a *visita*, or inspection tour, by a trusted servant of the crown, and the first venue was Mexico, Spain's richest colony by far. The inspector chosen for the task was José de Gálvez. Gálvez had not been born to great wealth or distinction, nor had he attended an elite university. He was the scion of a poor provincial family of minor nobility, a man who had worked his way up through the ranks of Spain's legal profession—just the sort of man Charles III tended to favor. As a self-made man who lacked both aristocratic connections and pretensions, Gálvez was assumed to be beholden to no faction, and thus could function as a reliable servant of the king. He would serve as visitor-general to Mexico (1765–1771) and later in the all-important post of minister of the Indies (1775–1787).

Gálvez was an apparently humorless man of considerable talent, energy, and intensity. He suffered from mental illness—what he called "fevers in his head"—which helped to account for occasional incapacitation and bizarre conduct, but even under normal circumstances he was uncommonly irascible, haughty, temperamental, and intolerant. He thoroughly assessed the colonial situation before departing Spain, and only allowed himself to see the things that confirmed his prejudices. Perhaps his firmest and most noxious conviction was that all creoles were vain, dull-witted, and untrustworthy people who should be deprived of any say in the governance of the colonies. As minister of the Indies, he would see to it that the numbers of *audiencia* judges were increased and that Spaniards were appointed to fill all vacancies, thus reducing the creoles to minority status. The creoles were outraged. A 1782 letter, signed by, among others, the father of South American liberator Simón Bolívar, charged that Gálvez treated "all Americans, no matter their pedigree, rank or condition, as if they were vile slaves," leaving them no option but "to rise against such an infamous and unbearable oppression."[2]

Gálvez was instrumental in implementing another policy that alienated the Mexicans: overreacting to the potential challenge the church presented to royal control, Spain suddenly expelled the Jesuit religious order from Mexico. By tradition, the clergy had long enjoyed immunity from civil law, which was galling to would-be absolutists like the Bourbon kings of Spain, who preferred to think of the inhabitants of their realms as uniformly obedient subjects. The clergy of the Roman Catholic Church generally had tremendous moral authority with the population. One broadside went so far as to claim that the only thing needed to quell a riot was the placing of "a friar with a Holy Crucifix in the nearest plaza."[3] For the most part, the clergy used their moral authority in support of the established government, but there was always the disturbing possibility that they might use it to rouse the masses in opposition. As far as Charles III was concerned, no clergymen were more dangerous than the Jesuits.

A religious order born of the Catholic Counter-Reformation, the Jesuits saw themselves as soldiers for Christ and the pope as their commander in chief. Their success in dominating higher education and in amassing spectacular wealth gave them the wherewithal to act independently, making them appear a serious threat to civil government. Certain Jesuit writings argued that disobeying or even killing a ruler was, in some circumstances, justifiable. When antigovernment riots broke out in Madrid in March 1766, Charles III, with fairly scant evidence, charged a Jesuit conspiracy, and in 1767 he ordered that all Jesuits be immediately expelled from Spain and its empire. In Mexico, 678 Jesuits were precipitously rounded up, taken under armed escort to the port of Veracruz, and shipped off to the Papal States. Only two of them ever managed to return to Mexico. Nearly all of them were creoles.

The move, which took place while Gálvez was making his inspection tour, caused outrage among Mexicans of all social ranks and walks of life. The Jesuits were popular in Mexico, at least in part because they had played a prominent role in securing papal recognition of the cult of the Virgin of Guadalupe, Mexico's most popular religious icon. The expulsion not only removed from Mexico many revered priests, but it also disrupted the schooling of many creoles, including that of the future instigator of the independence movement, Miguel Hidalgo. In several Mexican cities, violent uprisings protested the expulsion of the Jesuits. Gálvez repressed those uprisings with a brutality that shocked colonial society: in San Luis de la Paz, in the province of Guanajuato, he had four ringleaders summarily executed and several more exiled; he ordered troops to besiege the city of Guanajuato and quarantined it for three months; in San Luis Potosí he conducted a series of summary trials that resulted in the hanging of eleven people. To hammer home his point, Gálvez had the homes of the executed men burned and the ground sowed with salt, while the men's severed heads were displayed on pikes. Other riots were punished with similar severity, till in the end some three thousand people had been tried, 85 executed, 674 sentenced to life in prison, 117 exiled, and 73 flogged. If the original cause of the riots failed to disgust all of Mexico's citizens, few were unmoved by the savagery of the riots' aftermath.

Having quelled the riots, Gálvez turned his attention to his primary ambition, helping Charles III achieve his goal of raising royal revenues to their "proper level." This he hoped to accomplish by improving colonial administration, raising taxes, and stimulating the economy. Gálvez believed that a key problem in colonial finances was caused by *alcaldes mayores*, district officials who made most of their income through a notorious system known as *repartimiento de mercancías* (distribution of merchandise). This system was ingeniously simple: a prospective *alcalde*, having bought his position at an exorbitant price in Spain, would, upon arriving in Mexico City, enter into a pact with a well-heeled merchant who would supply, on credit and at outrageously high rates of interest, an array of merchandise. Such merchandise might in fact consist of useful items such as livestock, seeds, and tools, but it might also include such items as fine linens and beaver hats, for which the Indians had no need. The *alcalde* would force his Indian charges to buy those goods or to accept loans, with the understanding that the highly inflated prices—perhaps 150 to 200 times the normal prices—were to be repaid in installments, and that failure to make the regular payments would result in imprisonment. As chief law enforcer for his region, the *alcalde mayor* could usually back up his threats. The *repartimiento de mercancías* was not invariably abusive: it sometimes provided Indians with much-needed goods and credit and was their only link to the larger market economy. It did, however, offer ample temptation to the unscrupulous and was the cause of several riots. Gálvez hated the *repartimiento* not for its inhumanity, but rather because the *alcaldes*, by his reckoning, pocketed half of all Indian tribute, and their *repartimientos* contributed to the Indians' continued impoverishment. The crown was thus deprived of both tax revenue and potential consumers of Spanish goods.

Gálvez proposed to supplant the *alcaldes* with reliable, well-remunerated royal servants, to be known as intendants (the concept and name were both borrowed from the French). Despite Gálvez's eagerness to make this reform, his proposal was quickly caught up in bureaucratic and interest group infighting. Only after a bloody Indian rebellion in Peru in the early 1780s, in which the *repartimiento de mercancías* was a major factor, did the Spanish government implement the intendancy system—some twenty years after Gálvez had first proposed it, and only months before his death. The reform involved dividing Mexico into twelve administrative districts, or intendancies, and placing a handsomely paid intendant in charge of each. The intendants were charged with awesome responsibilities: they were expected to stimulate the economy, collect taxes, oversee public works, reform local government, recruit soldiers and manage military matters, and keep tabs on the church. The intendants were recruited from among the most talented administrators Spain had to offer, and they generally were honest and efficient, but the intendant system had a fatal flaw: the intendants' responsibilities were clearly too great for one individual, and their local-level assistants—known as subdelegates—were not paid at all well. It proved difficult to find qualified applicants to take such positions, especially in the more remote areas. Not surprisingly, colonial officials were soon deluged with complaints that the subdelegates were even greater rascals than the old *alcaldes mayores* had been.

Increasing taxes was another priority of Gálvez's, and another source of bitter complaints from the colonists. He established a government monopoly on tobacco: the government would buy tobacco from licensed planters, and the tobacco would be rolled into cigars in government-owned factories. The monopoly, like all important public enterprises, was administered by Spaniards recruited in Spain. Gálvez also made tax collection more efficient by appointing salaried tax collectors and placing them in twenty-four Mexican cities, with a director-general stationed in Mexico City to oversee them all. Revenues also came from tribute charged of Indians and castes; duties on pulque, the preferred intoxicant of the Mexican poor; and government monopolies on salt, mercury, leather, various minerals, gunpowder, playing cards, stamped paper, snow, and cockfights. The results were immediately impressive, with tax revenues nearly doubling between 1760 and 1780. During the late eighteenth and early nineteenth centuries, as Spain's military fortunes ebbed precipitously, tax collection became ever more predatory, and the colonials became ever more enraged.

Gálvez was also keen to revive the mining of silver, a metal he believed gave "spirit and movement to all human occupations and to the universal commerce of the globe."[4] To that end, he halved the price and increased supplies of mercury, a necessary ingredient in the amalgamation process that separates pure silver from ore. (Mexico's miners were entirely dependent on Spain for their supplies of mercury, which were mined at Almadén in central Spain.) He also granted a variety of tax reductions and exemptions to miners, set up special courts to hear mine-related cases, created a credit bank and a mining college, issued a new mining code, and rewarded successful miners with titles of nobility.

The results were spectacular. Although mining remained a notoriously risky and expensive enterprise—only two out of every ten speculators in Mexico's silver mines ever realized a profit—for the lucky few who succeeded the rewards were handsome indeed. The Count of Valenciana spent a fortune and several decades sinking the world's deepest mine shafts into a forlorn hill in Guanajuato, eventually striking veins that alone yielded more silver than the combined output of Peru and Bolivia. The Count of Regla, who began his career as a poor Spanish immigrant, became the wealthiest man in the world: so wealthy he was able to make the Spanish government a gift of two fully equipped warships, and could boast that, should the king ever visit Mexico, he would travel the nearly three hundred miles from the coast to the capital on a road paved entirely with silver ingots. By the late eighteenth century, Mexico was producing ten times more silver than all of the mines of Europe—fully two-thirds of all the silver mined in the world. Sixteen mine owners were elevated to the nobility.

Some reforms made by the Bourbons went beyond even the adventurous proposals of Gálvez, including fairly drastic reforms to the trading system. Spain had long been notorious for the rigidity of its trade, which featured privileged guilds, regular sailing fleets, authorized ports, and a byzantine roster of duties, fees, restrictions, and prohibitions. The system was based on the principles of mercantilism: that is, it was designed so that the state could enrich itself by controlling every detail of commerce. The thinkers of the Enlightenment criticized the old prescriptions. In 1776, the Scottish economist Adam Smith published his famous book *The Wealth of Nations*, which sweepingly judged the principles of mercantilism to be wrong and suggested that economies work best when they are left free and unregulated. The Spanish Bourbons were not prepared to go that far—the enrichment of the state always remained their priority—but Spain's increasing backwardness with respect to the rest of Europe did indicate that a more relaxed approach might bring benefits. The principal beneficiaries of the restrictive trading system, it seemed, were foreign smugglers, who developed an impressive repertoire of tricks to evade Spain's restrictions.

The changes in the commercial system came about gradually, beginning in the 1770s with the lowering of duties on some items, the legalization of trade between Mexico and other viceroyalties of the Americas, and the opening of new ports. In 1789, the Spanish crown decreed "free trade" throughout the empire, meaning that all ports were opened to trade and the monopolies previously enjoyed by the merchant guilds of Cádiz (in southern Spain) and Mexico City were broken. The economic reforms encountered considerable resistance from those who found their privileged positions under assault, but they also had much support from new groups who benefited. The cotton textile industry of Catalonia, in northeastern Spain, received a tremendous boost, and that in turn stimulated Mexican production of cotton and dyestuffs. In 1795, new trade guilds were established at Veracruz and Guadalajara, and these guilds were able to oversee the construction of new roads that further stimulated commerce. The valley of Puebla-Tlaxcala, located on the Mexico City–Veracruz axis, emerged as a substantial producer of cotton textiles for the domestic market, while Querétaro developed into a major producer of woolens. The quickened pace of industry and trade, in turn, stimulated agriculture, which at least in the central valleys became more commercial and competitive.

Harder Times for the Poor

The quickening pace of the economy during the eighteenth century created new pressures on Mexico's poor, especially the peasants, whose lot had improved somewhat during the previous century. With the revival of mining and trade, cities such as Guadalajara, capital of the wealthy province of New Galicia, grew at a spectacular pace. In 1700, Guadalajara had seven thousand inhabitants, and its chief industry was livestock grazing. By 1820, it had become a vibrant city of some forty thousand, a commercial center supplying imported goods, manufactures, and credit to much of west-central Mexico. Cotton plantations and mills sprang up in the city's environs, and the hinterlands became a major supplier of grain.

The acceleration of the region's economy was accompanied—and partly fueled by—a dramatic increase in population. The Indians, whose disease-ravaged population had bottomed out in the mid-1600s, now recovered their numbers impressively. Villages that had virtually disappeared during the 1600s were reborn. The greater abundance of Indians meant, for Spanish and creole farmers and manufacturers, a greater abundance of labor, one that spared them the need to experiment with labor-saving technologies and allowed them to increase production by simply exploiting their workers more ruthlessly. Land values shot up, wheat became immensely profitable, and haciendas expanded, often at the expense of Indian villages. Indians found themselves lacking sufficient land for their needs, and conflicts between Indian villages and haciendas over land and resources became endemic. There were also new conflicts within the villages themselves, pitting villagers against their own leaders, who often connived with outsiders to enrich themselves and despoil their fellows. The buyers' market for labor meant that wages and working conditions deteriorated. Villagers who had been accustomed to farming in order to feed themselves and their families, perhaps selling a bit of surplus corn on local markets, now found themselves obliged to work as day laborers for pitiful wages on sprawling haciendas. One result of all this was a steep rise in banditry—mostly highway robbery and cattle rustling—in the Guadalajara region, especially after 1780. The miscreants tended to be poor, illiterate, and landless young men. When the wars for independence broke out, some bandit gangs morphed almost seamlessly into rebel gangs.

Just to the east of Guadalajara lay a large area of fertile basin land known as the Bajío (comprising the modern state of Guanajuato and parts of Querétaro and Michoacán), the site of rich silver mines. Before the eighteenth century, the Bajío had presented a marked contrast to much of the Mexican countryside, where miserable Indian villages surrounded vast estates owned by whites. Large estates had existed in the Bajío, of course, but before the mid-eighteenth century there had also been a fair representation of modest commercial farmers, known as rancheros, who grew food for the towns. Even day laborers on the haciendas had been relatively well paid, for estate owners were fairly desperate to attract workers from among the sparse population. The Bajío's silver miners were among the best compensated of all Mexican workers, for in addition to a standard wage double that paid to farm workers, the miners were able to keep whatever ore they mined in excess of a prescribed quota. The *partidos*, as these payments were called, made silver miners the elite of Mexican workers. For mine owners, this was the price they had to pay to attract and keep workers, though most of them bitterly resented the system. But whenever they tried to put an end to the *partidos*, they had to face the wrath of the famously unruly and belligerent miners.

During the second half of the eighteenth century, the enviable situation of farm and mine workers in the Bajío deteriorated quickly. Silver mining, greatly stimulated by Bourbon policies, boomed; commercial farming, set up to supply the mine regions, also boomed. As in Guadalajara, the population increased perhaps fivefold between 1700 and 1810. Successful mine owners, flush with funds from their risky mine ventures, sought to secure their fortunes by purchasing haciendas, seeing them as safer, more predictable investments than mining. They bought out the small-scale rancheros, thus eliminating much of the local middle class. Ordinary workers, their bargaining power eroded by the burgeoning population, faced unemployment and poverty. Farming in the region was also reoriented to serve the needs and desires of a newly powerful elite, who tended to prefer wheat, vegetables, and fruits. Corn and beans—the staple foods of the less well-to-do—were relegated to small plots of poor land worked by impoverished tenants who combined their own meager farming with irregular day labor on the commercial estates.

The dire consequences of these changes became brutally clear in 1785 and 1786 when two years of drought and late frosts wiped out the corn crop. Some 85,000 people—15 percent of the population of the Bajío—starved to death in the resulting famine. Yet even in the darkest days of famine, the large haciendas continued to concentrate on producing the lucrative crops favored by the wealthy rather than retooling to relieve the hunger. Charges were rife that the large haciendas took advantage of the situation by price gouging. The government and church undertook some relief efforts, but these concentrated mostly on provisioning the poor of the towns and cities while leaving rural people to their own devices. Some poor people managed to flee to Mexico City, where the viceroy—Bernardo de Gálvez, brother of José de Gálvez—fretting that they might succumb to the "detestable and prejudicial vice of idleness,"[5] put them to work building roads or consigned them to a recently established "Poor House."

Famine, of course, is not such an uncommon event in peasant societies. Sometimes the sufferers can plausibly blame their plight on the caprices of nature. In 1785–1786, however, the poor of the Bajío understood that their suffering was not the fault of nature, but was part of the same man-made arrangements that had brought such a boon to the wealthy. Moreover, that famine was hardly the end of the poor people's suffering: there were serious famines in 1789–1790 and again in 1809–1810, and even in between those hardest of times, hunger was a fearful phantom stalking the poor. The Bajío would later be a key epicenter of rebellion: the rage of the region's poor against Spaniards, rich creoles, and their profitable estates was as vicious as it was predictable.

Enlightened Despotism

Some of the Bourbons' efforts were probably well-intentioned, but their effects were cruel. Mexican elites of the eighteenth century, enamored of trendy French customs and manners and styles of thought, looked with disdain on the exuberance of the Baroque era, a time when gaudy display was believed to connect somehow to godliness but which now appeared only as the excesses of a superstitious and superficial culture. Prosperity and progress, reason and order: these were the proper goals of a modern, civilized people.

Royal officials—in particular, the Second Count of Revillagigedo, who was viceroy from 1789 to 1794—focused considerable attention on Mexico's capital city, which they hoped to transform from the loud, boisterous place it had become into a model of modernity and decorum, a sort of urban French garden with everything in its place, laid out with both mathematical and aesthetic rectitude. Stinking canals were cleaned, trash collection was improved, streets were cobbled, sidewalks built, trees planted, streetlights installed, feral animals slaughtered, street entertainments curtailed, and drunks and vagabonds rounded up. (The German traveler Alexander von Humboldt described how each morning carts would reconnoiter the city's streets gathering insensate drunkards as if they were dead bodies, later shackling them by the ankles and making them perform street-cleaning duties.) The wealthy soon had places—the Alameda Park downtown, Chapultepec Park at the outskirts—where they could take leisurely strolls on Sunday afternoons, untroubled by the sight of beggars and vagrants.

The poor found these changes quite irritating, and the poor accounted for perhaps 80 percent of the city's population. Of that 80 percent, some 10 percent—perhaps fifteen thousand people— lived by begging or petty thievery. The poor people of the cities— whose ranks were continually swelled by migrants escaping the calamities of the countryside—lived appallingly unglamorous lives, and the ways in which they endured their hardships now came under official scrutiny and attack. Such diversions as bullfights, which had evolved from chivalric beginnings into rowdy popular entertainments, were increasingly seen by elites as savage and bloody spectacles that must be suppressed. *Pulquerías*—cantinas that sold pulque, the fermented maguey juice that was cheap enough to intoxicate the poorest of citizens—also came under the reformers' scrutiny. Drunkenness, lewd dancing, and fighting were standard fare at the *pulquerías*, something that elite reformers saw as a blight. They raised taxes on pulque, increasingly regulated the conditions of its sale, and policed the *pulquerías* to make sure no one had too good a time.

Worst of all, the authorities took aim at popular religious festivities such as the carnival that preceded Lent and the ceremonies of the Day of the Dead. Carnival often involved dancing, drunkenness, strange rituals, and the wearing of costumes that offended the elite. Men dressed as women, the poor sported the frock coats of the rich, and peasants dressed as priests, all to challenge the social order symbolically and to remind everyone that, in the eyes of heaven, all are equal. Ordinances banning such costumes, and prescribing harsh punishments for violators, appeared as early as 1731. Later edicts prohibited religious celebrants from using fireworks or alcohol, or dancing if it involved mingling of the sexes.

These efforts were by no means restricted to the cities. Bourbon reformers sought to suppress anything they deemed to be scandalous, irreverent, wasteful, absurd, or unseemly. Into that broad category fell many of the people's most cherished events: fiestas and carnivals, graphic reenactments of Christ's passion, and parades at Holy Week and Christmas that involved lurid costumes or the brandishing of weapons. The message to the poor seemed to be that not only must they endure increased repression, but they were not even allowed to have fun.

As the eighteenth century drew to its close, many people of all classes in Mexico had cause to complain: creoles were taxed and frozen out of public life, comfortable arrangements were altered in new and uncomfortable ways, the poor got poorer. Perhaps the country would have encountered a serious crisis of some sort in any event, but no one anticipated the bloody outbreak in the offing. Misery in Mexico, though it worsened in the eighteenth century, had been a fact of life for generations; something more was required for discontent to turn to violent and widespread upheaval. That something came in the form of a major meltdown in the mother country.

THREE

CRISIS

In early summer 1809, the rural people of Mexico's highlands sensed the onset of a recurring nightmare. The so-called rainy season was proving to be bone-dry, and their prayers for divine succor went unattended. Corn—the staple food of Mexico's poor—had long since been relegated to the most marginal lands, to be cultivated by the most primitive methods, while the richer soils and irrigation works were reserved for wheat and other grains favored by the well-to-do. Corn, and the hundreds of thousands of lives that depended on corn, were entirely at the mercy of the rain.

This had happened many times before. Older folks had bitter memories of the "year of hunger," 1785–1786, but knowing what to expect did not make the coming famine any easier to endure. By midsummer, stored supplies of corn began to run out, and in November and December, the usual harvest time, the cornstalks were parched and barren. People grew gaunt and weak, ghostly skeletons barely able to move. Some died of starvation or succumbed to disease; others abandoned their homes and villages to scour the countryside for edible weeds, seek work in the cities, or live by begging, crime, or prostitution.

Although Mexico's wealthy folk derided corn as food fit only for the poor, they could not escape the effects of the crisis. High corn prices brought on a general rise in the cost of living. Mine owners and textile manufacturers lacked the funds to buy needed tools and machinery or to replace broken parts. The cost of transportation rose, since most goods were carried on mule trains, and with dwindling food supplies mules could not be fed. The shortage of mules, combined with the general inadequacy of roads, meant there was little hope that food could be brought from regions unaffected by the drought. Livestock perished in the fields, raising the price of meat and depriving farmers of their beasts of burden. Dearth drove wild animals of the forests and mountains into the towns and cities in a desperate search for food. Indians, with no corn to sell and stressed by rising prices, could not make their tribute payments, and the treasury suffered. Bandit gangs multiplied, and armed escorts were needed to protect shipments of corn to granaries. In a perverse twist of fate, the famine happened to coincide with a shortage of mercury, which brought work at the silver mines to a standstill and led to massive unemployment. And, as during previous famines, greed made everything worse as big landowners and shopkeepers sought to profit from the crisis. Some officials—such as Miguel Domínguez, the corregidor (district governor) of Querétaro, and José Antonio Riaño, the intendant of Guanajuato—did what they could to provide relief and to punish speculators, but there were limits to what they could do.

By 1809, the living standards of the people of central Mexico had already been deteriorating for at least two generations, and famines were a dreaded but familiar part of rural life. The poor had endured earlier famines, growing angry at the rich, whom they held responsible for their suffering. But except for the occasional village riot, they had kept their peace, knowing that the authorities could and would crush any uprising with consummate brutality. This time was different. As the poor starved, the Spanish empire began to disintegrate from its center outward, affording the poor an opening to wreak a bloody vengeance upon their oppressors.

According to a curious logic, the vast numbers of poor and oppressed people inhabiting the Spanish empire were a key reason why that empire held together. Their existence meant that, although Mexican creoles chafed under the despotism of the Bourbons, few of them were inclined to challenge the Bourbons' right to rule them. In other parts of America, the recent past furnished sufficient cautionary tales to dim the ardor of most would-be revolutionaries. In the early 1780s, a movement in Peru that had begun as a protest against certain unpopular Bourbon policies spiraled into a nightmarish race war that cost one hundred thousand people their lives. At about the same time, a tax revolt in New Granada (now Colombia) had blossomed into a widespread popular uprising. In the 1790s, a falling-out among the planters of the French West Indian island colony of St. Domingue—later known as Haiti—gave way to a bloody slave rebellion that ended in the death or exile of the colony's entire white population. Mexican creoles were keenly aware that any movement they might start could slide quickly out of their control, and they might themselves be consumed in whatever conflagration ensued.

So, for the most part, the creoles grumbled and bided their time, even as Spanish rule became more and more intolerable. As it happened, the sparks that ignited Mexico's revolution for independence flared on the far side of the ocean.

Spain: War and Weakness

Spain's troubles began in earnest in 1761, when the Spanish Bourbons signed a "Family Compact" with their kinsmen in France and followed them into a losing war against Great Britain. The enmity that developed between Spain and Britain caused the Spanish Bourbons much anxiety. Charles III of Spain complained to his French counterpart that Britain would not be satisfied "unless

they despoil us entirely of the commerce and the riches of the Indies."[1] Britain already controlled several territories—Jamaica, Be-
lize (or British Honduras), the Mosquito Coast of Central America,
the Eastern Seaboard of North America—that, to the consternation of Spain, appeared to have Mexico practically encircled.

In 1779, Spain joined its French allies in aiding Britain's North
American colonists to gain their independence. It was certainly
not admiration for the rebellious colonists' cause that inspired
Spain's intervention, but rather a fear that Britain, should it defeat
the colonists, would have a large army in place in America which
it could easily use to menace Spain's own American possessions.

As it turned out, however, the triumph of the American Revolution brought Spain no relief. Britain did not cease its scheming
to relieve Spain of its New World possessions, and the erstwhile
colony soon emerged as a still more worrisome predator. Even
as the ink was drying on the Treaty of Paris, Spain's top diplomat,
the Count of Aranda, fretted famously that "this federal republic
[the United States] has been born a pigmy, so to speak . . . the
time will come when she will be a giant, and even a colossus, much
to be feared in those vast regions." Events soon justified this
anxiety. In 1787, aspiring Mexican revolutionaries approached
Thomas Jefferson in Paris to request U.S. aid in revolutionizing
Mexico—a request Jefferson, convinced that the Mexicans were
unfit to govern themselves, refused. In 1792, George Rogers
Clark, a hero of the American Revolution who felt his services had
been slighted by the United States, took part in a scheme abetted
by France to liberate Louisiana and New Mexico from Spanish
domination. Eight years later an American mustang smuggler
named Philip Nolan assembled a private army—known as filibusters—and invaded the northern Mexican province of Texas,
where he was killed by Mexican troops in early 1801. And in 1805,
former U.S. vice president Aaron Burr hatched yet another
scheme to seize Texas from Spain.

The American Revolution was also a harbinger of trends that

threatened not only Spain's vast empire, but the very foundations of its political and social order. The most fearsome manifestation of those trends erupted in 1789, when revolutionaries in neighboring France made King Louis XVI—cousin of the Spanish king—a prisoner and published a plan to destroy nearly every vestige of the "old regime." Spain's ruling classes shuddered at the thought of what might become of them should that contagion spread. It threatened to put an end to several cherished institutions and customs: the absolutist monarchy ordained by God, the special privileges of the nobility, the religious monopoly of the Catholic Church.

To further darken Spain's prospects, the competent King Charles III died one year before the French Revolution erupted and was replaced by his son, Charles IV. The most brilliant statesman would have been overmatched by the events that the new king was forced to confront, and Charles IV was far from brilliant. Badly educated, weak-willed, and callow, he seldom allowed affairs of state to interfere with his several hobbies and was content to leave most decision making to his wife and advisers. That might have been a workable method of governance had Charles had a keener eye for talent. As it happened, however, he chose to entrust his government to one Manuel Godoy, who was only twenty-five years old in 1792 when the king made him secretary of state and the most powerful figure in the Spanish government. Godoy had first come to the attention of the royal family in 1788 when, as a member of the palace guard, he had been thrown from his horse as the queen looked on from her coach. The queen apparently admired the aplomb with which the young man picked himself up and remounted, and, according to a widely accepted rumor, she took him as her lover. The king, to his great discredit in the eyes of his subjects, did not seem to mind. In fact, he became perfectly convinced that Godoy—a hardworking but venal and unimaginative man—was a political genius and the only person who could save Spain. The king and queen lavished lands and money and honorary titles on their "favorite." The people of Spain and its colonies quickly grew to despise Godoy, resenting his undeserved rise to wealth and power and the unseemliness of his relations with the royals. The institution of the monarchy, the symbol of all political legitimacy for Spaniards, fell into scandal and disrepute.

Under Godoy, Spain was plunged into a period of unrelieved catastrophe. The French Revolution, from its relatively moderate inception in 1789, grew steadily more radical. In January 1793, the French revolutionaries sent King Louis XVI to the guillotine, Queen Marie Antoinette following him in October. Godoy energetically protested the executions, inspiring the French revolutionaries to declare war on Spain with the avowed intent to "leave no Bourbon on a throne." Spain was in no way prepared for that war. An attempt at alliance with Britain was predictably strained, and by July 1795 Godoy had no choice but to negotiate a peace with France. The new understanding with France left Spain in the humiliating and ruinous position of France's perennial junior partner, forced to supply soldiers, ships, and money to aid the French in their war with Britain.

The alliance with France destroyed Spain's military power and severed it from its empire. A year into the alliance, Britain handed Spain a terrible naval defeat at the Battle of Cape St. Vincent off the coast of Portugal, then went on to blockade the Spanish port of Cádiz and commandeer Spanish ships on the high seas—186 of them in 1798 alone. From that point onward, Spain was effectively cut off from its main source of wealth. Mexican silver could not be reliably imported to Spain, and Spanish mercury—needed by silver miners to refine metal from ore—could not make it to Mexico. Nor was Spain able to supply its colonists with essential goods. In late 1797, Spain grudgingly acknowledged reality by legalizing trade between its American colonies and neutral merchantmen, most of which hailed from the United States. Spain could only watch helplessly as the foreigners' trade with its colonies boomed: in 1798 and 1799, the volume of goods shipped into and out of the port of Veracruz tripled, with Spain benefiting only from the sale of licenses and the collection of duties on neutral shipping. In 1799, Spain tried to revoke the authorization of neutral trade, but could not break through the British blockade, and all parties cheerfully ignored its unenforceable decrees. Spain had forever lost the trade monopoly it had so jealously guarded for almost three hundred years.

Spain continued its debilitating alliance with France after Napoleon Bonaparte came to power in 1799. In October 1804, a British naval squadron captured four Spanish ships bound from Argentina to Cádiz carrying nearly five million pesos in silver. The next year, the British virtually destroyed Spain's fleet at the Battle of Trafalgar. Meanwhile, the Spanish people suffered shortages, high prices, famine, and horrific epidemics of yellow fever and cholera.

In order to pay for its disastrous wars, Spain taxed its colonists mercilessly, seized lands from the church, and contracted loans. The government issued state bonds, known as *vales reales* (royal vouchers), in such massive quantities that they soon became practically worthless. All the while, the royals and Godoy refused to consider scaling back their own lavish lifestyle, nor would they entertain the notion of annoying their aristocratic supporters with new taxes. At long last a group of wealthy nobles and churchmen took to conspiring to replace Charles IV with his son and heir, Ferdinand, Prince of Asturias. Ferdinand's main qualification for the throne seems to be that he despised his parents and Godoy, though he offered no improvement either in wisdom or in virtue. In the words of Spanish historian Salvador de Madariaga, Ferdinand "behaved with all the base stupidity which is his only claim to an unwelcome corner in the memory of men."[2]

The feud within the Spanish House of Bourbon might well have brought the royals to grief in any case, but it was Napoleon who finally brought them to their inglorious—albeit temporary— end. Napoleon had followed up the disaster at Trafalgar by attempting to punish the British economy. His "Continental System" was an effort to reduce Britain to penury by cutting off all of its trade with Europe. By 1807, only two European countries—Sweden and Portugal—were defying the boycott. Napoleon got permission from Charles IV to send his troops into Spain on the pretext of subduing Portugal. In reality, Napoleon's army was an army of occupation. In March 1808, at the behest of Prince Ferdinand, a mob of peasants, workers, and soldiers rioted against Charles IV and Godoy, forcing Charles to abdicate. Ferdinand—now King Ferdinand VII—made a triumphal entry into Madrid. He soon discovered, however, that he was no match for Napoleon in treachery. Surrounded by French troops, Ferdinand could not decline when Napoleon summoned him to the town of Bayonne in southern France and informed him that he, like his father, must abdicate the throne. On that vacant throne Napoleon placed his own elder brother Joseph.

Although many top government officials in Madrid swore allegiance to King Joseph I, the Spanish people were not so acquiescent. They gave the new monarch the rude nickname "Pepe Botellas" (Joe Bottles), in honor of his alleged fondness for strong drink. On May 2, fierce street fighting erupted in Madrid. The fighting in the city was eventually contained, but the violence soon spread to the provinces, launching the Peninsular War, which raged for the next six years.

Meanwhile in Mexico: Hard Times and Drastic Measures

In Mexico as in Spain, the authorities' first reaction to the news of the French Revolution was to stifle it. French merchants and tradesmen operating in Mexico were automatically suspected of seditious intentions and subject to vicious harassment. In 1794, for instance, Mexican authorities arrested a pair of Frenchmen, a doctor and a sea captain, and treated them so harshly that both committed suicide in prison. The authorities went on to subject the hapless Frenchmen to a posthumous auto-da-fé, burning them in effigy and condemning them as heretics, deists, and materialists. The regime even permitted its paranoia to affect important matters of diplomacy, as in 1806, when a clergyman commissioned to make a study of the new boundary formed between the Spanish colony and the United States by the Louisiana Purchase asked permission to seek vital information in some books that had been banned by the Inquisition: permission was denied. No one, it seemed, could be presumed immune from the seductive power of those heretical ideas.

But in fact the threat from the French Revolution to Mexico was probably less philosophical than economic. Spain was embroiled in costly European wars, and those wars had to be paid for somehow. Spain was also desperate to defend its American colonies, most especially Mexico, its treasure chest. The threat was very real, as evidenced in 1806, when a British force of 1,600 men invaded and occupied the South American port city of Buenos Aires, forcing the viceroy to flee for his life. Although the British were eventually evicted from the port by a creole militia—a feat that quickly entered patriotic folklore for creoles throughout Spanish America—it was not far-fetched to imagine that the British might try their hand at invading Veracruz next. Spain came to understand keenly that it would have to beef up its defenses or bid farewell to its American dominions.

Since Spain's treasury was in dire straits, the crown had little choice but to demand that the colonists foot the bill for their own defense. Taxes, which had long been a source of irritation for the colonists, now became positively extortionate. Those exactions affected people of every rank in colonial society, from titled noblemen to impoverished Indian peasants. While Charles IV and Godoy refused to tax their aristocratic supporters in Spain, they had no qualms about attacking the fortunes of the Mexican nobility. The Mexican nobility was a small but fairly bumptious group, and fully fifty-one of the sixty-three titleholders in Mexico in the early 1800s were creoles. One of the chief perquisites of nobility was the entail (*mayorazgo*), a holdover from medieval times, which provided legal assurance that a nobleman's estate would not be sold or divided, but would pass intact down through the generations. Beginning in 1789, the crown tried to raise funds by increasing the cost of establishing an entail, and the price continued to rise until only the richest of the rich could afford it. By 1800, even the richest of the rich had given up.

Spain's troubles created other irritations for the Mexican elite. Silver miners complained that the British blockades disrupted their supplies of mercury, leaving them unable to refine their ore and depriving them of profits. The crown imposed special war taxes on silver, as well as duties on refining and coinage. Livestock raisers were burdened by irksome taxes and bribes at nearly every stage of their operations—when they moved animals through a town, again when they sold them, yet again when they slaughtered them. Farmers who produced sugar or pulque complained loudly of the high taxes on intoxicating beverages. And Spain chronically had its hand out, begging the wealthy to make patriotic donations to help defeat the British foe.

Irksome as such taxes were, they were all outdone by the notorious Law of Consolidation of 1804, a decree that helped make Manuel Godoy one of the arch villains of Mexican history. In the depths of its financial desperation, the crown looked covetously to the wealthiest institution in its realms, the Roman Catholic Church. The 1804 decree ordered the church in Mexico to sell its properties and turn over the proceeds to the crown as a loan. The crown, in turn, planned to use those funds to redeem its royal vouchers—the state bonds it had issued to help finance the wars—and it guaranteed the church a 3 percent return on the money loaned. The crown reckoned that this decree would have benefits beyond the obvious one of providing much-needed funds to the treasury. It expected that renters and mortgage holders would jump at the chance to own their properties outright, causing land to fall out of the inefficient hands of the church and into the eager hands of ambitious entrepreneurs.

The scheme was based on an entirely erroneous assumption, revealing the Spanish government's appalling ignorance of conditions in its own colonies. The church's principal wealth did not consist of land. It consisted, rather, of loaned capital. The church was the only banking institution in the colonies. People from every station and walk of life borrowed money from the church with the expectation that they would pay for their loans at the customary and agreeable rate of 5 percent interest. The economy of colonial Mexico was based almost entirely on such credit, for the voracious mother country had for centuries drained away most of the colony's silver for its own purposes, and hard money was always difficult to come by. The holders of church loans were by no means all rich. Churches and convents in rural areas controlled their own funds, and they lent money to struggling small farmers as well as to miners and land barons. Church capital comprised some two-thirds of all the capital circulating in Mexico, and perhaps 90 percent of all enterprises in the viceroyalty were indebted to the church. The Law of Consolidation, in effect, called in every loan in Mexico and raised the threat that essential credit—practically the only thing that enabled the economy to operate at all—would dry up.

Mexicans, facing unimaginable payments and possible ruin, howled in protest. Some officials in other parts of Spanish America had the good sense not to enforce the noxious decree. Mexico had the misfortune to be governed at the moment by José de Iturrigaray, a creature of Godoy. Rivaling Godoy himself in greed and corruption, Iturrigaray was known to permit and participate in smuggling operations, graft, illicit sale of offices and military ranks, and other improprieties. He, along with the archbishop and royal tax collector, was permitted to keep a certain percentage of the funds collected—in effect, a commission for enforcing the decree. Together, these officials managed to appropriate for them-

selves a half million pesos out of the twelve million collected between 1805 and 1808, when the decree was suspended. Adding
insult to injury, Godoy handed some five million pesos in Consolidation funds over to Napoleon Bonaparte. Manuel Abad y Queipo,
the reformist archbishop of Michoacán, made a dire prediction:
"Enforcement of the Consolidation will cause insurrection inevitably."[3] An overstatement, perhaps, but the Consolidation policy surely caused many Mexicans to wonder what benefit they
derived from a mother country that seemed to have become an in-
satiable leech.

The Problem of Defense

The goal of Spain's tax policies—to acquit the country well in its
wars in Europe and to defend its colonies—went unmet even despite the policies' voracity and arbitrariness. As late as the 1750s,
Mexico's defenses consisted of only a palace guard at Mexico City
and handfuls of soldiers at the ports of Veracruz and Acapulco.
Britain, had it taken a notion to do so, could easily have overrun
the colony. Even as late as 1794, while Spain fought revolutionary
France, fewer than five thousand soldiers defended Mexico. In addition to defending its coasts against foreign incursion, Mexico
needed to shore up its defenses on the northern frontiers, where
hostile Indians and foreign interlopers constantly threatened.

Had its fortunes been less tormented, Spain might have realized
its ideal of stationing a sizable professional army of Spaniards—
or at least one led by Spanish officers—in the colonies. But that
was an expensive proposition, and Spain was broke. Spanish officers, for their part, had no desire to serve in faraway places among
people they derided as miserable savages. And in any case, Spain's
leaders reckoned it was far more urgent to rebuild Spain's naval
forces for use in the European wars, so colonial defense had to be
accomplished on the cheap. The only real alternative was to create a tiny force of regulars and supplement it with much larger

forces of provincial militias and reserves, which at least theoretically could be quickly mobilized in case of emergency. The units were to be paid for with highly unpopular taxes on grain, flour, liquor, and chocolate, plus occasional "special" taxes in cases of shortfall. Landowners complained that they were often required to provide expensive and onerous upkeep for the military's animals.

After 1796, when Spain went to war with Britain, military concerns and expenses escalated rapidly, and taxes rose accordingly, as did the size of the colony's military forces. In 1806 and 1807, when there were genuine fears of a British invasion, Viceroy Iturrigaray had the satisfaction of being able to muster an army of sixteen thousand troops. Yet despite the stepped-up taxes, Mexico's military forces were perpetually underfunded. Soldiers went unpaid, wore rags for uniforms, rode on worn-out saddles, and carried shoddy or dysfunctional weapons cast off by the more advanced armies of Europe. In 1798, to cite one instance, Mexico was hoodwinked into buying a large shipment of rejected British muskets that weighed a whopping twenty-one pounds each. The muskets could barely be hoisted, let alone accurately aimed.

Worse yet, the regulars and the militias both had to be staffed with the only personnel available, namely creoles and castes (Indians, blacks, and some castes were not allowed to serve). The dangers of such a policy were grave and manifold: the militias would inevitably be dispersed among the various regions of Mexico, which could put power in the hands of local interests that could end up challenging the royal government. Officer commissions, according to the militia plan that was eventually adopted, were to be sold for hefty fees to well-heeled creoles eager to add a status-enhancing military title to their name. That would help defray the costs of the militias, but as far as conservative royal officials were concerned it would be placing weapons, men, and authority in the hands of persons whose loyalty to the crown was suspect.

Then there was the serious problem of recruitment. Mexicans, by and large, had little taste for military life. Most had heard horror stories about conditions at Veracruz, the most vulnerable point in the country and hence the one most in need of defending. Tropical diseases made Veracruz a death sentence for a shockingly large percentage of people sent there (a yellow fever epidemic in 1799 killed some 875 men out of a garrison of 4,000; another 358 deserted). The appearance of recruiters in a village was enough to send able-bodied men scurrying to the hills. To fill the ranks, authorities took to rounding up vagabonds, petty criminals, gamblers, drunkards, and even children as young as eight years old. Not surprisingly, these conscripts did not make the most impressive fighting men. Forced levies also alienated people, especially given that recruiters often brutally mistreated and extorted money from their unfortunate victims.

The matter of recruitment also exacerbated class resentments. Wealthy people were able to purchase exemptions from service, and venal subdelegates were eager to sell them those exemptions at scandalous prices; nobles, government officials, students, mine workers and technicians, muleteers, and churchmen were exempt from service. By 1807, Viceroy Iturrigaray was desperate enough to order that, if sufficient recruits could not be found, castes that had previously been considered racially unqualified, and even Indians, would have to be mobilized. Meanwhile, Spanish and creole officers scorned their dark-skinned recruits as lazy, drunken, immoral flotsam—Félix Calleja, who led the royalist forces during the early phases of the independence wars, described Mexico as a "desert . . . filled with monsters"[4]—and fretted that they would prove unreliable in defending the kingdom against foreign foes. Colonial authorities also feared that the army's other chief concern—defending Mexico against internal uprisings—was quite possibly hopeless. Far from being a defense against internal uprisings, the regulars and militias might instead become the means for such uprisings.

Crisis in Mexico

Unofficial word of Godoy's downfall and the abdication of the Spanish kings arrived in Mexico in June 1808, during the annual Pentecost festivities. Viceroy Iturrigaray, who at the time was amusing himself at the cockfights at San Augustín de las Cuevas, waited three days to order public demonstrations in honor of Ferdinand VII.

The delay was irksome to partisans of Spanish imperialism. Rumors ran that Iturrigaray was less than pleased to hear of Godoy's misfortunes, for Godoy had been his chief patron in the Spanish government. He was also allegedly heard to mutter, in a tone of satisfaction, that the king would never return to the throne. Suspicion was kindled that perhaps the unpopular viceroy harbored treasonous designs. Still, on July 28, when news of the abdications was officially confirmed by dispatch from Madrid, Iturrigaray was quick to declare, very much in accordance with the general wishes of the people of Mexico, that the Mexicans would never recognize Joseph Bonaparte as their sovereign. Celebrations were noisy and prolonged, complete with the firing of guns, the ringing of bells, the singing of Te Deums, shouts of allegiance to Ferdinand VII, and the hanging in effigy of Napoleon and Godoy.

But if Mexicans were largely in agreement as to what they would *not* do, precisely what they *would* do was an open question. Some Mexicans—especially creole patriots—held that Mexico should follow the example of several provinces of Spain, which, upon hearing of the Napoleonic usurpation, had formed provincial juntas to govern autonomously until Ferdinand VII could be restored to his throne. But the people of Mexico were experiencing something altogether unprecedented, a moment both exciting and terrifying. Tradition counted for a great deal. The knowledge that there was a king in Madrid was as natural and as comforting as the thought that God was in heaven. And even though the institution of kingship had suffered its share of calamities recently—

the executions of the king and queen of France by revolutionaries and the debasement of the monarchy by Charles IV and his adulterous queen—the legitimacy of king and church was something that few Mexicans of any race or station questioned. Mexicans also generally agreed that they despised Napoleon and the godless French. Beyond that, however, disagreements were profound— and the crisis of 1808 made them impossible to suppress or ignore.

First to act was a faction that advocated Mexican autonomy. The leading, and most radical, theorist of autonomy was a Mercedarian friar from Peru named Melchor de Talamantes, who made some bold proposals in a series of pamphlets. He argued that Spanish political tradition anticipated the possibility that a king might be absent or incapacitated. In such a circumstance, Talamantes said, sovereignty should fall to the people of the empire. The upshot was clear: Mexicans, said Talamantes and his fellow autonomists, were now free to govern themselves as they pleased. Talamantes ventured further into dangerous territory by proposing that Mexicans take advantage of the current crisis to effect some necessary reforms: they should abolish the Inquisition, as well as the special privileges enjoyed by the clergy; they should also introduce free trade and adopt reforms to promote industry and agriculture. To conservatives, making such crucial decisions without the blessings of Spain was simply treasonous. Some conservatives went so far as to charge that the formation of a junta would be an inevitable step toward the eventual destruction of the monarchy, which in turn would open the way for Protestantism and all manner of other heresies and immoralities.

On July 19, the *ayuntamiento* (city council) of Mexico City, which was composed mostly of creoles, asked Viceroy Iturrigaray to assume provisional leadership of Mexico and to convoke a junta, or committee, composed of representatives of the cities of Mexico, to advise him. Iturrigaray found the suggestion agreeable enough—he was, in fact, open to just about any suggestion that would maintain him in power and thus protect his large illicit fortune—but the proposal was instantly rejected by the *audiencia*, which was dominated by Spaniards. The *ayuntamiento* and the *audiencia* represented the two principal currents of elite opinion in Mexico, and the fault lines between them were made glaringly evident by the crisis. Each group figured that, if change was coming, it should be the one to lead it and benefit from it. While few at this time made so bold as to speak openly of independence, some surely entertained that sinful thought.

On August 9, 1808, Iturrigaray convoked an open meeting of prominent citizens—both creole and peninsular—to advise him on how to proceed. The debate was heated and the viceroy was memorably cranky. The representatives could not agree on the fundamental points. Some wanted to recognize the sovereignty of the Junta of Seville, the most prominent of several provisional bodies that had established themselves in Spain to oppose Bonaparte and govern in Ferdinand's name. Others wanted to form a junta of their own. Still others argued that they should wait until they had more information before doing anything at all. In the end, all they could agree upon was that Ferdinand VII was their rightful king and that they would reject any decree or representative from the French usurper.

Tensions grew sharper when a pair of representatives of the Junta of Seville arrived in Mexico City at the end of August and demanded that Iturrigaray swear his allegiance or face immediate arrest. Iturrigaray explained to the representatives that he found their tone impolite, that the Junta of Seville was but one of several contending provincial juntas, and that he would await further developments before swearing allegiance to anything. This was a perfectly reasonable attitude to take, but under the circumstances it aroused much suspicion from conservatives, who were coming increasingly to believe that the viceroy's apparent caution was inspired by ambition. Iturrigaray increased their suspicions when he sent out circulars to the *ayuntamientos* of Mexico's principal cities asking them to send representatives to a provisional congress. To conservatives, it appeared as though the viceroy was moving more and more in the direction favored by the creole autonomists.

Conservatives had grave misgivings even apart from the matter of the viceroy's apparent defiance of all Spanish authority. The viceroy had made himself unpopular with his blatant graft and favoritism. Some suspected he was playing a cynical game, hoping that events might develop in such a way that he could, with creole support, end up on the throne of an independent Mexico. The matter of gravest concern, however, was that Iturrigaray's vacillations gave people the impression that the government was in disarray, and conservatives were acutely aware that disarray among the ruling classes could invite upheaval from below. Should the poor decide to take advantage of the confusion for their own ends, the results would surely be disastrous for the whites of the kingdom. Conservatives, accordingly, decided to overthrow the viceroy.

To pave the way for their intended coup, conservatives created military units known as the Volunteers of Ferdinand VII. A wealthy Spanish meat and sugar merchant named Gabriel de Yermo somewhat reluctantly accepted command of the conspiracy. Yermo assembled a small army of conspirators supplemented by freed slaves from his own plantations. A little after midnight on September 15, the conspirators quietly assembled under the portals of the capital's main plaza, across from the viceroy's palace. They had previously taken care to assure themselves of the cooperation of the officers of the palace guard, a unit that the merchants of the capital had financed. Despite this precaution, as they entered the palace, one young guard, who was unaware of the plan, challenged the conspirators and was shot dead—the night's only bloodshed. The invaders discovered Iturrigaray asleep, arrested him, and sent him to the headquarters of the Inquisition along with his two eldest sons. He was soon dispatched to Spain, where he was tried for and later cleared of treason charges, though he was still being investigated for embezzlement and an assortment of other crimes when he died in 1815. The Volunteers chose as interim viceroy a doddering eighty-year-old field marshal named Pedro de Garibay. Conservatives claimed a victory for themselves and for Spain, but by this time the forces of rebellion were already gathering.

A general mood of panic and uncertainty overtook Mexico. Armed groups roamed the streets of Mexico City, and rumors were rampant. The new authorities ordered the arrest of several prominent creole advocates of autonomy, two of whom—Melchor de Talamantes and José Primo de Verdad—died days later in prison, giving the creoles the first martyrs to their impending struggle and adding considerably to their outrage. The new rulers hurriedly summoned the royalist dragoon regiment to Mexico City with instructions to restore public order, and they created a governing junta that they hoped could control the increasingly volatile situation.

Conspiracies

No one imagined that the elderly General Garibay was genuinely in command of the situation. Although he was considered honorable and was well liked, Garibay was so feeble that he could not hold a pen and had to sign documents with a stamp, and he suffered a stomach ailment that obliged him to lean on a servant whenever he sallied forth into the streets. His long military career had reduced him to dire poverty, and despite his high military rank, he was weak-willed and vacillating. But the conservatives figured that Garibay would serve their purposes well enough until Spain saw fit to honor their request that it send an energetic and resolute viceroy—preferably one accompanied by five or six thousand crack Spanish troops. In the interim they would make do with a puppet, and Garibay was willing to play that role. He granted the conservatives their every wish: ordering creole militias out of the city, sending funds to the Junta of Seville, abolishing taxes on meat, and ordering all residents of Mexico City to sport badges bearing the name of Ferdinand VII.

But Garibay and his handlers confronted a situation that grew constantly more menacing. Mexicans had certainly done their share of grumbling in the past, but their abiding respect for their distant king and their august traditions had tended to keep their more mutinous inclinations in check. But now a threshold had been crossed. A common rallying cry for Spanish American rebellions was a seemingly contradictory sentiment: "Long live the king! Death to bad government!" The king, in this conception, was a remote, semidivine figure who would surely right all wrongs if he only knew about them. "Bad government" meant those venal local authorities with whom people were obliged to deal in their day-to-day lives, mere mortals who abused their power at every turn. Now the king was a hostage, and the mere mortals had taken charge. In the capital, anonymous fliers and broadsides ridiculing or excoriating the authorities began appearing on the walls of buildings or were found scattered on the floors of cathedrals. Mexico City residents would awaken to find scurrilous graffiti and vulgar caricatures of Mexico's most prominent men painted on the walls of churches, and coins circulated on which the king's likeness had been grossly disfigured. There were similar stirrings in the provinces. The government did its best to assert its control, sending ragged and illiterate workers to whitewash the offensive slogans and pictures from the walls, meanwhile issuing harrowing decrees threatening harsh consequences for any who would "alter the peace and fidelity of the Kingdom." The Inquisition set up a force of detectives to chase down malefactors; hand-operated printing presses were outlawed; and rewards were offered for information leading to the arrest of dissidents. Garibay issued proclamations instructing the public to show their loyalty to Spain by contributing money to Spain's defense and ignoring the exhortations of traitors.

Such initiatives did little to cool the growing fervor. During Holy Week of 1809, when news reached Mexico of reverses suffered in Spain by the Spanish army, some creoles celebrated openly. As the conservative regime grew more paranoid, it re-

sorted to increasingly harsh and desperate measures, most of
which only inflamed the situation further. Garibay created a special tribunal to hear cases of sedition, and a handful of people
were arrested and tried under its jurisdiction.

In view of the manifest fact that Garibay was not effectively
squashing the growing agitation, the junta removed him in July
1809 and replaced him with the archbishop, Francisco Javier de
Lizana y Beaumont. Lizana, like Garibay, was genial and virtuous,
and his loyalty to Spain seemed beyond doubt—he even contributed his salary as viceroy to the defense of Spain. But also like
Garibay, Lizana was old, colorless, and ailing, often forced to dispatch his viceregal duties from a sickbed. Carlos María de Bustamante, a prominent lawyer, statesman, and historian of the day,
considered Lizana's most notable characteristic to be that he was
"as ingenuous as a child"—not, perhaps, the most auspicious trait
for a head of state under such perilous circumstances.[5]

It fell to Lizana to handle the first genuine conspiracy aimed at
overthrowing the conservative junta. The conspiracy was centered
in the provincial town of Valladolid, some two hundred miles west
of Mexico City. Its leader was José María Obeso, captain of the
town's militia regiment. Obeso was joined by an assortment of
modestly distinguished provincial creoles: priests, monks, military
men, and lawyers. Their aim was to overthrow the Mexico City
junta and form their own caretaker government in the name of
Ferdinand VII. They set the date of December 21, 1809, for the
outbreak of the uprising. The conspirators were assured of the cooperation of a fair number of both regular military and militiamen, and they expected to raise an army of perhaps twenty
thousand Indians by promising them relief from tribute payments.
Unfortunately for the Valladolid conspirators, the plot was betrayed to the authorities, and a young army officer named Agustín
de Iturbide, later a major player in the independence drama, arrested them. They were put on trial and ably defended by Carlos
María de Bustamante, who argued that the conspirators' only of-

fense was that they were plotting to save Mexico from a French invasion. Lizana listened sympathetically to Bustamante's prescient argument that "the day the first insurgent is hanged, Spain must abandon any hope of holding on to America." The viceroy ordered only very mild punishments: the militia officers were assigned to different units, and the rest were set free, though they were instructed not to leave Valladolid.

The Valladolid conspirators clearly had few reservations about mobilizing the impoverished masses. Many creoles, however, had the same apprehensions regarding Indians and castes that had inspired Gabriel de Yermo to overthrow Viceroy Iturrigaray. Provincial creoles were well aware that, even while the Spanish regime came unraveled, the provincial poor were suffering the devastating impact of a horrible famine, that their living conditions had been deteriorating steadily for years, and that they held white people responsible for their plight. The poor, in the view of many creoles, were ignorant, bitter, vengeful, and ruled by the basest passions. The essential question was troubling indeed: If the Indians and castes were given weapons and license to fight, just who or what would they fight for?

FOUR

THE QUERÉTARO CONSPIRACY

The disruption of the Valladolid conspiracy did nothing to discourage other plotters intent on overthrowing the junta at Mexico City. The most serious conspiracy was centered in the city of Querétaro, on the eastern fringe of the Bajío. Like their predecessors, these schemers planned to exploit Indian and caste discontent in order to build an army, as there simply were not enough disgruntled creole soldiers to form a credible force. When, for logistical reasons, they had to abandon their initial plan to launch their revolution from the popular religious festival of San Juan de los Lagos, they took to discussing other means of appealing to the poor.

They were well aware that they could not hope to attract an army of Indians and castes by trumpeting their true motivation for the rebellion, namely, to put political power in the hands of creoles like themselves. They also knew that few of those Indians and castes would fight in the name of independence from Spain: the poor, while they hated Spaniards, had great reverence for king and church, which were the very essence of the imperial system. Worse yet, the devotion of the poor to the Spanish king made perfect sense, and for reasons that were unlikely to work in the creoles' favor. During the long colonial centuries, the poor had been constantly assured that their king was a benevolent father who was solicitous of the needs of the lowliest of his subjects, even as God tended to all souls, loving and judging them equally. From time to time, instructions to protect the lives and property of the poor drifted down through the byzantine colonial bureaucracy, and invariably such orders bore the king's imprimatur and were executed in his name. If corruption and venality entered into the process, the poor usually blamed lesser creole and Spanish officials for perverting the royal will.

The conspirators planned, like their predecessors in the Valladolid conspiracy, to promise relief from the hated tribute payments, but that alone was unlikely to inspire the poor to risk life and limb. They were left with only one real option: they would have to make their revolution in the name of the rightful king, Ferdinand VII, and the Holy Catholic Church, both of which were imperiled by the radical, atheistic French. They would sell their revolution as a war in defense of religion and tradition.

The conspirators made a catastrophic miscalculation: they expected to topple the junta with a quick and decisive blow. The war would be over, they hoped, before the common folk had time to realize that their own cause had little to do with that of their leaders.

The Rebel Priest

At the center of the conspiracy was Miguel Hidalgo y Costilla, a fifty-seven-year-old parish priest. Hidalgo's résumé seemed to make him the ideal choice to lead the revolt. As a parish priest in a densely populated region, he had clout with the common people. Hidalgo, in fact, had a greater claim to credibility among the poor than most of his colleagues, many of whom routinely derided the poor as the *chusma*, the unredeemed rabble. Hidalgo had been raised in the country, having spent most of his formative years on his father's Bajío hacienda, San Diego Corralejo, near the rich silver mining city of Guanajuato. As a boy he had been surrounded by Indian servants and field hands and their children, and he was remarkably free of the racial prejudice common to many whites in Mexico. While all rural priests were supposed to learn native languages, in practice most spoke those tongues badly or not at all. Hidalgo, apparently, was quite competent in Tarascan, Náhuatl, and Otomí, the indigenous languages of his home region. During the 1790s, while he was parish priest at San Felipe de los Herreros, a small village to the south of Guanajuato, his home was nicknamed "La Francia Chiquita" (Little France), not so much because Hidalgo was a notorious Francophile, but because he had a custom of inviting Indians and castes into his drawing room to mingle and dance with creoles and Spaniards on terms approaching *égalité*. He continued this practice in all of his other priestly postings.

But Hidalgo's appeal was not restricted to the poor, and this is why his fellow conspirators chose him unanimously to lead the revolution: Hidalgo seemed to offer something for everyone. As a man of the cloth and a former university rector, he should prove reassuring to conservative creoles who feared the revolution might take a radical turn, wrecking tradition, property, and propriety. Hidalgo got along with peninsular Spaniards as easily as he did with creoles, castes, and Indians. He was a close friend of the Spanish archbishop of Michoacán and of the Spanish intendant of Guanajuato, the highest-ranking representatives of church and state in his region. He had been born into a respectable if not wealthy family, and his own racial "purity" was undisputed. He was an established member of the Bajío elite. Surely he would think twice before betraying his own social class.

Hidalgo's biography, in fact, contained some details that might have proved troubling to creoles of a conservative turn of mind. As a young student at the Jesuit College of San Francisco Javier in the town of Valladolid, which he entered in 1765 at the age of twelve, he had come under the influence of the creole historian

Francisco Javier Clavigero, who would later run afoul of the Spanish authorities when he published his *Ancient History of Mexico*, a book that lauded Indians and portrayed the Spanish conquistadors as brutal savages. Although Clavigero left the college shortly before Hidalgo arrived and the two men never met, his influence there remained strong. Thanks largely to Clavigero, the Jesuit fathers at San Francisco Javier attacked the hidebound scholasticism that was so characteristic of the Spanish empire, with its stultifying dread of straying too far from the holy writ and the philosophers of antiquity. Hidalgo studied mathematics, biology, experimental physics, geography, modern languages, and history, as well as more routine topics such as theology and rhetoric. In 1767, Hidalgo's schooling was rudely interrupted by the sudden expulsion of the Jesuits from Mexico, which forced the College of San Francisco Javier to close its doors. The expulsion of the Jesuits surely had a lasting impact on Hidalgo.

Hidalgo next enrolled in the College of San Nicolás Obispo in Valladolid, where he devoted himself to his studies for the next twelve years. In 1770, he received his bachelor of arts degree, and three years later he took a degree in theology. In 1776, he joined the faculty of San Nicolás Obispo, and in 1778, at age twenty-six, he was ordained a priest. After fourteen years as professor and treasurer, Hidalgo ascended to the position of rector of the college. His salary was handsome enough to enable him to buy three haciendas, and his prestige was at its height. He was able to reform the college's curriculum along the same lines that Francisco Javier Clavigero had done at the Jesuit College of San Francisco Javier: that is, he de-emphasized musty scholasticism in favor of a more dynamic and "positive" approach to pedagogy.

Hidalgo's adventurous ideas regarding religion and the church may have angered his more conservative colleagues, which could partly account for his next, and most puzzling, career move. In 1792, he abruptly resigned his prestigious post as rector of the College of San Nicolás Obispo and took a job as parish priest of Colima, a city some 240 miles west of Valladolid. Parish priests were the least prestigious—and lowest-paid—members of the secular clergy. Hidalgo's penchant for controversial ideas was likely not the sole reason for this strange demotion, however. He also seems to have mismanaged the college's funds as treasurer, turning a healthy surplus of two thousand pesos into a deficit nearly four times that amount. More damning yet was his lifestyle, which showed a blithe indifference toward spiritual matters and a hearty appetite for the things of this world. He was an inveterate gambler who racked up an impressive amount of personal debt. During his time at San Nicolás Obispo he had an affair with one woman who eventually, complaining of his "unrestrained" conversation, left him to enter a Carmelite nunnery; lived openly with another mistress who bore him a son and a daughter; and fathered yet another son by yet another mistress.

It is possible, of course, that Hidalgo's sudden departure from his rectorship was his own idea—the available documents say nothing to indicate it was a disciplinary measure. Perhaps he craved a less stressful existence, one that would allow him to indulge his various passions far from the censorious scrutiny of colleagues. At Colima, and during later posts in Guanajuato, Hidalgo gave free rein to his earthy predilections. He indulged his love for music by assembling a full orchestra, which performed for events both sacred and profane. He created a theater where he directed performances of his own translations of Racine and Molière, meanwhile finding the time to sire a pair of daughters with his lead actress. At his home he hosted dances, card games, and *tertulias*—informal discussions of literature, science, art, and industry—with the local intelligentsia.

Occasionally, discussions would range into dangerous territory. While visiting friends during Easter Week in 1800, he apparently tried to have a bit of fun with some very literal-minded friars by making a few purposely unsettling statements. He announced that popes were not merely fallible, but some of them had been downright stupid, and the church on the whole was led by ignoramuses; he questioned the virgin birth of Christ and opined that fornication was not necessarily sinful; and he read from a French book that claimed the Koran contained more truth than the Bible. The friars, apparently a mirthless pair, were unamused. One of them reported Hidalgo to the Holy Inquisition, which immediately launched an investigation.

The inquisitors were able to gather some titillating hearsay about Hidalgo: that he routinely derided kings and popes, for example, and that he was known to lament the superstitious nature of Mexico's Indians. His ex-mistress even emerged from her nunnery with a lurid tale of how she used to help the padre procure women with whom he could "sin." But few of Hidalgo's critics were willing to testify under oath, and the charges failed to stick. The Inquisition cleared Hidalgo in 1801, but the mere fact of having been investigated was enough to tarnish his reputation. Hidalgo lived circumspectly for a time, perhaps partly owing to the investigation but also because he was in a financially embarrassed condition. In 1803—the same year that José de Iturrigaray assumed his duties as Mexico's viceroy—Hidalgo's brother Joaquín died. Joaquín had been parish priest of Dolores, a dusty town of some 15,000 residents in the intendancy of Guanajuato. It was to Dolores that Miguel Hidalgo now relocated, to assume the priestly duties of his late brother.

Hidalgo moved into his brother's old house, a block from the town's main square and practically in the shadow of the elegant Cathedral of Nuestra Señora de Dolores (Our Lady of Sorrows), with its facade of rose-colored limestone and twin bell towers decorated in the intricate churrigueresque style. The town, situated some forty miles northeast of the intendancy seat at Guanajuato, was surrounded by hilly, dry scrubland that had long served only for grazing cattle and sheep but which, at the time of Hidalgo's arrival, was being used increasingly for precarious corn crops, a hopeful hedge against the bitter famines that periodically ravaged the region. In Dolores, Hidalgo—prompted, perhaps, by the rigors of life amid so harsh a landscape—took to delegating nearly all of his religious duties to his assistant while he concentrated on ambitious projects to improve the local economy, as well as his own fortune. He founded a ceramic workshop to create colorful *talavera* pottery, a product for which the town is still famous. On an hacienda close to town he planted a grove of mulberry trees and began experimenting with silk making. He founded a tanning workshop that made leather for shoes, an industry that was gaining importance in Guanajuato. He established shops for carpentry, harness making, blacksmithing, and wool weaving. He imported swarms of bees from Havana and began producing significant quantities of honey. He even dabbled in some areas—winemaking, olive growing—that threatened to run afoul of Spanish economic policy, which discouraged colonials from making products that would compete with those of Spain. Hidalgo surely did play an important role in stimulating the local economy, even though, with the qualified exception of ceramics, none of his enterprises enjoyed spectacular financial success.

Despite a demonstrated flair for theology, Hidalgo's interests clearly inclined more toward the material than the unseen world. His priestly vocation gave him ample free time, social respectability, and at least a modest income, but it was hardly a calling. He was nevertheless a figure of some standing in the Bajío, a man with solid connections to the government and oligarchy of the region. Lucas Alamán, who later became the dean of Mexico's conservatives, lived as a youth in Guanajuato with his comfortable creole family, and clearly recalled seeing the priest—a family friend—up close. He later provided a vivid description:

> [Father Hidalgo] was of middling stature, stoop-shouldered, dark-complexioned, and with lively green eyes, his head a bit slumped over his chest, his hair very white and balding, as if he had already passed the age of sixty, but vigorous, al-

though neither active nor quick in his movements: a man of few words in ordinary dealings, but animated when arguing in the collegial style, as when he entered heatedly into some dispute. Rather disheveled in his dress, he did not wear anything but what the small town priests normally wore at that time. (This was a cloak of black wool with a round hat and a large walking stick, and a suit of knee breeches, waistcoat, and jacket made from a kind of wool that came from China and was called Rompecoche.)[1]

His several qualifications notwithstanding, Hidalgo did not look or act much like a man who would shortly launch a bloody revolution.

The Conspirators

At Dolores, Hidalgo made the acquaintance of a number of individuals who shared with him some crucial traits and attitudes. They were creoles who felt that their hard work and extraordinary ambitions had netted them only the most meager rewards, while peninsular Spaniards dominated trade, the administration, the professions, and the choicest properties. Those creoles, though not exactly impoverished themselves, resented the rich and denounced the policies that seemed to perpetuate the glaring and growing divisions of class. The crises unfolding in both Spain and Mexico seemed to offer them a brilliant opportunity to correct those divisions by making a revolution.

Among Hidalgo's comrades in sedition were military men, merchants, farmers, ranchers, and priests. Ignacio Allende, who became second-in-command of the movement, was born in 1769 in the town of San Miguel el Grande, in the very heart of the Bajío, the son of a respected Spanish merchant who, by the time of his son's birth, was in straitened circumstances. The elder Allende died while Ignacio was still young, leaving him, his two brothers, and his widowed mother nearly destitute. Fortunately, his father's business partner, who was executor of the estate, was able to satisfy the elder Allende's debts and set up a trust to support the surviving family members, if not in high style, at least with sufficient funds to live "honorably." With little hope of serious affluence, Allende opted for a military career. In 1795, when Spain's increasing difficulties in European power politics had inspired a new preoccupation with defense of the colonies, new militia units were organized throughout Mexico, including the Eighth Brigade of Querétaro. That same year, Allende joined his hometown regiment of that brigade, the Queen's Provincial Dragoons. By 1808, he was captain in command of the regiment.

Allende cut a striking figure. He was tall and powerfully built, with curly red hair, robust whiskers, blue eyes, and a prominent, slightly crooked nose. He had a passion for bullfights and rodeos, and loved to dress in the gaudy *charro* outfit of the Mexican cowboy. A bullring mishap had left him with only partial use of his left arm, but even so he remained the prototypical Mexican macho: it was said he was strong enough to hold back a bull by the horns; his skills in horsemanship and military exercises were unparalleled, his amorous adventures the stuff of legend. He is known to have fathered several children, though he publicly acknowledged only one son. None of his children was born to his wife, who died shortly after he married her in 1802, leaving a fortune that was immediately tied up in tortuous litigation. Ignacio Allende was dashing, somewhat reckless, at least moderately well-to-do, and forty years old at the time he began conspiring to overthrow the government.

Among the other prominent conspirators were thirty-eight-year-old Juan Aldama, like Allende a captain in the Queen's Provincial Dragoons, and his thirty-year-old brother Ignacio, who had abandoned his law practice to engage in commerce, bankrolled by a rich Spaniard who apparently admired his honesty and dedication. The Aldama brothers, like Allende, were sons of a

Spanish immigrant who had done reasonably, but not spectacularly, well in Mexico—he was manager of an *obraje*, or textile workshop, owned by the Canal family, the richest in San Miguel el
Grande. Together, the brothers owned a small store, and by the
1790s they were able to purchase a modest and struggling hacienda called Charco de Araujo.

The youngest of the major conspirators was Mariano Abasolo,
also a captain in the Queen's Dragoons. Abasolo was twenty-six
years old in 1810, a resident of Dolores. He had inherited a substantial fortune from his father and supplemented that fortune by
marrying the daughter of a rich Spanish landowner. He owned
two haciendas as well as a two-story home in Dolores. Abasolo's
wealth seems to have been his principal virtue as far as his fellow
conspirators were concerned, for he played only a tangential role
and would later end up saving himself from execution by testifying
against his comrades. His wife vehemently opposed the conspiracy
and tried to talk Abasolo out of it.

Easily the most prominent and distinguished of the conspirators was Miguel Domínguez, the corregidor (district governor) of
Querétaro. The city of Querétaro, the seat of a prosperous district, had enjoyed tremendous growth during the eighteenth century, emerging as Mexico's fourth-largest city. By the end of that
century, Querétaro and its environs had become Mexico's principal manufacturer of woolen textiles, a major grower of wheat and
corn, a leading producer of tobacco products under the government's tobacco monopoly, and home to some of Mexico's wealthiest convents and most opulent churches. Yet despite the city's
wealth and importance, the creoles of Querétaro had many complaints. Peninsular Spaniards, who accounted for only a quarter of
the city's white population, overwhelmingly dominated commerce
and the professions, and they held most of the prized positions in
the colonial bureaucracy—the customs office, the post office, tax
collections, and the tobacco monopoly and factory. Spaniards also
monopolized the highest ranks of the regional militia. With the

fortunes they made in trade, they were able to buy *obrajes* and the best haciendas.

Miguel Domínguez, a creole, was appointed corregidor of Querétaro in 1801 by the viceroy. That appointment placed Domínguez among the most powerful and most handsomely paid men in Mexico, for a *corregimiento* was on par with an intendancy and its top official was responsible for a vast array of responsibilities: he oversaw tax collection, military recruitment, and the administration of justice; monitored economic activity; and attended to public works. Domínguez was, in fact, among the very few creoles to earn such an exalted position, and by all accounts he acquitted his duties with admirable honesty, efficiency, and compassion. In the bargain, he acquired his share of powerful enemies. Early in his tenure he was commissioned to investigate working conditions in the *obrajes*, woolen textile shops that were virtually all owned by peninsular Spaniards. Conditions in such establishments were infamous, and Domínguez's report pulled no punches. The *obrajes*, he reported, were among the last redoubts of slavery in Mexico; black slaves were joined by convicts, vagabonds, and debt peons who traded their freedom for desperately needed advances of cash. Some hard-pressed parents even sold their children to the *obrajes*. *Obraje* workers lived on the premises, behind double doors that remained locked except on Sunday, when married workers were allowed leave to visit their families. They lived in appalling conditions, half-naked, emaciated, and disfigured, pale from lack of sunlight, and subject to harsh punishments for the smallest infractions. "Forced into these prisons," Domínguez wrote, "and considering so distant their freedom and so meager the fruits of their labor, . . . some workers fake illness to get out of work, and according to the *obraje* owners some get to such extremes of desperation that they try to flee, whatever the cost or danger. Some even provoke the masters and overseers into injuring them, thus gaining their freedom even at the high cost of losing their health and risking their lives."[2] The unvarnished report,

and Domínguez's efforts to improve working conditions in the
obrajes, did not endear him to the *obraje* owners and their fellow
Spaniards. Domínguez also made enemies when he took on the
problem of corruption in city government, and he ran afoul of
Viceroy Iturrigaray when, in 1805, he authored a strenuous protest against the hated Law of Consolidation. Iturrigaray, who was
busy enriching himself through the enforcement of that law, removed Domínguez from his post. Happily for Domínguez, the *audiencia* ordered Domínguez reinstated, and it held Iturrigaray liable
for paying Domínguez's salary for the time he was suspended, plus
damages.

Along with his critics, Domínguez had his share of friends and
admirers: with the help of a generous contribution from a wealthy
hacienda owner, he was able to upgrade the city's police force and
to carry out widely appreciated public improvements. And when
famine hit the region in 1808–1810, he worked hard to find stored
grain to ease the crisis. He was a popular figure with the impoverished Indians and castes of the region.

He was also, from 1808 onward, a staunch advocate of autonomy for Mexico. When news arrived of the abdications of the
Spanish Bourbon kings, Domínguez went before the city council
of Querétaro to plead for the convocation of a Mexican congress
to rule the country until Ferdinand VII could be restored to the
throne. When the hard-liners deposed Viceroy Iturrigaray, Domínguez took to supporting plans to depose the hard-liners. The meetings of the Querétaro conspirators, which masqueraded as literary
societies, took place in the home of a priest named José María
Sánchez. Domínguez himself did not attend the meetings, but he
offered protection to the conspirators and kept abreast of their
progress with regular reports from Ignacio Allende. Although
Domínguez's commitment to the revolution ultimately proved
tepid, that of his wife, Doña María Josefa Ortiz—later celebrated
as "La Corregidora"—was unrivaled. She was a devoted mother
of fourteen children, but it was clear that the great passion of her
life was revolution, and she played a pivotal role in events.

To supplement the Querétaro junta, revolutionary juntas formed in all of the principal towns and cities of the Bajío— Celaya, Guanajuato, San Felipe, San Luis Potosí, and San Miguel el Grande. In San Miguel el Grande, conspirators gathered on the first floor of the two-story home of Ignacio Allende's brother. They took care to hold a dance on the home's second floor during their meetings so that no one would be alarmed by excessive comings and goings. They let it be known that the penalty for betrayal was death. They discussed strategy, of course, but they also were at pains to justify their impending actions. Virtually all seethed with hatred for the *gachupines*. Some, especially the militiamen, forgetting Viceroy Iturrigaray's many faults, elevated him to the status of martyr to the greed and ambition of Spaniards, and determined that his humiliation would have to be avenged. The plotters were unanimous in deciding that their first move would be to arrest and deport all the Spaniards they could find, and execute any who resisted.

The revolutionaries' planning appeared to benefit from events in Spain and Mexico. Throughout 1810, the Spanish and British armies had been suffering a series of setbacks at the hands of Napoleon's forces, and practically all that remained to the independent Spanish government was a small area around the southern coastal city of Cádiz. The Central Junta of Seville was dissolved in January 1810, replaced by a five-member regency which gamely issued a call for the formation of a parliament, known as the Cortes. Mexicans hardly knew what to make of the extraordinary news that continually arrived from the mother country like artillery salvos. News of Spanish military reverses reached Mexico in April 1810, convincing many that it was unlikely that the Bourbons would recapture the throne any time soon, if ever, and increasing the fear among patriotic Mexicans that their leaders might capitulate to the French.

Mexico City seemed to be in turmoil. Well-heeled merchants there, having grown increasingly disgusted with the bumbling regime of Viceroy Lizana y Beaumont, petitioned the Spanish regency to remove him and find a more vigorous replacement. Lizana surrendered without a fight in February 1810, leaving the *audiencia* in charge. The new viceroy would not arrive until September. The *audiencia*, meanwhile, desperate to retain some semblance of control, mixed naked repression with clumsy attempts to play on popular sentiments. In May, when lightning struck the cupola of a popular shrine near Mexico City that housed the revered image of the Virgin of Los Remedios—a statue that had been brought to Mexico by the Spanish conquistadors—the government took advantage of that divine serendipity to have the image taken on a ten-week pilgrimage around central Mexico, hoping to drum up patriotic sentiment. In August, they ordered that three days of fiestas be held to honor the anniversary of the Spanish conquest. The impression they gave was likely that of a crumbling regime trying desperately to stay afloat, albeit with a tin ear for the popular mood. As has often been the case in history, the specter of a crumbling regime tended to further encourage sedition.

Precisely when Hidalgo joined the Querétaro conspiracy is not clear, but by early summer he was fully committed. He had his workers fashion crude weapons like slingshots, machetes, lances, and primitive artillery pieces in clandestine shops, and he worked to turn as many military men as possible in favor of the rebellion, especially the provincial infantry battalion of Guanajuato. Hidalgo was far less fearful about mobilizing the masses than his fellow conspirators, but he also saw the good sense in cultivating a solid core of military professionals. If enough of them backed the rebellion, perhaps a high degree of popular participation would be unnecessary. Such an outcome had already happened in Argentina, where in May 1810 a creole militia was able to depose and imprison the viceroy and form a new governing junta without recourse to either bloodshed or mass mobilization. To that end, Hidalgo invited the Guanajuato regiment's drum major and band leader, whose name was Juan Garrido, along with a couple of sergeants, to one of his famed fiestas in Dolores. There, on September 12, he explained to them his plans and promised them high rank in the liberating army. He also gave them seventy pesos with which to suborn their fellow troops. The three men seemed agreeable to the seduction, but upon returning to Guanajuato the next day Garrido reported the entire conversation to his captain, who in turn passed the word up the chain of command that ended with the intendant of Guanajuato, Juan Antonio Riaño. Garrido was so eager to be helpful that he surrendered the seventy pesos Hidalgo had given him and begged the intendant to throw him in jail so as to allay the suspicions of the conspirators. Riaño, a longtime friend of Hidalgo's, ordered that the alleged conspirators be placed under surveillance.

The Plot Unravels

Unfortunately for Hidalgo and his colleagues, their plot had begun hemorrhaging from multiple points long before Garrido's treachery. Back in mid-August, the secretary of the Querétaro junta, one José Mariano Galván, had told his boss—the postal administrator of Querétaro, a certain Joaquín Quintana—some details of the plot, and was rewarded with the post of warehouse keeper for the local cigar factory. Quintana passed the information along to his Mexico City counterpart, who in turn alerted the *audiencia*, where the information seems to have entered a bureaucratic netherworld. On September 10, Captain Joaquín Arias of the Celaya militia, a fairly high-ranking member of the conspiracy who was to have the primary responsibility for launching the revolution in Querétaro, decided the plot had already been betrayed and thought to save himself by informing his superiors, who dispatched a messenger to inform the new viceroy. That new viceroy, Francisco Javier Venegas, was a military man who had landed in Veracruz on August 28 and was, as the conspiracy unraveled, enjoying a slow and needlessly ceremonial journey from the port to the capital.

All of this certainly boded ill for the conspiracy. But the series of events that precipitated the final crisis began on September 13, 1810, when a priest, Manuel Irriaga, one of the architects of the proposed plan of revolution, became gravely ill and made a death-bed confession to a Franciscan friar named Francisco Bueras, a Spaniard. Bueras clearly thought the news momentous enough to warrant a violation of his sacred vow to keep confessions confidential: he breathlessly told the ecclesiastical judge, Rafael Gil de León, that the plan involved no less than four hundred conspirators, that the revolution was set to break out that very night, and that it would begin with the beheading of all Spaniards. He was also able to provide two more intriguing details. One was that there were large stashes of weapons in two Querétaro homes, one belonging to an individual named Sámano, another to one Epigmenio González, a grocer. The other was that one of the leading conspirators was none other than the corregidor of Querétaro, Miguel Domínguez.

Gil de León, although not personally involved in the conspiracy, was, like many prominent citizens of Querétaro, a friend and admirer of the corregidor. He therefore made haste to inform Domínguez of the new revelations. Domínguez realized that he was suddenly in a perilous predicament. He evidently concluded that the conspiracy was doomed, and that his only hope was to find a way to keep himself and as many of his co-conspirators as possible alive and out of prison. He had no choice but to proceed with a search of the homes of Sámano and Epigmenio González, knowing he would have to feign surprise at what he found there. He also decided at this moment of crisis that his impetuous wife, Doña Josefa—of the two, by far the more zealous revolutionist—was not to be trusted: he locked her up inside the house, taking the key with him.

He next went to the office of the court clerk to relay what he had heard. Arriving at the clerk's office at eleven at night, he told him that a priest of good reputation had revealed a conspiracy and weapons stashes. It was a high-stakes game of nerves, for as it happened the clerk already knew of the plot, and was aware that the corregidor was complicit in it. The clerk shrewdly determined, nevertheless, to play along with the corregidor's feint in the hope of gathering solid evidence. Fearing treachery, he armed himself with a sword and dagger before leaving to carry out the searches. Going first to the headquarters of the local militia brigade, the clerk gathered forty soldiers, half of whom were sent to search the Sámano home while the other half accompanied him and the corregidor to the home of Epigmenio González.

Corregidor Domínguez, upon arriving at the González home, rushed at once to the door, apparently hoping that by quickly rapping on that door he could alert González in time to allow his escape. The clerk, however, impeded him from knocking until he had his troops placed in strategic spots on the ground and on the surrounding rooftops. Epigmenio González soon appeared at a window, refusing to open up until he saw the soldiers and was informed that the searchers were prepared to enter by force. The corregidor, still hoping for a less disastrous outcome, walked quickly through the González home and pronounced himself satisfied that there was no stash of weapons. The clerk insisted on a more careful search. He noticed that an opening leading from the dining room to a bedroom was hidden by cotton blankets. The soldiers entered the bedroom and found a man stuffing gunpowder into cartridges, surrounded by sturdy sticks waiting to be fashioned into lances. Still more cartridges and lances were stockpiled in other rooms. The corregidor had no choice but to order the arrest of all of the home's occupants. Soon he would have to proceed with the tedious business of pretending to interrogate them.

Meanwhile, "La Corregidora," the indomitable Doña Josefa, was hardly ready to abandon the cause. Apparently having foreseen the possibility of finding herself locked up in her house at such a critical moment, she had arranged an emergency signal with the city's jailer, the elderly Ignacio Pérez, who lived directly below her room and who was a fully committed member of the conspiracy: she would stomp three times on the floor to get the jailer's attention and relay whatever message might need relaying. Remarkably, she was by this method able to tell Pérez, who appeared at once outside her window, that the plan was betrayed and that arrest orders would soon be issued for all of the principal conspirators. In the small hours of the night, Pérez set out on the forty-mile trip to San Miguel el Grande and alerted Ignacio Allende and Juan Aldama. Allende and Aldama then set out for Dolores—about twenty miles to the north—to inform Father Hidalgo of the catastrophe.

On the evening of September 15, while Allende and Aldama rode their horses furiously northward, Miguel Hidalgo was enjoying a relaxing evening at the home of the subdelegate of Dolores, playing cards with several of the town's most distinguished residents, some of them Spaniards. Hidalgo retired at eleven o'clock, as was his custom. That same evening, back in Querétaro, the corregidor and corregidora were arrested. A search of the corregidor's coat pocket turned up several letters he had exchanged with Hidalgo and Allende, one of which set the date for the start of the uprising as October 1. Official arrest orders were issued for the known conspirators.

Aldama and Allende reached Dolores at about two o'clock on the morning of September 16. They went straight to Hidalgo's home and woke him, delivering the sobering news. Hidalgo remained calm before the unattractive options he faced. The conspirators could flee and hope to make it safely to exile; wait around to be arrested; or begin the revolution—which had been scheduled to break out in two weeks' time—at once. Some of the conspirators thought flight worth a try, but it was hardly a sure thing. The authorities had much better evidence against these conspirators than they had had against those of Valladolid, and given the hardening mood of those authorities there was no reason to expect leniency should they be captured.

Hidalgo decided on the third option, even though not all of the preparations had been made. He sent street watchmen with orders to summon his pottery and silk workers, who were already committed to the revolution and who numbered roughly fourteen. Allende could deliver an additional thirty-one soldiers from the Queen's Dragoons at Dolores, and there would be more soldiers available in San Miguel. As rumors spread, people began to gather at the priest's home. Some made ready the weapons that had been fashioned in the padre's secret workshops, while others emptied the town jail and began rounding up the local Spaniards, perhaps twenty in all, including some of the very people Hidalgo had amicably played cards with the previous evening. Hidalgo sent emissaries to the principal cities—Guanajuato, Querétaro, Guadalajara, and Mexico City—to raise the cry of revolt. He ordered that the church bells be rung early, as if calling the people to mass. The town would have been crowded that day in any case, for Sunday was the traditional market day. By eight o'clock there were perhaps six hundred men in the town center, and all were aware that something extraordinary was happening.

At some point on this remarkable morning, Hidalgo spoke some words that have come to be immortalized as El Grito de Dolores (the Cry of Dolores). Accounts of what precisely Hidalgo said vary, but the best sources indicate that he told the people that the Mexico City junta was actively planning to surrender Mexico to the French, and they must rise up to defend church and king; most likely he promised the Indians an end to tribute payments; and he probably assured that all who joined the cause would be paid wages. He closed his oration with the cry, "Long live Fernando VII! Long live America! Long live religion, and death to bad government!"[3]

Hidalgo and his confederates had embarked upon a hazardous course, though it seems doubtful they grasped the true extent of the danger. Their hope on that fateful September day was most likely that such an overwhelming mass of people would join in the fight that the entire revolution could be accomplished quickly. If it went well, the popular uprising might deliver a decisive shock to the already floundering junta, culminating in a festive march upon

Mexico City to take over the reins of government. The longer the revolution took to triumph, the more the creole leadership would have to accommodate the masses of Indians and castes, and the more the interests of those masses would become paramount.

By eleven o'clock, Hidalgo rode at the head of a column of some eight hundred men. Accompanying the column were the twenty or so Spaniards who had been removed from the jail and loaded onto pack mules—a common means of transporting the lowliest of delinquents. After some discussion it was decided that, rather than march directly on Guanajuato, capital of the intendancy, the rebels would tour the Bajío in hopes of attracting more recruits. The first stop would be San Miguel el Grande. Along that route, Hidalgo stopped at the church of a small village called Atotonilco, where there was a well-known oil painting of the Virgin of Guadalupe. He made the painting into a banner, which he attached to a lance. Guadalupe thus became the banner and patron saint of Hidalgo's revolution.

No sooner had the rebels arrived in San Miguel than the troops commenced to satisfy their twin hungers—for food and vengeance. They arrested and abused Spanish store owners and ransacked their shops. Allende managed to discipline them that evening, but early the next morning agitated people roamed the streets shouting, "Death to the *gachupines!*" and throwing stones at the properties of Spaniards. Allende, watching the mayhem from the balcony of his home, became enraged. Grabbing his sword, he mounted his horse and furiously managed to restore some semblance of order.

At nine o'clock that morning, the leadership of the rebellion held a strategy session, and a major rift appeared for the first time. Hidalgo began the meeting by upbraiding Allende for his harsh methods of restoring order, arguing that such methods were counterproductive. Allende responded that there was no chance of success without discipline, but Hidalgo persisted, and the argument grew heated. Sacking and plundering, said Hidalgo, were rights of war, and unless the common folk were permitted to do such things they would have no incentive to support the rebellion. The people of the Bajío had, after all, just endured two years of extreme drought and famine, which followed upon generations of humiliation and abuse, and they had their reward coming. At length something of a compromise was reached. Allende was placed in charge of organizing the army, while Hidalgo grudgingly agreed to speak to the troops, urging them to maintain discipline and moderation. The dispute was papered over, but hardly resolved.

On the morning of September 18, the army was again on the march through a land that, after two years of drought and hardship, was exuberant. Corn and wheat ripened in the fields, fruit hung heavy in the trees, cattle grazed peacefully on pasturelands still moist from frequent rains. The army that wound its way through that landscape was a sight to behold. It consisted of creoles, castes, and Indians; there were army deserters in uniform, cowboys resplendent in their *charro* outfits, and peasants dressed in rags, barefoot or wearing crude leather sandals. They carried old muskets, farming tools, garrotes, machetes, bows and arrows, clubs, lances, axes, and slingshots. Some banged on large wooden war drums or blew into sackbuts and trumpets, while others held effigies of Ferdinand VII or improvised images of the Virgin of Guadalupe. There were women and children as well. Conservative writer Lucas Alamán later insisted that Hidalgo's army "looked more like barbarous tribes migrating from place to place than like an army on the march."[4] At the head of the army rode the rebel priest, Miguel Hidalgo, his drab priestly garb now embellished with a wide-brimmed hat and a large, military-style sash, a saber, and two pistols.

FIVE

THE HIDALGO REBELLION

The creole rebels hoped for a quick and decisive victory, but it soon became apparent that the haphazard manner in which the rebellion had begun, coupled with the maddening complexities of rural Mexican society, made such an outcome unlikely. Further dimming the rebellion's prospects was Father Hidalgo himself. Although he is celebrated as one of Mexico's greatest patriotic heroes, he proved woefully deficient as a military leader, for it was apparent that he could not control his troops and, in fact, made little effort to do so.

The rural rebellion that Hidalgo unleashed was a violent but undirected affair. Those who participated did so for a variety of reasons: some for vengeance, adventure, or curiosity; some for the pay; others because they were pressed into service; still others because it afforded them opportunities for crime, corruption, and mayhem. Most of the rebels, it is fair to say, had little conception of a world that stretched much beyond their home region. Like most peasants, the social transformations they fought for were limited by the myopia and parochialism of village life. They could dream of resurrecting a golden age that lay somewhere in the mythical past; they could destroy the people who had harmed their traditions or stolen their land; they could fight for the glory of exalted abstractions like God and king; and they could envision a world made more just through liberating violence. What they could not imagine was the very thing their putative leaders aimed to achieve: an autonomous or independent nation-state called Mexico, governed by an enlightened creole elite. To the poor, separating their homeland from the Spanish king would be tantamount to doing away with all hope of justice and placing all power in the hands of mortal tyrants. The objectives sought by leaders and followers in this tortuous rebellion were not merely irreconcilable, they were mutually unintelligible.

The Siege of Guanajuato

After leaving San Miguel el Grande on the morning of September 18, 1810, Father Hidalgo and his army, with their Spanish prisoners on mules, marched south along the Laja River to Celaya. As they went, enthusiastic recruits flocked to the banner of Guadalupe, till they numbered nearly fifty thousand. Panicked royalist officials shared the anxieties of Puebla intendant Manuel de Flon, who fretted that "there is not an Indian or creole who does not join the insurgents when they go to attack some town."[1] Hidalgo and Allende sent word to officials in Celaya telling them that if they offered resistance, the Spanish prisoners would be executed to a man. The threat worked: on September 21 the rebels entered Celaya unopposed.

Once again, Hidalgo's troops went on a rampage of wanton destruction, especially targeting the homes and shops of Europeans. And once again, Hidalgo defended the mayhem on the grounds that Spaniards had abused the Indians for centuries, stealing their land and wealth. There was also the more mundane consideration that Hidalgo as yet had little money to pay his troops, and was satisfied to let them take their pay in plunder. But his second-in-command, the professional military man Ignacio Allende, clearly doubted the wisdom of ever having roused the restive masses, and tensions grew. For the time being, Allende more or less held his peace. At Celaya, he formally became second-in-command, assuming the rank of lieutenant general while Hidalgo was accorded the grandiose title of Captain General of America.

The authorities in Mexico City were woefully unprepared for the outbreak of the rebellion. As recently as 1808, Viceroy Iturrigaray had been able to assemble 16,000 troops to meet a rumored British invasion, but his successor, Garibay, had dispersed that force in the name of economy. Mexico's military had long been severely underfunded. Its poverty forced it to rely on a token force of professional fighters garrisoned at the capital and widely dispersed militias made up, for the most part, of the very sorts of people who now flocked to join Hidalgo's ranks. With the outbreak of the rebellion of 1810, the Prince's Cavalry Regiment of Guanajuato boasted only twenty-five men, while the Infantry Regiment of Celaya hemorrhaged so many troops to the rebellion that it disbanded altogether.

The newly arrived viceroy, Francisco Javier Venegas, had been informed of the Querétaro conspiracy midway in his journey from the coast to the capital. He arrived in the capital and formally took the reins of government on September 14, only two days before the start of the rebellion. In contrast to his most recent predecessors, Venegas was relatively young at fifty-six, and he was a seasoned military man who had helped the Spanish army to trounce Napoleon's forces at the celebrated Battle of Bailén in 1808. In Mexico, he was at a considerable disadvantage, for he did not know the country and was wisely skeptical of the abilities and loyalties of its army.

Venegas was correct in assuming that he enjoyed only lukewarm popular support as he faced the Hidalgo rebellion. Considering the dire situation, he acted decisively. He offered a prize of ten thousand pesos to anyone who captured or killed Hidalgo,

Allende, or Juan Aldama, and he soon issued a decree abolishing Indian tribute payments (that decree had in fact originated with the Spanish regency in May). His next priority was to concentrate all available forces in the city of Querétaro, and he entrusted those forces to the intendant of Puebla, Manuel de Flon, who had accompanied him on his journey to Mexico City. Flon led two battalions of infantry with four cannons to Querétaro; they were soon followed by two battalions of grenadiers. In Querétaro, the royalists would have a convenient beachhead from which to retake the towns lost to the rebels, San Miguel el Grande, Dolores, and Celaya. Seeing that Querétaro was well defended, Hidalgo decided to turn northward and attack the rich silver mining city of Guanajuato, a city that had virtually no defenses.

Guanajuato's intendant, the highly capable Juan Antonio Riaño, kept closely abreast of developments. It was clear by now that this was no mere mutiny, for people throughout the Bajío had been flocking to the rebellion as though in the grip of some sanguinary religious rapture. Riaño also knew well that the common people of Guanajuato had suffered grievously in the recent famine, and had no good reason to risk their lives in defense of the status quo. Although later much criticized for his decision, Riaño reasoned that the common people of Guanajuato would join the rebellion no matter what he did, and that his only hope was to find some defensible place, hole up there with his fellow Spaniards, and pray that help would arrive quickly.

The strongest building in the city was the Alhóndiga de Granaditas, a public granary that Riaño himself had ordered built between 1798 and 1809 to store grain against the frequent shortages. A large, perfectly rectangular and unadorned stone building—easily the city's most imposing structure—the Alhóndiga seemed well nigh impregnable. On September 24, Riaño, together with roughly five hundred Spaniards and wealthy creoles, moved into the Alhóndiga. They shared the space with the stored grain, which was to be made into tortillas by servant women; and they brought with them roughly three million pesos as well as stacks of gold and silver ingots, the intendancy and municipal archives, a small amount of gunpowder, some notoriously brittle swords, and a few mended muskets. The few militiamen who had not been seduced by the rebellion were dispatched to man hastily built barricades at the three most likely points of attack, but no one had any illusions that they would be able to hold back the advancing throngs for long. Some Spaniards fled to Guadalajara, but Riaño and his supporters determined to put up a fight.

When the common people of Guanajuato realized that Spaniards were taking steps to save themselves and their treasure, they drew the obvious conclusion, namely, that the Spaniards did not trust them to defend the town and that they were now abandoned to their fate. Riaño, in a halfhearted bid to win hearts and minds, published a decree abolishing tribute payments. Under other circumstances that might have earned him gratitude, but in the gathering crisis it seemed no more than a cynical ploy, done from desperation rather than compassion. If there had been any real doubt before September 24 who the common folk would support, those doubts were put to rest by the Spaniards' own panicked bid for self-preservation. The infantry commander at San Luis Potosí, General Félix Calleja, heard Riaño's desperate pleas for aid, but could offer only encouragement and a vague assurance that, at some point, he might have reinforcements to send.

Though obviously terrified, the defenders of the Alhóndiga voted to reject Hidalgo's invitation to surrender on the morning of September 28, and all vowed a fight to the death. Riaño's son Gilberto, a military man, had the idea of creating makeshift grenades by stuffing sturdy iron flasks, which were normally used to transport mercury for the mines, with gunpowder and grapeshot and fitting them with wicks. The defenders set about making as many of these as they could. They were as prepared as they could possibly be, but they were also keenly aware of the perils they faced. Not only were they poorly armed and vastly outnumbered, but geography was an enemy. Guanajuato is situated in a hollow, sur-rounded by craggy hills and rocky ravines, with the Cata River flowing to the east. The Alhóndiga itself was dominated to the north by a high hill called El Cuarto, and to the south by one called San Miguel. Without control of the high grounds, the defenders would have been vulnerable even had they enjoyed the backing of the city's population.

On the morning of September 28, townspeople gathered on the heights of El Cuarto and San Miguel as if to watch a pageant. Shortly before noon the rebel army appeared with their slingshots, lances, clubs, bows and arrows, and stones. Gilberto Riaño, who had assumed command of the resistance, ordered his men to open fire from the roof of the Alhóndiga, causing the insurgents to fall back briefly. But the rebels soon regrouped, some gaining entrance to the city and emptying the city jail. Insurgents took up positions on the hills around the Alhóndiga; some hastily gathered stones from the riverbed, and those stones would be the rebels' chief weapon in the siege. Soon Hidalgo gave the order for an all-out assault. Many rebels were killed at close range by gunfire from the troops manning the barricades, but they soon overwhelmed the tiny garrisons and began to pelt the Alhóndiga with a ferocious barrage of stones. Intendant Riaño was an early casualty. He imprudently left the Alhóndiga to help organize the defenses of the barricade at Los Pozitos Street; upon returning to the Alhóndiga and mounting the stairs, he was shot in the head.

With the elder Riaño dead, the defenders fell to bickering over who should inherit his supreme authority, leading to further confusion. The siege continued, furious and irresistible: the royalist troops who had been manning the barricades all fell back to the Alhóndiga, while troops that had been stationed on the building's roof found they could no longer withstand the barrage of stones that rained down from the surrounding hills. The defenders hoped they could wait out the siege in the building's interior, lobbing their makeshift grenades out the portals into the encroaching crowd. The grenades made tremendous noise and smoke and blew bodies apart, but they stifled the assault only momentarily.

Unfortunately for the Alhóndiga's defenders, among the attackers were mine workers with considerable experience of blasting through stone. According to legend, one strong young man named Juan José de los Reyes Martínez, nicknamed "El Pípila," after tying a flat stone to his back to protect him from the gunfire, crawled to the door of the Alhóndiga and smeared it with pitch before setting it ablaze. (El Pípila is today memorialized in the city of Guanajuato with an enormous, torch-wielding statue.) Troops inside opened fire as the rebels rushed in through the flaming door, but they were soon overwhelmed by the sheer numbers of attackers. In desperation, some of the defenders threw money at the crowds, hoping to distract them; others donned disguises and tried their best to flee; still others surrendered in the hope of receiving humane treatment. Some merely muttered prayers, which, they no doubt believed, would be their last. Nearly all were slaughtered without mercy. By five in the afternoon Guanajuato had gone almost silent but for the shrieks and moans of the wounded or dying. Numbers are unreliable, but it seems likely that nearly all of the five hundred or so Europeans and creoles who defended the Alhóndiga were killed, while perhaps as many as two thousand attackers lost their lives.

The aftermath of the massacre was as telling as the massacre itself, a hideous drama revealing the burning hatred and mutual incomprehension that prevailed between rich and poor. For the workers and peasants who had joined the siege or watched it from the hilltops, this was a cathartic moment, as though the rebel priest had authorized an impromptu religious fiesta, a rowdy ritual of blood, fire, liquor, and plunder; for the Spaniards and well-heeled creoles, it was as if the earth had rent itself asunder and spewed forth all the demons of hell. "The sad scene on that mournful night," wrote the conservative historian and statesman Lucas Alamán, an eyewitness to the events, "was lit by many torches of candlewood and pine tar, and nothing was heard but the blows of doors being battered down, and the ferocious howls of the rabble who applauded upon seeing them fall, and then charged as if in triumph to steal merchandise, furniture, clothing, and all kinds of things."[2] As in their religious festivals, the poor took the opportunity to lampoon the rich and their pretensions. Barefoot, drunken Indians sported clothing looted from the homes of gentlefolk— gilded hats, uniforms with epaulettes, embroidered dresscoats. "On the twenty-ninth," Alamán continued, "Guanajuato presented the most lamentable aspect of disorder, ruin, and desolation. The plaza and the streets were full of fragments of furniture, the remains of the goods looted from the stores, and liquor that had been spilled once the people had all drunk their fill."[3]

The violence and disorder of the sacking of Guanajuato seems to have shocked even Father Hidalgo, who had been defending mayhem as a legitimate tool of the insurgency. Once the insurgents had taken possession of the Alhóndiga, Hidalgo had hastened to claim the gold and silver for his army's treasury, but found himself unable to prevent looters from absconding with much of that bloodstained booty. He was also dismayed that his September 30 order to cease the looting was disregarded. Once all of the homes of Spaniards had been plundered, the looters began tearing down wrought iron from balconies and window grates, and raiding the homes of creoles, some of whom might at one time have supported the rebellion. Eventually, the priest rode out to the main square to try to quell the ardor of the crowd. Finding his orders disobeyed, he ordered soldiers to open fire in the direction of a group that was busily tearing down a balcony. He was also obliged to hide a large portion of the treasure he had managed to recover, lest his own people steal it.

The taking of Guanajuato was a triumph for the insurgents, but it was in many ways a Pyrrhic victory. Not only did the rebels lose many men in the siege, but the sacking of Guanajuato soon became an item of folklore, a cautionary tale that, to moderate and conservative creoles, revealed the horrors that would ensue should they place their fate in the hands of the unwashed masses. To make the matter worse still, Hidalgo, upon occupying Guanajuato, began a practice of dispensing military commissions so promiscuously that they became virtually meaningless. As Alamán put it, "There was scarcely a vagabond or knave in the city who failed to obtain the rank of captain"[4]—and indeed, many an unsavory character came to claim high rank in Hidalgo's forces. Many would-be supporters concluded that the rebellion was a hideous, dangerous, and disreputable farce, something no respectable person could endorse.

The Counterattack

The man charged with putting an end to the rebellion was Brigadier General Félix María Calleja del Rey, First Count of Calderón, a Spaniard who had served in Mexico since 1789. He gained combat experience in expeditions against Algiers and Gibraltar in the 1770s and 1780s, as well as in wars against nomadic Indians and Anglo-American filibusters. In 1810, he was commander of the infantry brigade of San Luis Potosí, and from that position he moved rapidly and impressively to respond to the fast-spreading insurrection. Unable to communicate with the viceroy because of the disruptions occasioned by the uprising, Calleja was largely on his own. News of the massacre and plunder at Guanajuato immensely aided his cause, for it galvanized a general will to resist among supporters of the colonial regime, as well as creoles who feared what the massacre might portend.

With Querétaro apparently slated for imminent attack, Calleja held frantic meetings with his officers and influential locals to discuss the best ways to respond. "My troops are short in numbers and of the same quality as yours," he wrote the commander at Querétaro, Manuel de Flon, who was a brother-in-law of Juan Antonio Riaño, the late intendant of Guanajuato. "I lack artillery, infantry officers, and I am in a country so undermined by sedition that I cannot abandon it without exposing it."[5] He ordered a halt to silver shipments to ensure they would not fall into rebel hands, offered higher pay to soldiers, and saw to the recruitment of new infantry and cavalrymen. He mobilized artisans to found cannons and manufacture lance points under the direction of military officers, and he decreed special taxes to support the counter-insurgency, even confiscating tithe income from the church. He solicited donations from the wealthy, and although he would have ample cause to bemoan the lack of patriotism of his fellow Spaniards in Mexico, he did manage to gather some meaningful donations. He did his best to win over the populace by placing a portrait of King Ferdinand VII under a canopy and insisting that all swear to him their allegiance. He also issued a proclamation hinting that Napoleon was somehow responsible for the insurrection and demanding that all rise up to defend that which was most sacred, namely, religion, the law, and the fatherland—the very things, in fact, that Hidalgo claimed to be fighting for. "Let us disperse that gang of bandits who, like a destroying cloud, lay waste to our country because they have encountered no opposition."[6] Calleja was proving himself resolute and capable, but he also soon acquired a reputation for cruelty that inspired one independence supporter to label him, with much hyperbole, "the new Tamerlane."

Meanwhile, in Mexico City, a propaganda war was shaping up. The church contributed to the demonization of Hidalgo by declaring him excommunicated, and the Inquisition hurriedly dredged up the charges it had dismissed a decade earlier, painting the rebel priest as a heretic and an apostate and warning that all who followed or supported him would be his companions on the road to perdition. The press—which at this point in the rebellion was controlled entirely by the royalists—weighed in with lurid tales designed to create revulsion toward Hidalgo and his cause.

The defenders of the royalist regime cannot rightly be accused of overconfidence. They were alarmed by the mass desertions and the dispiriting ease with which the rebels gained new recruits, leading Calleja to compare the rebellion to a "hydra reborn as fast as one cuts off its heads."[7] But they were well aware that they were not facing anything close to an organized, disciplined, professional fighting force. This, they reasoned, was an army of plunder. Unschooled, poorly armed, inexpertly led, the rebels would likely beat a panicked retreat at the first hint of stout resistance—a sharp cavalry charge, say, or a well-aimed cannonade. The action on the outskirts of Querétaro on October 6 appeared to confirm this hypothesis. Aware that a band of rebels was approaching the city, Flon sent about 600 troops under the command of Sergeant Major Bernardo Tello. Believing that the rebel forces consisted of no more than 300 men, Tello was horrified to encounter no less than 3,000 rebels holding an easily defensible position. Most of Tello's division broke and ran, but a core of about 180 remained to mount an attack. The royalists found that their opponents, though outnumbering them seventeen to one, were easily crushed. Reliable eyewitnesses later retailed incredible stories of Indians so innocent of the machinery of war that they tried to stop up cannon barrels with their straw hats. The insurgents were put to flight, suffering around 200 dead while the royalists lost only one man— and he to friendly fire. Calleja and Flon were emboldened by their understanding that, if they could only stanch the hemorrhaging of men to the rebels and maintain a core of disciplined warriors, the rebels would be badly overmatched.

But for the moment, both insurgents and royalists were in flux. Commanders on both sides were unsure how far to trust their raw recruits or how strong their opponents might ultimately prove to be. Hidalgo's forces controlled Guanajuato, which was situated between the two royalist positions at Querétaro and San Luis Potosí. Had the royalists been more confident of their troops, they might have moved swiftly on Guanajuato, trapping Hidalgo's forces and finishing them off. Had Hidalgo been surer of himself, he might have attacked Calleja at San Luis Potosí, then doubled back on Querétaro, the principal obstacle between his army and the ultimate prize, Mexico City. Instead, the royalists bided their time, and on October 8 Hidalgo began to march west to Valladolid, the city where he had once been a distinguished college rector. He left Guanajuato with only the most meager defenses. En route, again, his forces were swelled with enthusiastic new recruits, and his coffers were now fairly bursting with silver and gold bullion looted from the Alhóndiga.

Valladolid was a city committed to education and religion, and its defense was entirely in the hands of priests, particularly Bishop Manuel Abad y Queipo, Hidalgo's erstwhile friend who was now his harshest critic (it was he who had issued the writ of excommunication against the wayward curate). The defenders of Valladolid were handed a terrible setback when insurgent guerrillas captured three royalist units that had been dispatched from the capital. Most of the provincial regiment of Valladolid was either committed to the rebellion or suspected of disloyalty, and the townsfolk were likewise suspect. In view of their perilous circumstances, the leaders of Valladolid's defense opted to abandon the effort and seek refuge in Mexico City. The first company of insurgents entered Valladolid unopposed on October 15, and Hidalgo's forces arrived on October 17 to cheers and the raucous clanging of church bells.

At Valladolid, the familiar problems arose. The rebel soldiers, hungry from their campaign, gorged themselves on fruit and vast quantities of liquor. Several fell ill and died, and the rumor ran that they had been deliberately poisoned at a Spanish cantina. Once again the rebel troops set about looting and plundering, though the townspeople had been assured in advance of Hidalgo's arrival that such doings would not be permitted this time. Allende ordered a cannon shot at the looters, leaving several dead and injured and quelling the disturbance. The swaggering Allende took a few ostentatious swallows of the allegedly poisoned liquor, thus proving it was not the cause of the maladies.

At Valladolid, Hidalgo's ranks were swelled by the provincial infantry regiment, consisting of two battalions, eight more infantry companies that had been formed by Abad y Queipo to defend the city, and an entire dragoon regiment from Michoacán. His forces now numbered around eighty thousand, an army that might well enable him to take the capital city if he could get there before Calleja and Flon rushed to its defense. Viceroy Venegas entrusted the capital's defense to Lieutenant Colonel Torcuato Trujillo, a Spanish officer who had arrived in Mexico along with Venegas only a few weeks earlier. A notoriously cruel man with little knowledge of the terrain or people of Mexico, and counting on only seven thousand troops, Trujillo was not an ideal choice to lead the defense, but Venegas simply did not trust any of the available Mexican officers. Trujillo stationed garrisons at several bridges along the Lerma River, some thirty miles east of Mexico City, then fell back with his main contingent to a mountain pass called Las Cruces. It was there that the two forces met in a bloody battle on October 30, 1810.

Allende proved himself an able strategist at the Battle of Las Cruces. His men took possession of the heights surrounding Trujillo's flanks, while another force secured the road to Mexico City, cutting off retreat. At 11 a.m. Hidalgo's column mounted a frontal attack on Trujillo's forces, only to be thrown into a panic by a blast from a cannon Trujillo had ordered hidden in the brush. Hidalgo's army had four cannons, though two were made of wood and all were virtually useless; his main column consisted of Indians armed with the usual lances, stones, and clubs, along with sacks for hauling off the anticipated booty of Mexico City. There were experienced soldiers from the provincial regiments manning the flanks and rear guard, but they had lost most of their leaders and, finding themselves obliged to fight alongside such an amateur army, their morale was low. Still, they managed to rally the troops after the initial shock of the artillery blast, and the fighting was fierce on both sides. At three in the afternoon it appeared the combat had reached a stalemate, and since Trujillo's forces were still surrounded and cut off from retreat, Trujillo decided to parley, indicating he might consider joining the rebel cause. But as the insurgents came within range to begin the discussions, Trujillo ordered his men to open fire, killing more than sixty rebels in one devastating blast. The battle resumed more fiercely than before, till around five in the evening when Trujillo, his ammunition nearly gone and a third of his men dead or wounded, had no choice but to abandon his artillery and fight his way eastward. He made it back to Mexico City with a battered contingent of two hundred survivors. He claimed to have won a glorious victory, a claim that most citizens found implausible.

In a sense the Battle of Las Cruces was indeed a victory for the royalists. It stiffened the resolve of the capital's defenders, especially that of Viceroy Venegas. Although he briefly pondered the option of fleeing to Veracruz, in the end he was resolute. "I will never be able to survive the disgrace of having been conquered by such vile and perfidious people," he wrote.[8] But the residents of Mexico City, who were keenly aware that the rebel army had made rapine and devastation their standard procedure, were understandably uneasy. Many hid their money and precious possessions and barricaded their homes; others sought refuge in monasteries and convents in the hope the pious rebels might respect such places. Disturbing rumors circulated, painting the rebels as better armed and even more numerous and bloodthirsty than they actually were. The prospect that the city's wretched homeless population—some 20,000 of the city's 150,000 inhabitants—might join the rebellion caused the city's better-off residents no small amount of anxiety. But that nightmare did not materialize. A stark cultural divide separated Mexico's cities from its hinterlands, and even though the urban poor suffered tremendous hardships, they remained at least nominally loyal to the Spanish regime.

In preparation for the anticipated attack, Venegas stationed troops at strategic points around the city, had the streets barricaded, distributed weapons to the city's residents, and fortified his own viceregal palace at Chapultepec with artillery. Gabriel de Yermo, the man who had led the overthrow of Viceroy Iturrigaray in 1808, now provided five hundred black workers from his sugarcane haciendas to defend the capital (soon styled "Yermo's blacks," they went on to distinguish themselves in the royalist cause). Earnest volunteers formed several corps, but they were of limited utility as all were poorly armed and devoid of military experience. There were still barely two thousand experienced, well-armed troops defending the city, leading Venegas to send urgent communications to Calleja and Flon to undertake a forced march to the capital.

Always alive to the symbolism of the struggle, Venegas ordered the statue of the Virgin of Los Remedios, which lay astride the rebels' path to the city and which he understood to be much venerated by Mexicans, moved to the metropolitan cathedral of Mexico City on November 31. Laying his truncheon at her feet and adorning her with a sash of the royal army, he solemnly bestowed on her the rank of generalíssima and captain general of the royal army. Women formed themselves into a group called Patriotas Marianas and set about sewing banners of the Virgin, while other creative souls authored solemn proclamations they pretended had come from the Virgin's own lips. The villages of the Mexican provinces quickly followed suit, festooning their most sacred images with martial sashes and granting them the most exalted military ranks. (The Virgin of Los Remedios was brought to Mexico by the Spanish conquistadors and was seen by many as the protector of Spaniards; given that the rebels had adopted the Virgin of Guadalupe as their patron, the rebellion conjured the strange spectacle of dueling Virgins.)

On November 1, a rebel agent approached the city to demand its surrender, and he was rebuffed. In these anxious moments, every cloud of dust that appeared on the distant hills seemed a fearsome portent that sent people scurrying to the relative safety of their homes. But, strangely, the attack never came. Soon the city's residents learned that the rebel army had withdrawn and the city was, for the time being at least, safe.

Historians have debated the reasons for Hidalgo's failure to attack ever since. Some have seconded the opinion of Ignacio Allende, that the priest erred badly in not pursuing his advantage and laying siege to the city. Others credit Hidalgo with wisdom, if not great boldness. The Battle of Las Cruces had given most of Hidalgo's men their first taste of pitched combat, and they were mortally terrified by it—especially by their daunting disadvantage in weaponry. Even their relatively meager stores of weapons and ammunition had been severely reduced by the battle, and some forty thousand men—fully half of the rebel force—had been lost to death or desertion. In addition, Hidalgo had been troubled to find that, in stark contrast to his peregrinations in the Bajío, when people had flocked to his cause en masse, the country people of central Mexico generally remained aloof. Few new recruits showed up to replace the men lost at Las Cruces. Many of the agents Hidalgo had sent to scour the local villages for new recruits had themselves deserted the cause. Hidalgo might well have ordered the siege had it been clear that local peasants and the city's poor would support the rebellion, but they remained quiescent.

It is not easy to understand why the rebellion did not attract the poor of central Mexico, but several explanations have been put forward. Villagers of the Valley of Mexico enjoyed greater autonomy than those of the Bajío, and accordingly their thirst for vengeance against white society was not so acute. Moreover, the royalists still controlled all of the country's printing presses and most of its pulpits, and their propaganda campaign was having its effect. Typical were the rantings of Manuel Abad y Queipo, who compared Hidalgo's rebellion to the bloody slave uprising in Haiti and accused the rebels of "insulting religion and Our Lady, and also insulting our Sovereign, scorning and attacking the government that represents him, oppressing his innocent vassals, disturbing the public order and violating the oath of fidelity to the Sovereign and to the government."[9]

There were other sound reasons for Hidalgo's hesitancy. Venegas had managed to disrupt Hidalgo's communications by intimidating his secret agents, making coordination difficult. Hidalgo had been kept apprised of the movements of Calleja and Flon, who were marching as hurriedly as possible to the capital to reinforce its defenses. He knew that reinforcements were also on their way from Veracruz. It was highly likely, given his lack of manpower and arms and the inexperience and indiscipline of his army, that a rebel attack on the capital would be suicidal. And even if the attack were successful, Hidalgo and his confederates understood that the battle would inevitably be followed by a ferocious plunder party, and Calleja's royalist army would make short work of a rowdy, drunken mob.

Contemplating these distressing realities, Hidalgo lingered three days at the small village of Cuajimalpa, fifteen miles outside the city, and then he ordered his forces to move northward. From this point onward, Allende took to referring to Hidalgo as "that knavish priest," and the schism between the two men became unbridgeable. Both Hidalgo and Allende were probably correct in their assumptions: an assault on Mexico City at this point likely would have been a bloodbath and a disaster for the insurgents; but it was also the rebellion's last, best hope of victory. The insurgency would never again seriously threaten Mexico's capital.

The Retreat

After leaving Cuajimalpa, Hidalgo and his army, now numbering only forty thousand, moved toward Querétaro. A force jointly led by Félix Calleja and Manuel de Flon caught up with them at the town of Aculco on November 7. Although the royalists had only seven thousand troops, they were better armed and disciplined than the rebels. The rebels were still smarting and demoralized from the battering they had taken at Las Cruces. The royalists, advancing in five orderly columns, struck terror into the ranks of the rebels, causing them to scatter in hopeless confusion. The rebels lost virtually all of their artillery, arms, supplies, livestock, and even eight prostitutes who had been traveling with the army.

Following the disaster at Aculco, Hidalgo and Allende split their forces, with Hidalgo going to Valladolid and Allende to Guanajuato. The plan was to patiently manufacture arms and ammunition, recruit troops, and generally regroup and strengthen the rebel army in preparation for an eventual attack on Mexico City. At Valladolid, Hidalgo received the good news that one of his lieutenants, José Antonio Torres, had taken the city of Guadalajara, and he decided to go to that city despite Allende's desperate pleas that Hidalgo bring his troops to reinforce Guanajuato. Torres, a mestizo peasant, proved to have not only considerable military talent but also the ability to prevent his troops from committing the kinds of depredations for which Hidalgo's army was now justly famous. His occupation of Guadalajara was remarkably orderly and dignified. He quartered his troops on the outskirts of the city, permitting no looting or drunkenness or violent reprisals against Europeans. By contrast, in Valladolid Hidalgo secretly ordered the summary execution of some sixty Spaniards.

Meanwhile, Calleja was, with relative ease, retaking the towns of the Bajío—Celaya, Salamanca, Irapuato—one by one (in Allende's recounting, the royalists were "entering the towns we've conquered as if they were entering their own homes"). As the royalist forces approached Guanajuato, a frightened mob broke into the now infamous Alhóndiga and massacred 138 Spanish prisoners, afterward desecrating their corpses. Allende was not at the scene, and though his officers made a valiant effort to restrain the slaughter, the crowd was beyond anyone's ability to control.

On November 24, the combined forces of Calleja and Flon attacked Guanajuato. The leaders of the attack were as yet ignorant of the latest massacre at the Alhóndiga, but they were nevertheless eager to avenge the many horrors that city had suffered at rebel hands. Allende dispatched desperate pleas to several insurgent chieftains, including Hidalgo. Allende's letter to Hidalgo clearly reveals the growing rift between the two leaders, for he bluntly accused the priest of seeking his own security at the expense of the progress of the revolution, and he painted a dire picture of the consequences of Hidalgo's inaction. Calling Guanajuato "this precious city, the most interesting in the kingdom," Allende suggested that allowing it to fall to the royalists would greatly embolden the enemy and doom the rebel cause. "It seems to me that we are bound to lose all that we have achieved," Allende predicted, "the entire enterprise, and we shall likewise forfeit our own lives and security, for they will seek us out even on the most miserable little ranch and judge us to be cowards and fugitives; they will become our executioners."[10]

Allende was prescient enough. In a six-hour siege, the royalist army took the city at a cost of only four dead and seven wounded, while the rebels lost some 1,500 men and twenty artillery pieces. Allende's army was destroyed, and Allende was forced to flee to San Luis Potosí.

Upon taking Guanajuato, Calleja learned of the recent massacre at the Alhóndiga, and he determined to make an example of the unfortunate city. His first instinct was to order the entire city "put to fire and sword," but he quickly rescinded that draconian command. He nevertheless decreed the pain of death for any who refused to surrender their weapons, engaged in seditious speech, or failed to provide information on the perpetrators of the massacre. On the morning of November 26, while carpenters erected gallows in every corner of Guanajuato and in the surrounding towns, Calleja conducted hasty interrogations of about seventy prisoners, randomly selecting twenty-three for immediate execution. Those unfortunates were permitted to hurriedly confess their sins, then forced to stand one at a time against an interior wall of the Alhóndiga and shot. In the evening the gallows were put to use in public, almost ritualized hangings by torchlight of eighteen prominent citizens; eight more met their fate the following day, and still more the day after that, until finally Calleja, having dispatched sixty-nine citizens, magnanimously decreed a general pardon. The executions coincided with an epidemic of typhus and a general exodus from the city. Guanajuato, which not so long before had been the wealthiest and most opulent city in the empire, was scarcely more than a depopulated ruin, its mines abandoned and its agriculture devastated.

Hidalgo, along with about seven thousand followers, arrived at Guadalajara on November 27, where he was greeted by cheering crowds, garish decorations, martial music, artillery salvos, fireworks, and ringing church bells. In the cathedral, a local priest sprinkled him with holy water, and a solemn Te Deum was sung in his honor. After that, he repaired with full entourage to the city's municipal palace, where he got down to the business of organizing a rebel government. Unfortunately, in this, his first attempt to place a veneer of formality over what had so far been a hasty and haphazard affair, Hidalgo proved in the most important respects to be surprisingly tepid. Although there is no doubt that he considered the ultimate aim of his rebellion to be complete separation from Spain, he refrained from declaring this, but rather continued the fiction that he was fighting for King Ferdinand VII. Instead of devising new institutions and offices, he set up a regime that merely aped the offices and institutions of the Spanish government as it had existed under Charles IV. This was bound to be confusing to the rank-and-file soldiers in Hidalgo's rebel army. Most were willing to fight to save King Ferdinand and the Catholic Church from Napoleon's unholy minions. But the royalists *also* claimed to be fighting in the name of Ferdinand VII, and they not only had a stronger claim to the mantle of Bourbon legitimacy, but they had better propaganda organs with which to denounce Hidalgo's forces as hypocrites, blasphemers, and frauds. There was something sterile, vacillating, confusing, even a bit pathetic about Hidalgo's continuing insistence that he was the champion of the old regime at a time when his private correspondence revealed that his most cherished hope was to demolish that regime.

Also at Guadalajara, Hidalgo greatly enhanced his growing reputation for savagery, making the last weeks of 1810 and the first weeks of 1811 among the most troubling of the entire revolution. Hidalgo had already ordered the summary executions of sixty Spaniards at Valladolid. At Guadalajara, he met a man named Agustín Marroquín and bestowed upon him the rank of captain, making him a trusted bodyguard. Marroquín was a sadist and career criminal who had spent the last five years in jail on charges of stealing royal funds. In determining his sentence, Marroquín's judges took into account his lifelong history of involvement in nearly every crime imaginable. At the time of the rebels' arrival, Marroquín was preparing to begin ten years of hard labor at a military fortress in Havana. The granting of an officer's commission to such a notorious delinquent disgusted the polite society of Guadalajara and became another element in Allende's growing disdain for Hidalgo. On the night of December 12, Marroquín and some of his fellow rebels led a group of Spanish prisoners to a hill a few miles from the city, beheaded them, and threw their mutilated corpses into a ravine. In the ensuing month, such executions became an almost nightly ritual, eventually ending the lives of some 350 defenseless Spaniards. Mariano Abasolo, one of Hidalgo's chief collaborators, was apparently so appalled by this unrestrained barbarity that he took to hiding Spaniards and helping them to escape. Even the impetuous corregidora, Doña Josefa Ortíz Domínguez, was scandalized by the savagery. She scolded Hidalgo in a letter, warning that terror could only lead to more terror.

Despite its brutality and lack of direction, Hidalgo's revolution was at something of a high tide, at least superficially. The treasury was enriched with funds confiscated from government and church offices of the rich intendancy of Guadalajara, and even despite the loss of Guanajuato and several Bajío towns, the rebellion's military fortunes were improving. José María Mercado, a parish priest who had only recently joined the rebellion, had managed to take the important city of Tepic and the port of San Blas to the west; to the northeast, another rebel priest, Luis de Herrera, took San Luis Potosí; in the far north, rebel troops took San Antonio, Texas, and Saltillo, Coahuila, and they controlled the provinces of Nuevo León and Nuevo Santander (Tamaulipas); and in the south, yet another parish priest, José María Morelos y Pavón, was beginning a remarkable campaign that would soon make him the rebellion's most successful general. What was more, Guadalajara was home to one of the viceroyalty's four printing presses, and that press now fell into rebel hands. The rebels lost no time in establishing a newspaper, *El Despertador Americano*, to broadcast their side of the story.

Curiously, Hidalgo's propaganda seemed to reflect his assumption that there was now little hope of attracting much additional creole support. There were the almost perfunctory charges that the Spaniards had long trampled the legitimate rights of the Mexican people with discriminatory and unfair policies, that they were desecrating the holy religion, and that patriotism and self-preservation demanded adherence to the rebellion. But at the same time, Hidalgo threatened to put to the sword any Spaniard or Mexican who spoke against or opposed the rebellion; any Spaniard unlucky enough to be held captive by the rebels when the royalists attacked; any Spaniard or Mexican who refused to free his slaves; and any Mexican who gave shelter to a Spaniard in order to aid the royalist cause. If a Mexican gave refuge to a Spaniard out of simple compassion, his property would be confiscated and he would be exiled. The harshness of such threats undoubtedly only increased the already profound fear and prejudice that most creoles felt toward the rebellion.

Rather, Hidalgo's pronouncements seemed aimed more at Indians and castes than at creoles. No doubt this reflected the priest's compassion for the poor, but it also betrayed the sense that, since all hope of widespread creole support was lost, the poor were the rebellion's only hope. Hidalgo decreed an end to slavery, Indian tribute, government monopolies on gunpowder and tobacco, restrictions on industry and agriculture, and taxes on liquor. He also issued a decree envisioning a rudimentary agrarian reform, wherein renters were to become landowners. And although Hidalgo gave at least some lip service to the idea of curtailing the looting and plunder that had so delighted his earliest followers, he seems still to have regarded looting and plunder—along with the image of the Virgin of Guadalupe—as his most effective recruiting tool. It also seems that Hidalgo reckoned that his appeal to the masses would be strengthened if he acted like royalty. He had traded his drab priestly garb for a magnificent military uniform, and was having a grand time attending banquets and dances and enjoying the adulation of the people, even if much of that adulation was feigned. He had taken to styling himself "Generalissimo" and "Most Serene Highness," and was invariably accompanied by a retinue of armed bodyguards.

Whatever the chief lure of the rebellion might have been, it was working. The ranks of Hidalgo's army increased steadily with new recruits throughout December, until he once again headed an army of eighty thousand men. Of that number, however, there were only six thousand cavalry with lances and only two hundred trained soldiers carrying firearms. A few hundred primitive muskets were available, but most of the soldiers had to make do with the usual lances, clubs, slings, and crudely fashioned bows and arrows. The rebels also counted on some 125 cannons, but most were homemade affairs of poor quality. Moreover, although detachments of recruits engaged in listless drills on the plains outside the city, the lack of discipline among Hidalgo's forces was scandalous. The recruits were quartered in private homes and inns throughout the city. They had lost none of their zeal for theft, vandalism, and general disorderliness, causing many of the city's more comfortable citizens to decry the rebellion. Ignacio Allende, who arrived in Guadalajara on December 9 after his defeat at Guanajuato, was more disgusted than ever by Hidalgo's pandering to the poor. He went so far as to consult a certain Dr. Maldonado and a local bishop about the possibility of giving the priest a dose of poison in order to prevent future crimes.

Tensions were high when news reached the rebels that two royalist armies were approaching Guadalajara. One, led by the brutal General José de la Cruz, boasted two thousand infantrymen; the other, led by Félix Calleja, consisted of six thousand. The relatively small number of soldiers was compensated for by the fact that these troops were mostly experienced, well-trained, well-equipped, disciplined fighters, half of them mounted, and they were led by talented, determined, and ruthless officers. The rebels should have been intimidated, but they were not. The majority, who had not yet been tested by combat, were buzzing with joyful anticipation of the coming contest, convinced that their superior numbers and enthusiasm would carry them to victory. Allende and Hidalgo once again bickered, this time over the proper strategy for meeting the royalists. Allende, loath to risk the entire army in a single battle, argued that Guadalajara should be evacuated and the army split into small tactical units, which would attack the royalist columns in successive waves. Hidalgo insisted that splitting up the army would demoralize the troops. The debate was long and heated, but once again Hidalgo prevailed.

Upon receiving news that Calleja's forces were approaching on January 14, Hidalgo led his army about thirty miles east of Guadalajara, to a stone bridge traversing the Lerma River known as the Bridge of Calderón, which lay astride the route from Mexico City to Guadalajara. His army occupied that position on January 15, optimistically packing enough supplies to ensure that once they smashed Calleja's forces they would be prepared for an assault on Mexico City. Toward nightfall on January 16, Calleja's army appeared in sight, but waited till dawn to launch its attack.

The fighting at Calderón was fierce, but the rebels—while predictably suffering far more casualties than the royalists—held their own for nearly six hours. Then, in the afternoon, a royalist grenade scored a dead hit on a rebel ammunition wagon, causing a tremendous explosion that immediately killed many rebels. But if the explosion was fearsome, the aftermath was a horrifying nightmare: a stiff wind blew fire swiftly through the dry grass and flora of the field, enveloping it in impenetrable black smoke and flames. Visibility was reduced to nothing, and many rebels were burned alive or smothered by the fumes. The rebel forces dissolved in a panic, while the royalists mowed them down without mercy, or took them captive for later execution. The losses in the battle were fearfully lopsided. Fewer than fifty royalists were killed, including Calleja's valued second-in-command, Manuel de Flon; the rebels lost at least 1,200, probably many more.

For all intents and purposes, the Hidalgo revolt came to an end at Calderón. Calleja entered Guadalajara on January 21, where he was greeted with wild enthusiasm by many of the same people who had but recently feted the rebels, a display of sycophancy indicating that many Mexicans had only the shallowest of allegiances, and hoped only to remain aloof from the conflict.

The Last Act

After the catastrophe of Calderón, Hidalgo's army simply evaporated, its leaders and followers alike scattered and left to fend for themselves in the hostile terrain. Hidalgo fled north, hoping to make it to Zacatecas, which was held by rebel chieftain Rafael Iriarte, who had thirty-two cannons and half a million pesos. Northward was the only feasible direction, since General José de la Cruz had gained secure control of Michoacán, cutting off Hidalgo and his dwindling forces from their southern confederates.

A few days after the calamitous battle, the rebellion's leaders rendezvoused at an hacienda called Pabellón, on the outskirts of the city of Aguascalientes. It was bound to be an explosive moment, for Ignacio Allende had accumulated an impressive list of grievances against Hidalgo. Allende was incensed that he had lost every debate over military tactics, even though Hidalgo's plans had proved consistently catastrophic. He was still livid that Hidalgo had ignored his pleas and refused to reinforce him in his desperate defense of Guanajuato. He reviled the priest for permitting and even encouraging pillage, as well as for his senseless brutality against Spanish prisoners, actions that had alienated nearly every potentially useful ally. The confrontation between the two men was the most heated yet, but this time Allende had solid support from the rebellion's other leaders. The choice that Allende and his allies now gave Hidalgo was simple enough: surrender his command or be killed. Their problem was, however, that only Hidalgo had the prestige and charisma to command the loyalty of the Indian and caste troops, and news of his ouster would surely exacerbate the already serious problem of desertion. Allende thus became the new generalíssimo. Hidalgo was made a prisoner and kept under close surveillance by guards with orders to kill him should he attempt to flee. But the rank and file of the rebel army were told nothing of this, and they continued to believe that Hidalgo remained at the helm.

Allende may initially have been confident that his more disciplined and professional approach might turn the tide of the rebellion. If so, he was quickly disabused. News of the rebels' humiliation at Calderón raced ahead of the army, reinforcing royalist propaganda declaring the rebellion decisively crushed. Demoralized troops deserted or fought listlessly, and as the main body of the army moved northward, key cities—Zacatecas, San Luis Potosí, Tepic—fell one by one to the royalists. The royalists wisely leavened their military successes with an offer of a general pardon for all rebels who voluntarily laid down their arms, and there were many takers. Even so, General Calleja constantly bemoaned the declining zeal and discipline of his army, brought on, in his view, by the "whores and the heat." (Both contending armies traveled with large contingents of prostitutes.)

As the prospect of returning southward and gaining ground in central Mexico seemed increasingly hopeless, a new plan presented itself to Allende. While the rebellion had been withering in central Mexico, insurgents had made significant gains in the north. In the first week of January, Lieutenant General José Mariano Jiménez had revolutionized much of what were known as the Eastern Interior Provinces and established a base at the town of Saltillo, capital of the province of Coahuila. Still farther to the north a royalist officer, Captain Juan Bautista de las Casas of San Antonio de Béxar, went over to the rebellion, arresting Texas governor Manuel María de Salcedo and all of his fellow Spaniards and confiscating their property. He sent an account of his deeds to Hidalgo, asking Hidalgo to confirm him as revolutionary governor of Texas. The rebels then established a provisional government at the town of Nacogdoches. Accordingly, it appeared to Allende that the rebellion's best hope was to strike out northward in hopes of eventually making contact with the United States, a potential source of money, weapons, and moral support for the rebellion. The United States, after all, was itself the product of a fairly recent revolution against an overbearing European power, and it represented itself as the very homeland and fountainhead of the revolutionary ideals of individual freedom and social equality. The prospect of such an alliance was something the royalists took very seriously, for Texas was a buffer against what they assumed to be an aggressive, expansionist foreign power. It was a practical certainty that, should rebel agents reach the United States, they would at the very least secure the aid of American mercenaries and adventurers. The royalist government sent a force to sail up the coast from Veracruz, while other royalist forces grouped at the border of Coahuila, with orders to prevent the rebels from reaching Texas.

The rebels had already tried once to interest the United States in their struggle, with tragic and inconclusive results. At Guadalajara back in December, Pascasio Ortíz de Letona, a young botanist from Guatemala, had been appointed minister plenipotentiary to the United States, fully empowered to sign whatever military alliances and commercial treaties he could persuade the Americans to support. Letona was captured en route to Veracruz, and the papers authorizing his mission were found under his saddle. While being taken as a prisoner to Mexico City, Letona took a fatal dose of poison. No one really knew how the Americans would respond to rebel pleas, but Allende and many of his fellows had a naive faith in the willingness of the United States government to support their cause.

Allende named Ignacio Aldama, one of the original conspirators from San Miguel el Grande, as the new minister plenipotentiary to the United States, and he was dispatched to Washington, along with Friar Juan de Salazar and a hundred bars of silver with which to purchase weapons and recruit mercenaries. While Aldama and Salazar were en route, the situation in Texas took an unfortunate turn. Captain Casas, the former royalist whose coup had secured Texas for the rebels, had managed to alienate his chief lieutenants. They, in turn, persuaded a local priest named Juan Manuel Zambrano to head a rebellion against Casas. That rebellion was still in its early stages when Aldama and Salazar arrived in San Antonio, and the arrival of the revolutionary agents accelerated events. Zambrano and his co-conspirators swayed the opinion of the local people by spreading the rumor that Aldama and Salazar were in fact agents of Napoleon. The elegant uniform that Aldama wore gave some credence to the charge in the minds of the townsfolk. Just before dawn on March 2, Zambrano's forces took Aldama and Salazar into custody and deposed Casas as governor. All three were executed soon after. The counterrevolution had triumphed in Texas.

The counterrevolution in Texas had enormous repercussions for the Hidalgo revolt, for it set in motion a chain of events that ended with the capture of the rebellion's top leaders. About 260 miles southwest of San Antonio, at the dusty desert town of Monclova, Captain Ignacio Elizondo—a retired militia officer who had defected to the rebellion only a few weeks earlier—was holding the deposed royalist governor of Texas, Manuel María de Salcedo, in

his custody. Elizondo had become an advocate of independence in
a moment of exuberance, and his convictions were shallow. Angered by Allende's failure to make him a general, Captain Elizondo proved an easy mark for his prisoner, who was able to
persuade him to rejoin the royalist side. Not only was Elizondo a
habitual turncoat, he also had a gift for treachery. When he received word of the counterrevolution in Texas, he was inspired to
carry out a counterrevolution of his own in Coahuila, deposing
Coahuila's revolutionary governor on March 17. He also discovered that Allende and virtually all of the principal rebel leaders
were approaching Monclova, and he decided to set a trap.

Feigning loyalty to the rebellion, Elizondo contacted the chief
of rebel operations in the north, Mariano Jiménez, offering to
greet the rebel leaders with an honor guard at a site just south of
Monclova known as Acatitas de Baján, where a series of wells
would provide the parched rebels with much-needed drinking water. Elizondo advised the rebels to spread their 1,500 troops out in
a long, thin line to ensure that the thirsty soldiers did not all drink
at once, exhausting the wells. Elizondo's forces were waiting in
ambush when, on March 21, the fourteen carriages bearing the
sixty top leaders of the rebellion appeared. The leaders were arrested one by one as their carriages rolled desultorily into Elizondo's trap. Allende realized too late what was happening and
tried to resist, but Elizondo's men opened fire on his carriage, killing Allende's son and Joaquín Arias, one of his most valued lieutenants. Hidalgo also briefly contemplated resistance, but in the
end surrendered peacefully. In all, 40 men were killed and 893
taken prisoner.

The leaders were taken first to Monclova; then they were
shackled hand and foot and loaded on mules—a mode of con-
veyance designed to demean—for the nearly four-hundred-mile
trek to the royalist stronghold of Chihuahua for trial. Viceroy
Venegas insisted that the trials and executions take place in the remote deserts of the far north, fearing that Hidalgo and his com-

rades were still popular figures in central Mexico and it would be risky to try them there. When the prisoners reached Chihuahua on April 23, Brigadier General Nemesio Salcedo (father of Texas governor Manuel), commandant of the Interior Provinces, ordered that the prisoners be paraded through the city streets. The townspeople were allowed to watch them, but were ordered to refrain from expressions of either sympathy or hatred.

A military court was established on May 6, and the trials went quickly. The majority of judges who heard and decided the cases were creoles who were unanimous in their condemnation of the revolution and the revolutionaries. The chief interrogator, Judge Angel Abella, baited the prisoners with such provocative questions that at one point Ignacio Allende burst out of his shackles and beat the judge about the head with his chains. Allende's testimony made abundantly clear that he held Hidalgo responsible for the disastrous course the rebellion had taken. Allende, Mariano Hidalgo (Miguel's brother), Juan Aldama, and several others were executed on June 26, 1811, with other executions both preceding and following. The only major figure who was spared was Mariano Abasolo, who testified against his comrades and swore that he had never wanted to be part of the rebellion in the first place. He was sentenced to ten years in prison and had his considerable property confiscated. He died in a Spanish prison five years later.

Hidalgo was not executed with his erstwhile comrades. The procedure for executing a man of the cloth was more complex, since before such a sentence could be carried out he had to be formally degraded from the priesthood, a fairly involved process. At his trial, Hidalgo did not try to deny or excuse his errors. Asked why he had sanctioned mass executions of Spaniards, Hidalgo could only respond that he "had no more motive than a criminal compliance with the desires of the army composed of Indians."[11] He confessed that "not one of those killed at his order were given a trial nor was there any reason to do so, since he knew perfectly well that they were innocent."[12] Although there were a few glim-

mers of defiance in his testimony, for the most part Hidalgo appeared genuinely contrite. On May 18, a document appeared
bearing Hidalgo's name, and although its authenticity has been
called into question, historian Hugh Hamill, after a close study of
the matter, concluded that, whether genuine or not, the statement
gives an accurate reflection of Hidalgo's state of mind. The most
fervid jeremiads of the rebellion's many critics seem subdued compared to Hidalgo's anguished confession. The priest bemoaned
"the evils I have caused America, now that the dream has been removed from my eyes and my penitence has left me prostrate in
bed: from here I can see, far off, the gallows upon which I shall be
executed, and with each moment I breathe out pieces of my soul
and feel that, before I die once and for all, I shall die a thousand
times of shame for my excesses."[13]

In a ceremony on July 27, Hidalgo was stripped of his priestly
garments. Three days later he was taken to the place of execution.
He died bravely, after passing out candies to his executioners and
placing has hand over his heart to help guide the aim of the
marksmen.

The heads of the rebellion's top leaders—Hidalgo, Allende,
Aldama, and José Mariano Jiménez—were severed and placed in
iron cages that adorned the four corners of the Alhóndiga de
Granaditas in Guanajuato, a warning to any who might be
tempted to follow their example. The heads remained there until
Mexico's independence was achieved a decade later.

Any assessment of Hidalgo and his revolt must reckon with the
fact that the rebel priest has been enshrined as perhaps the greatest hero of the Mexican nation. The canonization process began
not long after the deaths of Hidalgo and Allende, when Hidalgo's
successor, José María Morelos, called them heroes and proposed
making September 16—the date upon which Hidalgo called the
rebellion into being—a patriotic holiday. Hidalgo has been celebrated with monuments and statues, poems and paintings, and

fireworks and speeches. Historians have contributed to the hagiography, perhaps none more enthusiastically than the American Hubert Howe Bancroft, who rather glibly excused Hidalgo's cruelty and declared that all the adulation was richly deserved. "Let his memory be honored!" the historian wrote in 1885. "Let his name be enrolled among the world's champions of liberty!"[14]

There is certainly something romantic and appealing in the story of the relatively obscure parish priest who turned rebel in his fifty-seventh year, transforming himself in his final few months of life into the "generalíssimo" of a revolutionary army, hero to the downtrodden and scourge of the rich. But historians have by no means all been kind to Hidalgo. Opinions range from the terse judgment of the historian Timothy Anna—"Hidalgo accomplished nothing"[15]—to the more caustic views of the nineteenth-century conservative historian and statesman Lucas Alamán, who credited Hidalgo with accomplishing a great deal—albeit nothing positive. For Alamán, Hidalgo not only failed to achieve independence, but he caused it to be delayed for years. At the time the rebellion began, wrote Alamán, public opinion in Mexico overwhelmingly favored independence. But in raising an army with the easy enticement of vengeance and pillage, Hidalgo transformed the struggle from one pitting the supporters of independence against its foes into one that pitted a vicious and vengeful horde against decent people who hoped to defend their lives and possessions. Hidalgo's methods in effect forced the very people who should have been at the vanguard of the liberating struggle to support the imperial system they despised, simply in the interest of self-preservation. The resulting war visited immense devastation upon the country's agriculture and industry, deepened hatreds between Americans and Europeans, ruined the army, promoted immorality, and destroyed tradition. Not only did Alamán hold Hidalgo accountable for perverting the independence struggle itself, but he charged that the enduring echo of his hateful revolution was responsible for many misfortunes Mexico suffered in the decades after independence was achieved.[16]

Hidalgo's critics cannot be hastily dismissed. Hugh Hamill, in a judicious assessment, maintains that Hidalgo headed two failed revolutions, one to secure Mexico's independence from Spain and another to redeem the oppressed masses.[17] Both revolutions failed for the simple reasons that their objectives were incompatible and that the natural constituencies of the two revolutions were separated by a wide gulf of suspicion, hatred, and misunderstanding. In order to rally troops, Hidalgo maintained the fiction that his revolution was made in the name of the legitimate king of Spain and the Holy Catholic Church, both of which were menaced by the evil Bonaparte. This was a calculated lie, predicated on the assumption that the masses had very meager powers of comprehension. Beyond that, Hidalgo offered his would-be followers the shallowest enticement imaginable: the chance to gather loot and wreak vengeance on the oppressor. Some of his proclamations in the area of social reform—the abolition of Indian tribute, for instance—were concessions that even the royalists were willing to make in the name of attracting troops. His agrarian reform plan was moderate and vague. In short, Hidalgo did not appeal to his recruits with a well-developed vision of how they might be uplifted and how Mexico's glaring inequalities might be lessened. His message was more expedient, not to say demagogic. Hidalgo ordered the brutal slaying of hundreds of defenseless prisoners he knew to be innocent of any crime, which stains his reputation indelibly. As a military leader, Hidalgo made a series of disastrous decisions, and the allegiance of his soldiers weakened with every defeat.

Hidalgo cannot be held accountable for the yawning chasm in Mexican society that separated rich and poor, powerful and powerless, white and nonwhite—the chasm that rendered meaningful communication and shared objectives between the rebellion's leaders and the common folk a practical impossibility. But by any measure, his revolution failed, and in the process it did indeed delay the achievement of Mexico's independence while visiting enormous destruction and hardship on the Mexican people, rich and poor alike. It also provided conservative and moderate Mexicans with a harrowing cautionary tale, a vivid and terrifying example of what might happen when the restive masses were roused. The moral they drew from the rebellion was simply that the common people must be kept in their proper place, and power must be restricted to men of learning, wealth, and breeding. In short, Hidalgo's rebellion may not only have delayed Mexico's achievement of independence; it may also have been a factor in delaying the achievement—or even the attempt to achieve—greater justice for Mexico's poor.

SIX

WAR, THE CORTES, AND THE CONSTITUTION

The years 1812 and 1813 witnessed some remarkable developments. In Mexico, the rebellion continued under the able leadership of another parish priest, José María Morelos, who brought
rebel power to its apogee. In Spain, Spaniards and Spanish Americans created a new parliament—known as the Cortes—and wrote
a new constitution for Spain and its dominions. Both developments gave hope to Mexicans who longed for autonomy or independence, but they also brought bitter frustrations and hardships.
These were exciting times, but they were probably also the cruelest
years of the rebellion.

The Rebellion Continues Under Morelos

The capture and execution of the first group of insurgent leaders
heralded dark days for the rebellion, but the movement was by no
means extinguished. Other leaders appeared to carry the movement forward. One was Ignacio López Rayón. Back in Guadalajara, Hidalgo had elevated Rayón to the office of secretary of
state. A thirty-eight-year-old lawyer and miner from Michoacán,

Rayón had joined the movement early on, establishing his revolutionary bona fides by helping to create the rebels' first newspaper, *El Despertador Americano*. He had been at Saltillo when the other insurgent leaders had made their way northward, and thus escaped the treachery at Baján. Upon learning of the capture of the main insurgent leaders, Rayón moved quickly to claim Hidalgo's mantle. In August 1811, after politely notifying the viceroy of his intentions, he formed a governing junta in the town of Zitácuaro, about a hundred miles west of Mexico City.

Rayón did not share Hidalgo's concern and affinity for the poor. In fact, he fit neatly into the group of moderate creoles whose most cherished wish was to make Mexico self-governing and equal in stature to the provinces of Spain itself, but without major alterations in the social structure. Autonomy had been, and still was, the goal of many creoles who had abjured the revolution and chosen to work within legal channels to enhance Mexico's status within the empire. Rayón displayed his essential moderation when, in April 1811, he wrote to Calleja proposing that they end the revolution by establishing a new national junta to govern Mexico in the name of the captive king Ferdinand VII. Calleja refused even to consider the proposition, demanding unconditional surrender. Rayón then tried to unify the various insurgent chieftains under his central authority, an effort that met with much resistance. By late 1811, many rebel chieftains were already operating as independent warlords, some barely distinguishable from bandits. Some, like the notorious Chito Villagrán of Huichápan, clearly *were* bandits. Villagrán's conduct was so thoroughly ungovernable that, by late 1812, Rayón was fighting him nearly as vigorously as he was fighting the royalists. With some other rebel leaders, the problem was ideological. They objected to Rayón's moderation, especially his continued insistence on granting allegiance to Ferdinand VII. One of Rayón's most insistent critics was the man who was destined to give his name to the rebellion's second stage, José María Morelos y Pavón.

Morelos objected to making the revolution in the name of Ferdinand because, he believed, Spain had been lost to the French, and to continue pretending otherwise was dishonest and a distraction from the hard business of building a new government. Morelos's convictions may have stemmed from his difficult upbringing, for he was by no means a member of Mexico's elite. He was born in the city of Valladolid (now named Morelia in his honor) in 1765, the first of three children. His father was a poor carpenter, his mother a schoolteacher. Although his birth certificate declared the young Morelos to be a "Spaniard," his physiognomy suggested a mixture of Indian, African, and European blood. As an adult he was short and stocky, with a decidedly swarthy complexion and a misshapen nose bearing a prominent scar, the result of a youthful encounter he had had with a tree branch while riding in hot pursuit of a runaway bull. He nearly always wore a handkerchief on his head, which supposedly eased the pain from frequent migraine headaches. At the age of fourteen, Morelos was sent to live with an uncle on an hacienda near the town of Apatzingán, in the hot lands of Michoacán. The uncle, Felipe Morelos, was a man of some means. In addition to his hacienda, he was the master of a mule train that plied the China Road, a rude path stretching the three hundred miles from Mexico City to the port of Acapulco, where the Manila galleons unloaded goods from the Orient. José María Morelos began accompanying mule trains as an assistant, eventually becoming a muleteer in his own right. Muleteers figured prominently in the insurrection, for their occupation enabled them to develop a great familiarity with the landscape and people. Muleteers also had ample reason to resent the pretensions and practices of the venal Spanish merchants of Mexico City who controlled the trade, routinely shortchanging all involved.

In 1790, after eleven years as a muleteer, Morelos bowed to his mother's wishes and began studying for the priesthood. While Morelos's writings indicate that he was sincerely religious, his reasons for entering the priesthood owed more to material concerns: one of his forebears had established a benefice (*capellanía*), a sum of money donated to the church for the purpose of providing an income for descendants who entered the priesthood; those descendants were to say masses for their benefactor after his death. If Morelos could stake his claim to the *capellanía*, which had become vacant in 1789 when its previous claimant had married, he and his mother would be set for life. Accordingly, Morelos embarked on his studies for the priesthood. He enrolled at the College of San Nicolás Obispo in Valladolid at the very moment when Miguel Hidalgo had taken the reins as rector of that institution. Morelos was a diligent and gifted student who was much admired and encouraged by his professors. He was ordained a priest in 1797.

If Morelos supposed his priestly career would bring him security, comfort, and prestige, he was doomed to chronic disappointment. The original logic of his career choice became moot in 1791 when the *capellanía* was awarded to one of Morelos's rivals. And the task to which the church assigned him—the parish priesthood of a town called Carácuaro—was decidedly unglamorous. Like most of Mexican society, the priesthood was characterized by staggering inequality. At the top of the hierarchy were the bishops, who lived in great luxury. Priests who had the good fortune to practice in and around the major cities of the viceroyalty were also remunerated handsomely. Occupying the bottom rung were the parish priests of the many impoverished and remote villages that dotted the Mexican landscape. There were not many rungs below Carácuaro, some seventy miles south of Valladolid in the arid, hot country of Michoacán, where Morelos took up his duties as parish priest in 1799.

In Carácuaro, Morelos earned an annual salary of about 120 pesos, roughly one-thousandth what an archbishop made. Making matters worse was the fact that this meager recompense was provided by taxes paid by already desperately poor villagers, and those villagers resented it. They wrote to the bishop of Michoacán complaining that Morelos mistreated them; Morelos—expressing sentiments shared by many parish priests of the day—declared that the villagers were poor because they were lazy, insolent, and habitually drunk. Still, he eventually agreed to reduce his already small salary by a fourth, and had to turn to raising livestock in order to make ends meet. He remained quite poor even after 1806, when the holder of his family's *capellanía* forfeited his claim by marrying and, at long last, Morelos was awarded the funds. The *capellanía* was a disappointment, to say the least, for it netted him only a miserly 72 pesos.

Like Father Hidalgo, Morelos did not allow his priestly vocation to interfere with an active love life. His first son, sired with an Indian woman named Brígida Almonte in 1803, was named Juan Nepomuceno Almonte. Almonte would go on to achieve distinction as a statesman and military leader. Morelos is known to have fathered at least two, possibly three, other children during his time at Carácuaro.

Morelos entered middle age with few prospects of ever becoming anything more than an obscure country curate, but in 1810 his fortune changed suddenly and drastically. He first learned of the Hidalgo uprising in October of that year, when the newly elected bishop of Michoacán, Manuel Abad y Queipo, an erstwhile friend of Hidalgo's, ordered him to publish a ban of excommunication against Hidalgo and his associates. Morelos chose to demur until he had a chance to speak with Hidalgo, which he did on October 20. Hidalgo talked at great length about how the Spaniards in Mexico City were conspiring to turn the empire over to the French, who in turn would arrest priests and seize church property and "kill all Americans up to a certain age."[1] From that time onward, the impending and imminent loss of Mexico to the impious French was a staple of Morelos's thinking, the primary reason he habitually cited for his revolutionary activity. "We will not tire," he wrote to the bishop of Puebla in November 1811. "Spain is lost, and the Americas will inevitably fall into the hands of Europeans if we do not take up arms, because the Americas have been and remain the object of the ambition and greed of foreign nations. [Rebellion] is the lesser of two evils."[2]

Hidalgo persuaded Morelos to accept an officer's commission

and to carry the revolution southward. Specifically, he was detailed to conquer the vital port of Acapulco, a task for which Morelos was well suited, given his long experience as a muleteer and his intimacy with the terrain of the hot lands. Together with a mere twenty men, all poorly armed and untested, he set out toward Acapulco on October 25 and arrived near that port in early November. By later that same month his forces had swelled to three thousand—hardly the tens of thousands who had flocked to Hidalgo's banner in the highlands, but remarkable in view of the region's sparse population. Particularly enthusiastic were mulattoes and Indians from a region to the northwest of Acapulco known as the Costa Grande. In contrast to the peasants of the highlands, most of whom grew corn for subsistence, the coastal poor were mostly sharecroppers who grew cotton destined for sale in the country's interior. Spanish merchants from Mexico City made a regular practice of swindling the sharecroppers by forcing them to accept goods against future production of cotton. During the late colonial period, the Napoleonic Wars disrupted shipping, making the market for cotton extremely uncertain. There were good years, when conflict interrupted shipments of textiles from Spain and demand for cotton was high in the colony. But there were more bad years, when shipments from Spain depressed the colonial market for cotton, and the sharecroppers found themselves perpetually on the losing end of transactions, with little power to protest. Indians and mulattoes were also the only people in the colony forced to pay tribute. Their anger was palpable, and Morelos offered them a release for that anger.

Even with three thousand men, Morelos's task was daunting. Acapulco was among the best-defended cities in the viceroyalty, for it was the colony's lifeline to the lucrative Asian markets. Inland it was ringed by small towns that could be quickly garrisoned for defense from land attack, and facing seaward from the east side of the harbor was a stone fortress designed to be impregnable, with twelve-foot-thick walls and a hundred guns of large caliber.

Morelos spent much time preparing his siege. He issued a proclamation designed to appeal to the region's poor. "With the exception of Europeans," it read, "inhabitants of this America will be known simply as Americans; they shall no longer be classified as Indians, mulattoes, or castes. None shall pay tribute, nor will there be slavery in the future, and all who have slaves shall be punished. There will be no local taxes, and the Indians shall receive the profits from their own lands. All Americans who owe any quantity of money to the Europeans are not obligated to pay, while debts owed by Europeans will be rigorously enforced."[3] The proclamation had its intended effect, even enticing some royalist troops to desert to the rebels. Morelos's forces were quickly able to take control of the towns around Acapulco, cutting communication between the port and the capital. When royalists tried to drive them out in January 1811, the rebels won an impressive victory, capturing valuable military supplies in the bargain. Unfortunately for the rebels, the port itself proved practically invulnerable. After laying siege for six months, Morelos finally was obliged to abandon the effort and move his forces northward.

Morelos's military fortunes soon improved. He was able to seize many of the key towns in what is now the state of Guerrero—Chilpancingo, Tixtla, Chilapa—capturing many military supplies along the way. Morelos soon proved himself a far more capable military commander than Hidalgo had been, organizing his army with a tight chain of command, and subjecting his men to rigorous drills and training. He strictly forbade plunder, which, along with insubordination, cowardice, treason, or "any disturbance which is opposed to the law of God, the peace of the kingdom, and the progress of our arms," was grounds for execution. Morelos was also able to add to his forces a couple of elite families, the Galeanas and the Bravos. The Galeanas were descended from a British pirate who had been shipwrecked on the coast in the early 1700s; by the late 1700s, they had become wealthy cotton planters. The Bravo brothers—Leonardo, Miguel, and Victor—were relatively well-to-do farmers of the Chilpancingo region who refused to contribute to the defense of the colonial regime. When the royalists seized their hacienda in retaliation, the entire family hid out in a cave for several months before joining Morelos's forces in May 1811. Leonardo Bravo's young son, Nicolás, also joined the rebellion; he would later serve as the first vice president of independent Mexico. Also joining Morelos were a number of other individuals who displayed formidable military talents. Manuel Félix Fernández, who took the nom de guerre Guadalupe Victoria, would become Mexico's first president; Vicente Guerrero, a man of mixed Indian, black, and white blood, would become its second. By late August 1811, Morelos had four battalions under arms, and the rebels controlled most of Mexico's southern coast. This effectively ended what is generally referred to as Morelos's "first campaign."

Autonomists and the Spanish Cortes

Most creoles disdained the movements of Hidalgo and Morelos because their extreme violence and the sorts of people who made up the rank and file of the rebel armies seemed to pose a serious threat to the established social order. That social order tended to work fairly well for prosperous creoles. As far as they were concerned, it merely needed tweaking, not a complete overhaul. If Spain's more obnoxious policies could be rescinded and greater opportunities for home rule provided, conservative and moderate creoles could abide quite happily within the Spanish empire. And, as it happened, events in Spain appeared to offer them the chance to realize their aims without participating in the bloodletting.

Back in January 1809, only four months after the coup that overthrew Viceroy Iturrigaray and set revolutionary conspiracies in motion, the Supreme Central Junta in Spain set a precedent that delighted those creoles: it declared that "the vast and precious dominions of the Indies are an essential and integral part of the

monarchy." Those dominions were declared to be of equal stature
with Spain itself, and all had the right to political representation. It
only remained to devise the mechanism through which such representation would be realized.

Further events made the matter appear more urgent. In early
1810, the Spaniards resisting Napoleon suffered a series of reverses and were forced to reassemble their government in the port
of Cádiz in the far south. While besieged by French armies and
yellow fever and fearing that Spanish nationality was likely lost forever, they nevertheless managed to form a five-man regency to
govern the empire in the name of Ferdinand VII. In the summer
they received alarming news from overseas: citizens in Venezuela
and Argentina, assuming Spain to be a lost cause, had forcibly deposed the Spanish authorities and formed their own juntas to
wield power locally, ostensibly until Ferdinand VII could be restored to his throne. The specter of colonists ruling themselves
seemed to herald the very real possibility that the entire empire
could disintegrate. The regency thereupon called for a meeting of
the Cortes, a parliament that had originated in the eleventh century, but which had fallen into a prolonged period of disuse with
the rise of royal absolutism in the fifteenth century. In February
1810, the regency issued a call to the Americans to choose representatives to the Spanish Cortes, one for each province.

The deputies were chosen by a quick and simple process: the
municipal council of each provincial capital met and chose three
men who were intelligent, honest, and native to the province. The
names were placed in a container, and one was drawn at random.
These procedures—the closest thing to a popular election Mexico
had yet seen—were attended by artillery barrages, martial music,
and the inevitable Te Deums. Virtually all of the men selected
were zealous advocates of Mexican autonomy. The American
deputies were unable to reach Spain in time for the September
convocation of the Cortes, so the Americas were represented in
the short term by Americans already living in Spain. Eventually,
twenty-one Mexican delegates took their seats in the Cortes.

Although in theory a venerable institution, the Cortes that met in 1810 was in reality something entirely new on the Spanish political landscape. Unlike its earlier incarnation, this Cortes included American representatives, claimed supreme authority during the king's absence, and set out to create a constitution that would establish laws of the land and place formal limits on the powers of the king, when and if he returned to the throne.

These were exciting times: in the midst of war, a group of bold men aimed at nothing less than the remaking of the entire Spanish empire. Most of the men who spearheaded the effort were young. They had grown up in the days of Charles IV and Godoy, so their reverence toward the monarchy was more tepid than that of their older and more traditionally minded counterparts. They had also come of age in the era of the French Revolution, and were inspired rather than horrified by the ideas it represented. At its first meeting, on September 24, 1810, even while recognizing Ferdinand VII as the legitimate king, the Cortes declared that it governed in the name of the people. It attacked some of the sacred institutions of the old regime, including the absolutist monarchy and the Holy Inquisition. In November it decreed freedom of the press, making an exception for religious dogma. These adventurous men came to be called "liberals"—the first recorded use of the term as a political label. Their opponents, the traditionalists, acquired the name "serviles."

Most of the American deputies to the Cortes fell squarely into the liberal camp, and they were hardly shy in arguing their cases. On December 16, 1810, the American delegation presented a list of American demands to the Cortes, arguing that only if those demands were met could Spain contain what one Mexican delegate, a parish priest named José Miguel Guridi y Alcocer, called the "fire which is spreading like a flood and burning up entire provinces."[4] The liberals who represented Mexico at the Spanish Cortes hated Spanish despotism and were as eager for reform as the rebels in arms. Miguel Ramos Arizpe, another prominent Mexican delegate, denounced the Spanish monarchy in terms that flirted with sedition, charging that kings were interested only in their own luxury. Guridi y Alcocer argued passionately, if futilely, for an end to slavery throughout the empire. And Pedro Bautista Pino, the delegate from New Mexico who did not arrive in Spain until November 1812, attributed the violence in his country to the existence there of millions of hungry, ill-clad people without land or hope. Even so, the demands the deputies made did not envision drastic social reform. They were essentially the same ones that creole autonomists had been making for years—reforms designed, not surprisingly, to make life better for the creoles. They wanted representation in the Cortes in proportion to their population; equal access to all civil, ecclesiastical, and military offices; the abolition of government monopolies; the return of the Jesuits; and full economic freedom. If those demands were met, most of the American deputies implied, then the Americas would be content to remain part of the Spanish empire.

The first and most important task that the American deputies set themselves was to secure equality of representation for Americans in the Cortes. Debate on the matter commenced immediately, and it naturally became a heated issue in the framing of the new constitution that the Cortes began to prepare in December 1810. Spaniards in the Cortes faced a dilemma: on the one hand, they were well aware that allowing representation for the colonists was essential if they were to forge the unity necessary to keep the empire together and to confront the French invasion; on the other hand, their census data told them that there were perhaps 16 million people living in the Americas and the Philippines, while Spain itself was home to only about 10.5 million. If they allowed true proportional representation, they would find themselves outnumbered perhaps three to two in the Cortes.

The Spanish delegates hit upon the issue of race as a means of assuring their continued political control. They proposed that all persons descended in any wise from Africa, with the exception of a few who would be granted special recognition by the Cortes for distinguished service or exemplary conduct, be excluded from political life. Race mixing had proceeded in the Americas for many generations, ensuring that race was a thoroughly ambiguous concept—so ambiguous, in fact, that no one could say with anything close to certainty how many people would be excluded by the proposed provision. One Mexican deputy, claiming as his authority the German traveler Alexander von Humboldt, insisted that 10 million of the 16 million inhabitants of the Americas had African blood. Other estimates were far lower, but in any case race mixing had effectively rendered it impossible to divine the true racial makeup of the American population. The proposal to exclude all those of African descent was clearly a ploy on the part of the Spanish delegates, and the Americans did not hesitate to make that charge explicit.

Of course, the American deputies undoubtedly had their own self-interest very much in mind as they delivered their impassioned pleas for racial justice. They pointed out that, as a practical matter, the denial of full citizenship rights would surely alienate the castes and perhaps drive them into the rebel camp. Several deputies went beyond practical considerations and made a powerful brief for racial justice, something that had been largely lacking during the three hundred years of the colonies' existence. The Colombian deputy José Mejía Lequérica—who, as the illegitimate son of a prominent lawyer, had felt the sting of prejudice—spoke out eloquently in favor of total equality, even for slaves: "Slaves too are men, and some day policy, justice and the Christian religion will show us how they also should be considered. As plants are improved by grafting, so too are the mixed castes of America . . . why should their blood be deemed impure?" The Mexican Miguel Ramos Arizpe, his eyes filled with tears, eloquently described the virtues of the colored castes, and presciently noted that overcoming Mexico's race problem was vital to the country's future: "I cannot but give way to emotion when I contemplate the fate that threatens such virtuous and worthy folk . . . Our great interest . . . consists in merging all these castes, in making one nation, one people, one family."[5]

Not all were so enlightened. Some American deputies opposed equal rights for the castes, and the zeal of some Spaniards to maintain control of the Cortes was bolstered by the most virulent racism. On September 16, 1811, the merchants' guild of Mexico weighed in with a memorial that was read in an open session of the Cortes. The memorial viciously denounced Indians, but reserved its harshest insults for the castes: "Inebriates, incontinent, lax, lacking honor, gratitude, and fidelity, without a sense of religion or morality, without elegance, cleanliness, or decency, they appear even more mechanical and immoderate than the Indian himself."[6] The American deputies tried to walk out of the Cortes en masse in response to the diatribe, but were restrained by the guards. In the end, the Americans' arguments failed to carry the day, and the constitution—which became law on March 12, 1812—did indeed exclude nearly all castes from political life. Despite all protestations to the contrary, it was clear that the Spanish Cortes had no real intention of recognizing the overseas provinces as truly equal.

Still more galling for the Americans, the Constitution of 1812 did not grant them all of the economic reforms they desired. There were at least some small victories in this area. Americans asked the Cortes to remove all restrictions on the development of agriculture, industry, and handicrafts, especially those irksome prohibitions on Americans engaging in enterprises—such as the cultivation of wine grapes and olives—that competed with those of Spain. These requests met with unanimous approval. They also demanded that all government monopolies, such as those on tobacco and salt, be eliminated and replaced with direct taxes. This too was done. But the victories on these points were ultimately less significant than the failure of the Americans to get meaningful reform of trade. The Americans wished to be allowed to sell any goods they produced to anyone who was willing to buy them, and to be allowed to ship those goods freely in either Spanish or foreign vessels. They wanted access to Spain's possessions in the Philippines, and by extension to all of Asia. They wanted to be permitted to trade directly with any nation that was not a frank enemy of Spain. These issues garnered the full and acrimonious attention of the wealthy and powerful merchants of Cádiz, Veracruz, and Mexico City, who stood to lose their extremely lucrative monopoly on trade. The Cortes's refusal to allow the Americans to become masters of their own economic destiny, along with the refusal to permit true proportional representation, clearly signaled again that the Americans were not truly equal. Ramos Arizpe warned that the Europeans would never enjoy "complete prosperity, if they do not make it transmissible to their brothers of America."[7] Others warned, more menacingly, that the obstinacy of the Spaniards would soon drive the Americans to separate themselves from the empire.

The American deputies achieved one other important concession. In response to the tireless pleas by Ramos Arizpe and others for greater home rule, the constitution allowed for the creation of two entirely new institutions. City councils throughout the empire, which traditionally had been dominated by hereditary elites, were now transformed into popularly elected bodies; and new institutions, to be known as "provincial deputations," were created. These were to be local governing bodies made up of several popularly elected members and an executive appointed by the central government. The provincial deputations originated in the many small juntas that had appeared in the wake of the French invasion, and they were enormously popular with Americans who were enthusiasts for regional autonomy. Unfortunately, the trend toward regionalism—which was exacerbated by the wars for independence—would become one of Latin America's greatest curses during the nineteenth century. But for the moment, at least, the constitution's allowances for regional autonomy seemed to liberals to be a signal victory.

With the new arrangements of power, the office of viceroy ceased to exist. Instead of a viceroy, the major overseas provinces were to be governed by superior political chiefs, and the smaller provinces by captains general. In Mexico, this meant that the former viceroy lost jurisdiction over those areas that already had captains general, an enormous swath of territory that included most of northern and southern Mexico. The *audiencias*—theretofore the highest governing institution after the viceroy—were transformed into high courts. Henceforth, declared the constitution, the Spanish empire would consist of provinces, all at least partially self-governing, all answering ultimately to the central government in Spain.

Although by no means a perfect instrument from the American point of view, the Spanish Constitution of 1812 was a decidedly liberal document, one that threatened to completely rearrange the balance of power within Spain and its dominions. It transformed Spain from an absolute monarchy into a constitutional monarchy, where the king was reduced from sovereign to a mere executor of the laws who had to share power with the elected representatives of the people. The hereditary powers of aristocrats were abolished, and all citizens were to become equal before the law, with the same guaranteed set of rights. From the perspective of the American deputies and their creole backers, these were very welcome changes, and they gave ample cause to hope that, in time, true equality might one day be attained.

The Monster of the South

Of course, the dramatic reforms outlined by the deputies in Spain had to be implemented in the real world of Mexico, something Viceroy Venegas showed little inclination to do. He rather seemed disposed to invoke a venerable formula in imperial relations that was summed up in the phrase *Obedezco pero no cumplo* (I obey, but do not carry out). This invocation solemnly acknowledged the authority of higher-ups in Spain while implying that those higher-ups were regrettably ignorant of colonial realities. Venegas refused to publish the Cortes's decree of freedom of the press, despite the angry and insistent demands of the Mexican deputies. He now deemed it unwise to test new freedoms and political schemes while facing a major and metastasizing popular insurrection.

The official order to enforce the new constitution reached Viceroy Venegas on May 10, 1812. The timing, in Venegas's view, could not possibly have been worse, for the rebellion was approaching high tide. To the north of the capital, rebels were able to obstruct trade, including the movement of vital mercury and gunpowder to the silver mines. Rebels had occupied many towns and haciendas to the east of Mexico City, and were able to keep up steady harassment of trade and travel between the capital and the vital port of Veracruz. They had secured a stronghold at the town of Apizaco, roughly fifty miles north of Puebla, and the villagers of that region supported the rebellion so enthusiastically that they donated their cherished church bells to be melted down and forged into cannons. At the end of January, rebel bands besieged Tepeaca, just to the southeast of Puebla, and were beaten back, but another band managed to take the town of Huejotzingo, to the northwest of Puebla. Venegas assumed that the fall of Veracruz to the rebels was imminent. Worse yet, between December 1811 and February 1812, José María Morelos with an army of some three thousand men had taken the towns of Taxco, Izúcar, and Cuautla, all within striking distance of Mexico City. Once again tension gripped the residents of the capital. For the government, the only unequivocal bright spot had been the disruption, in January 1812, of Rayón's Supreme National Junta, which involved the merciless destruction of the town of Zitácuaro. But that victory had only wounded the rebellion; it had not come close to finishing it off. For Venegas, promulgating a new constitution at this perilous moment was practically suicidal. It was a terrible time for the Spanish government to change the rules.

Morelos made Venegas's task somewhat easier by choosing this moment to commit the greatest strategic blunder of his career. From Izúcar, it would have made much sense to advance northward to take Atlixco, and then to lay siege to Mexico's second-largest city, Puebla, which was situated astride the all-important road connecting the capital to the port of Veracruz. In December 1811, when Morelos had his best shot at taking Puebla, the city was very vulnerable. Its intendant, the highly capable Manuel de Flon, had left to fight the Hidalgo revolt back in October 1810 and was killed at the Battle of Calderón three months later. The municipal government took charge of the city's defenses, recruiting battalions of patrician volunteers who delighted in their special uniforms but had little stomach for actual fighting. In early 1811, the city's defenses had been placed in the hands of royalist commanders García José Dávila and Ciriaco de Llano, but despite their firm leadership and contributions from wealthy merchants and landowners, the volunteer corps still had only a hundred rifles. Had Morelos struck quickly and decisively that December, he might well have taken Puebla and been poised for an attack on the capital. But Morelos, fearing that his conquests to the south were threatened with recapture by the royalists—a fear that was well founded, for that was precisely the strategy that Venegas and Calleja were plotting—left Izúcar and returned to Taxco, which he successfully defended against encroachments by royalist commander Rosendo Porlier, capturing many weapons and prisoners in the bargain. He then moved east to Cuautla, which, according to a royalist spy, he entered "as confidently as you would enter your own home." There he resumed plans for an assault on Puebla. But by then it was too late, for Puebla was by that time well fortified and defended. Venegas sent Calleja to Cuautla to bottle up the rebels there and prevent their movement northward. Venegas saw the siege of Cuautla as pivotal: "With the fate of Cuautla will be decided the fate of this kingdom."[8]

Morelos's forces at Cuautla, consisting of roughly four to five

The Mexican Bajío, a region comprising the state of Guanajuato and parts of Querétaro and Michoacán, was home to Mexico's richest silver mines and the cradle of the wars for independence. (Photograph by the author)

José de Iturrigaray (1742–1815), viceroy of Mexico from January 4, 1803, to September 16, 1808. His overthrow by conservative Spaniards set the stage for the creole conspiracies that eventually erupted into revolution. (*Los gobernantes de México*, by Manuel Rivera Cambas, 1873)

Ferdinand VII (1784–1833), king of Spain briefly in 1808 and again from 1813 to 1833. Although the rebellion in Mexico was initially incited in his name, upon assuming the throne he proved to be intransigent and autocratic, and was clearly no friend of the insurgents. (*Los gobernantes de México*, by Manuel Rivera Cambas, 1873)

Miguel Hidalgo y Costilla (1753–1811), the parish priest of the town of Dolores whose Grito de Dolores launched the insurgent movement. (Museo Regional La Alhóndiga de Granaditas)

Ignacio Allende (1769–1811), a captain in the militia unit known as the Queen's Provincial Dragoons, became Hidalgo's chief co-conspirator and second-in-command. (Museo Regional La Alhóndiga de Granaditas)

The Parroquia de Nuestra Señora de los Dolores (parish church of Our Lady of Sorrows). It was here that Miguel Hidalgo gathered the townsfolk and delivered his famous Grito de Dolores. (Photograph by the author)

The Alhóndiga de Granaditas, the municipal granary of Guanajuato, where frightened Spaniards took refuge during the early stages of the rebellion. The bloody and disorderly siege of Guanajuato persuaded many creoles to turn against the rebellion. (Photograph by the author)

Juan José de los Reyes Martínez (1782–1863), nicknamed "El Pípila," was the mine worker who set fire to the granary door during the siege of Guanajuato, and is celebrated as one of Guanajuato's great heroes. During the 1930s, when the leftward-leaning Lázaro Cárdenas was president, this huge, torch-wielding monument was built in his honor. The legend reads, "There are still other Alhóndigas to burn." (Photograph by the author)

José María Morelos y Pavón (1765–1815), a parish priest of mixed race who became the leading figure in the rebellion after the deaths of Hidalgo and Allende. (Museo Nacional de Historia, INAH)

Francisco Javier Venegas (1760–1838), a distinguished Spanish military officer who served as viceroy of Mexico from September 14, 1810, to March 4, 1813, the first phase of the wars for independence. (Los gobernantes de México, by Manuel Rivera Cambas, 1873)

General Félix María Calleja del Rey, First Count of Calderón (1753–1828), Spanish military man and eventual architect of the counterinsurgency in the rebellion's early stages. He served as viceroy of Mexico from March 4, 1813, to September 20, 1816. (Museo Nacional de Historia, INAH)

Francisco Xavier Mina (1789–1817), a liberal Spanish military officer who, with an army composed mostly of Anglo-American adventurers, invaded Mexico in 1817. His rebellion fizzled, and he was captured and executed at age twenty-seven. (Museo Regional La Alhóndiga de Granaditas)

Agustín de Iturbide (1783–1824), the royalist army officer who switched sides to lead the movement for independence in 1821. (Museo Nacional de Historia, INAH)

Juan Ruiz de Apodaca, First Count of Venadito (1754–1835). He became viceroy on September 20, 1816, and served until July 5, 1821, when ·conservative military men overthrew him, contending that he failed to take stern measures against the Iturbide uprising. (*Los gobernantes de México*, by Manuel Rivera Cambas, 1873)

Vicente Guerrero (1782–1831), the only prominent rebel leader still remaining in the field by 1821. After some intense persuasion, he agreed to unite his forces with those of Iturbide under the terms of the Plan of Iguala. (Museo Nacional de Historia, INAH)

Antonio López de Santa Anna (1794–1876). Later Mexico's great caudillo, in 1821 he was a young royalist army officer operating in the strategic region of Veracruz. He enthusiastically endorsed Iturbide's rise to power, but later led a revolt against the empire. (Museo Nacional de Historia, INAH)

The Angel of Independence, erected on Mexico City's Paseo de la Reforma by the government of the dictator Porfirio Díaz in 1910 in honor of the centennial of Hidalgo's Grito de Dolores. Since 1925, a mausoleum in the monument has housed the remains of Hidalgo, Allende, Morelos, Guerrero, Mina, and several other heroes of independence.

(Photograph by Greg Crider)

thousand troops, were outnumbered nearly two to one. But the two sides were evenly matched in firepower, and the city of Cuautla—located in the midst of rolling hills and abundant vegetation, with a thick defensive wall to the west and the wide Cuautla River to the east—was admirably situated to withstand attack. General Leonardo Bravo had busied himself fortifying the plazas and churches and digging a network of trenches around the town. Two cannons were stationed at each entrance to the city, and most of the town's defenders were armed with rifles. The rebels apparently felt little anxiety about the impending attack, for according to a royalist spy they made merry with constant "games, dances and amusements, such that many of the families who had fled now returned very happily to their homes."[9]

The royalists attacked on February 19 from four directions, but the rebels repelled them with cannon shots and heavy fire from the roof of a convent. Calleja, appalled at the carnage and having narrowly escaped being killed by a blast from his own cannons, ordered a retreat. He then opted for a patient policy, building up his forces and armaments and settling in for a prolonged siege. Later in the month his army was reinforced by troops from Puebla commanded by General Ciriaco de Llano.

On March 10, the royalists began a furious bombardment that went on for four days, demolishing much of the town but doing little harm to the rebels' confidence. But unfortunately for the rebels, time was on the side of the royalists. They surrounded the city, cutting off communications as well as supplies of food and drinking water. By the middle of April, corn supplies had been exhausted, and the town's inhabitants were reduced to eating insects, rats, cats, lizards, and worn rawhide stripped from the doors of homes. The only liquid that was abundantly available was cane liquor, which only weakened the defenders further and encouraged an onslaught of disease. The town church and many homes were filled with the sick and dying; by month's end twenty or thirty people were perishing daily, and many more were wracked with fever and dysentery. Even so, Morelos rejected entreaties to surrender, at times with taunts. He addressed a letter to Calleja on April 4 to "Mr. Spaniard," going on to say, "He who dies for the true religion and for his fatherland does not die unhappy. You, who wish to die for the religion of Napoleon, will end your days as others direct. It will not be you who determines the end of this army, but God, who has decided that the Europeans should be punished and the Americans should recover their rights." He ended his sarcastic missive by inviting Calleja to "throw some more little bombs at me, as I'm sad without them."[10]

On April 17, Venegas offered amnesty to any rebels who would lay down their weapons, but Morelos refused the bait. Calleja grudgingly confessed his admiration for Morelos's remarkable leadership, for morale remained high and desertion was minimal even during the darkest days of the siege: "If the determination and activity of Cuautla's defenders were in behalf of morality and directed to a just cause, they would one day merit a distinguished place in history. Pinned down by our troops and afflicted by privation, they manifest joy in all that happens: they bury their corpses amid the pealing of bells celebrating their glorious deaths; they shout, dance, and get drunk, imposing the death penalty upon any who speak of misfortunes or surrender. [Morelos] is a second Mohammed, who promises worldly resurrection and eventual paradise, feeding the passions of his happy Muslims."[11]

The royalists too were suffering from hunger, disease, unusually heavy spring rains, and declining morale. Calleja, himself in poor health, made plans to lift the siege, but before he could do that Morelos made a bold attempt to flee the town. At midnight on May 2, Morelos gathered his soldiers and townspeople in the main plaza and instructed them to march quietly out of town. The ploy nearly worked, for the rebels covered some distance before the royalists caught on. The royalist attack was swift and brutal, dispersing the rebel column in panic and confusion. Some three thousand rebels were slaughtered, their corpses clogging the roads and impeding the royalists in their efforts to chase down the few who escaped. The carnage inflicted upon the insurgents was so terrible that even some veteran royalist officers were sickened by it. H. G. Ward, who became the British chargé d'affaires years later, recounted having heard "officers, who were present at the siege, speak of [the slaughter], after a lapse of ten years, with horror."[12]

Among the few to escape was Morelos himself. Many of his stalwart fighters went to their deaths defending his life, and he was able to struggle on to Izúcar despite two broken ribs. The royalists seized Morelos's archives, virtually all of the rebels' armaments, and one of Morelos's most trusted commanders, Leonardo Bravo, who was garroted on September 13 after refusing Calleja's offer of a pardon if he and his son would renounce the revolution.

The indefatigable Morelos—"the Monster of the South," as Mexico City newspapers were now calling him—began his third campaign almost immediately, this time moving southward toward the important city of Oaxaca. The rebels took the towns of Chilapa and Huajapan, the latter after a siege of 111 days. But these conquests counted for relatively little, since the royalists were firmly in control of the region to the immediate south of Mexico City, effectively closing off the possibility of a rebel assault on the capital. Royalist Captain José Gabriel Armijo undertook extensive mopping-up operations in the region around Cuautla, including an assault on Yautepec that led to the capture of a notorious rebel commander named Francisco Ayala. Ayala, in addition to maintaining a cannon foundry, had been annoying Morelos by regularly sending him the severed heads of captured royalists. The practice did not endear Ayala to the Spaniards, either, so it is unsurprising that the royalists now executed him along with his two sons, publicly and with dispatch.

Mexico's First Elections

In November 1812, José María Morelos took the key southern city of Oaxaca, encountering only minimal resistance. Though still far from victory, Morelos's forces controlled most of southern Mexico, including what are now the states of Oaxaca and Guerrero as well as portions of the provinces of Veracruz, Puebla, and Mexico. From September he had been enjoying a new and invaluable asset, namely, a fifth column inside Mexico City. A group of people styling themselves "the Guadalupes," many of them prominent and wealthy creole lawyers, clerics, and journalists, had formed in the capital. Some among them were well connected enough to gain access to the viceroy's own correspondence from his secretary's office, and they were able to convey to Morelos news about royalist military plans and movements, the government's financial condition, political developments in the capital, and the rebels' ongoing search for overseas alliances. They also worked to set up an insurgent press, smuggle arms and munitions, shelter fugitive rebels and royalist deserters, and drum up pro-independence sentiment. The most famous of the Guadalupes was María Leona Vicario, the daughter of a wealthy Spanish merchant. From her comfortable Mexico City residence, Vicario managed to establish an efficient courier service that carried encoded communications to the rebels, furnishing them reports on royalist military maneuvers and the latest political developments. She also persuaded a large number of skilled armorers to relocate to Ignacio Rayón's encampment at Tlalpujuhua, Michoacán, where they set about manufacturing quantities of rifles and cannons.

Late 1812 was a heady time for the pro-independence movement. The liberal Spanish Constitution of 1812 decreed press freedom and called for elections of officials at a variety of levels. Of course, the Cortes had already decreed freedom of the press, a decree that Viceroy Venegas had been blithely ignoring for two years now. But he could not easily disregard a constitutional imperative, so after establishing a board of censors to watch for sedition, he published the new law on October 5, 1812. The Guadalupes were poised to take full advantage of the new freedom, for they had already been involved in producing clandestine propaganda. Soon Mexico City was inundated with pamphlets and broadsides produced by the likes of Carlos María de Bustamante, a lawyer and journalist, and José Joaquín Fernández de Lizardi, who styled himself "the Mexican Thinker" and was later credited with writing the first major Latin American novel.

The Guadalupes were also active in preparing for Mexico's first elections. The procedures set out in the constitution were indirect and byzantine in their complexity, but the Cortes's intentions were undoubtedly generous and sincere. All citizens of the Spanish dominions were eligible to vote; there was a literacy requirement, but it was suspended on the grounds that it would take time for public education plans to take effect. Excepted from citizenship were criminals, vagrants, debtors, domestic servants, and persons of African descent. The elections were to choose new constitutional city councils (*ayuntamientos*), provincial deputations to advocate for the various regions, and deputies to the Spanish Cortes, whose next session was slated to begin in October 1813. (Mexico was to have forty-one deputies at the Cortes.)

The initial round of voting, where electors were chosen to select the eventual officeholders, took place on November 29, 1812. The results were a huge shock to the viceroy and his fellow Spaniards. All of those elected were creoles, and they all favored some version of autonomy for Mexico, if not outright independence. None of them sympathized with the Europeans, and some were suspected of frankly treasonous activities, including two men who had been implicated in a plot to assassinate the viceroy and some who were known to have actively collaborated with the insurgency. Worse still, the raucous celebrations that followed the elections made it abundantly clear to the royalists that they and the system they defended were heartily despised by a majority of the Mexican people. "The city was flooded with crowds of people," wrote General Calleja, "who carried a great number of torches all during the night; they shouted vivas to Morelos, to independence, and to the electors, all of whom were unreliable Americans, and the greater part of them disloyal; they shouted death to the Europeans and to their government; they tried to break into the cathedral tower to ring the bells; and they had the audacity to appear before the palace and demand artillery."[13] The Guadalupes, of course, were elated, and they conveyed their elation to José María Morelos at his new base of operations in Oaxaca. In many parts of Mexico, rebels celebrated the results of the voting with artillery salvos and masses of thanksgiving.

The triumph was illusory. Although there is little convincing evidence that the elections were marred by fraud or violence, and although the outcome clearly reflected the true wishes of the people, the election of 1812 still set an unfortunate precedent for Mexican democracy. As in many subsequent cases, the people in power simply refused to abide by the results. Viceroy Venegas suspended the elections, charging voting irregularities. He also revoked freedom of the press, jailing a number of pamphleteers, including Lizardi, and forcing others to flee. General Calleja, a man renowned for his oppressive tactics, was named military governor of Mexico City, and in March, at the behest of European Spaniards who felt Venegas was too lenient, the Cortes ordered that Calleja replace Venegas as viceroy. This was nothing less than a coup d'état by the city's Spaniards, and it left the rebels and autonomists bitter and frustrated. Morelos claimed that treachery had been the real point of the election: "They call elections to draw out the electors in Mexico; they grant the license to print in order to seize the writers."[14]

General Calleja, who became viceroy (or "superior political chief," as the constitution would have it) in March 1813, refused to reinstate press freedom, but he did allow elections, first for the *cabildo* (city council) of Mexico City and later for deputies to the Cortes. Although he permitted the results of those elections to stand, he complained about them vociferously and did everything in his power to undercut whatever authority the elected officials might claim. He even went so far as to warn his superiors in Spain that two deputies elected to the Cortes—José de Alcalá and

Manuel Cortázar—were "pernicious subjects" who were bound
to "hasten the ruin of the Americas." Mexico City's constitutional
cabildo contained, in the view of the conservative *audiencia*, "not
one single individual of proven patriotism."[15]

The Terrible Year

José María Morelos began the year 1813 by committing another
serious military blunder. The Guadalupes, who hoped that 1813
would be the year the insurgency triumphed, urged Morelos to
head north and attack either Puebla, Veracruz, or the capital itself.
They also advised him to focus on disrupting the supply lines between Mexico City and Veracruz, and to make a more determined
effort to seek aid from foreign powers, especially the United States,
which, they supposed, was most likely to sympathize with the liberal project of independence. This was sound advice, but unfortunately Morelos chose a different course. Perhaps unable to forget
his original commission from Father Hidalgo, and imagining that
a thriving Pacific trade would be a boon to the rebellion, Morelos
resolved again to lay siege to Acapulco. After much careful planning, the attack began on April 6; the seemingly impregnable
fortress of Acapulco fell to the rebels nearly five months later, on
August 19.

Unfortunately, Acapulco, as it turned out, was not nearly the
prize Morelos had imagined it would be. The rebels controlled the
countryside around the city, so the port was already of little use to
the government at Mexico City. Planning and executing the siege
had used up a full seven months, and many men and resources
were lost in the effort. More importantly, the period during which
Morelos was preoccupied with the siege of Acapulco had allowed
Calleja to battle lesser rebel chieftains in the north of the country
and to shore up the defenses of the capital. Late 1813 was a high-
water mark in the sheer quantity of territory held by the rebels,
but appearances were deceiving.

The year 1813 might well have been a perfect time for the rebels to move in for the kill, for the people of Mexico City were suffering torments of biblical proportions.[16] Most of their misery could be blamed directly on the rebellion. It had disrupted supplies of food, leading to severe shortages and high prices. The price of corn had risen 300 percent since 1808, and the price of meat had quadrupled. Currency became scarce as the rebellion disrupted shipments of silver and mercury. Viceroy Calleja tried to compensate by ordering the minting of cheap copper coins, which increased inflation. Speculation, hoarding, and fraud added to such woes. A serious shortage of fuel was caused by the practice—initiated by royalist soldiers, but also engaged in by merchants and government officials—of waylaying Indians on the roads to the city and buying up their supplies of charcoal at their asking price, then selling the same charcoal in the city at wildly inflated prices.

While prices rose, tax revenues plummeted. At least part of the shortfall could not be blamed directly on the rebellion: the Cortes had done its part by ending Indian tribute payments, depriving the government of about a million pesos per year. Another principal source of revenue—a 6 percent sales tax and a tax on pulque—dropped by more than half between 1810 and 1813. Silver, which had long been the motor force of the economy, bottomed out in 1812, with production amounting to less than one-sixth that of 1809. To compensate, Calleja turned to Mexico's rich, collecting forced loans and inventing a variety of irritating new taxes. People with incomes in excess of three hundred pesos a year were subject to income taxes of up to 12.5 percent, and a 10 percent tax was levied on urban real estate. People were ordered to surrender their silver and jewelry with the promise that its value would be reimbursed with interest within a year—repayments that never materialized. Calleja also set up a novel lottery. Purchasing lottery tickets was voluntary for the first six months of the year, but during the second six months persons of means were forced to buy tickets. Despite all of this fiscal creativity, the treasury continued to suffer.

The total debt of the viceroyalty had risen to some 49 million pesos by 1813, and it would rise to 80 million by 1816.

Government penury meant that essential city services were lacking. In the absence of such services, crime increased to epidemic proportions, sanitation was neglected, and schools were shut down. During 1813, only about 5,000 children in Mexico City attended school at all, out of a total school-aged population of around 30,000. By 1819, only 2,773 children were in school.

As if hunger, shortages, bloodshed, and rampant sedition were not enough, in early 1813 central Mexico was hit by a plague of typhus. The epidemic began in Puebla and soon spread to Mexico City, despite attempts by authorities to quarantine the city, fumigate travelers, and suspend mail and commerce from the east. Mexico City was an unhealthy place during the best of times, built as it was on a former lake bed. Canals that flowed through the city were normally filled with rubbish, sewage, animal carcasses, and other pollutants, all of which dumped eventually into fetid salt marshes east of the city, the remnants of the once lush Lake Texcoco. Unsanitary conditions, rancid food, and hunger combined to make the plague uncommonly severe. By midsummer, more than half of the city's residents had fallen ill. The treasury, of course, was bare, and private charity was hardly sufficient to confront the crisis. Improvised hospitals were set up to treat the dying. Each day, two specially designated carts reconnoitered the streets to gather bodies and haul them to hurriedly dug mass graves. In some neighborhoods people simply buried their dead in the streets or vacant lots. The plague was harshest for the very people that the city fathers traditionally relied on to collect the garbage and clean the canals, namely, the poor. So many of them died or fled that even an offer to triple the customary wage for trash collectors found no takers, and convicts had to be mobilized for the task. The city council eventually took the dramatic step of prohibiting the tolling of church bells, on the grounds that they spread panic.

Unusually heavy rains in August flooded the streets, adding to the general sense that God had singled the city out for exemplary punishment. At the same time, the city was invaded by packs of wild dogs that scavenged the streets, raided homes and gardens, attacked chickens and livestock, and, most horrifying of all, dug up the mass graves of plague victims and feasted on their decaying flesh. The government sent out parties of men armed with guns, knives, and poison to slaughter the dogs by night. Mornings would find the streets red with blood, the drainage canals clogged with the animals' ravaged carcasses.

The plague eased up with the cooler weather of autumn, but its toll was fearsome: officially, 20,385 people died of fever that summer of 1813, one-eighth of the city's population. The plague in the capital city also meant that a traditional destination for those fleeing the harsh conditions in the countryside was effectively closed off. And yet conditions in the countryside were harsher than they had ever been. The royalist counterinsurgency campaign brought mass executions, the razing of villages, mass relocation of country people, conscription into royalist or rebel armies, confiscation of property, banditry, and general devastation. The only comfort for the people of central Mexico lay in the thought that things could not possibly get much worse.

The rebellion for independence might well have come to an end in 1813. At that time, the rebels controlled nearly all of southern Mexico and portions of the center and north. They had allies working actively on their behalf in the capital. Popular elections clearly demonstrated that the Mexican people overwhelmingly favored autonomy or independence, and that the royalists had virtually no support. Mexico City, the center of imperial power, was a mortally weakened organism, ravaged by hunger, disease, social unrest, and natural calamity. Had Morelos chosen the summer of that year to deliver the coup de grâce to the capital instead of attacking Acapulco, Mexico might well have been spared several more years of warfare. It is remarkable that the royalist regime did not collapse in that year.

Despite their setbacks, the rebels continued to plan for a brighter day. In June 1813, from Acapulco, Morelos issued a decree convoking a congress, which was to gather in the southern city of Chilpancingo in September. So even as the residents of Mexico's capital suffered through unspeakable horrors, rebels gathered to form a new government, write a constitution, and, at long last, declare Mexico's independence from Spain.

SEVEN

THE UNRAVELING REVOLUTION

During the years 1812 to 1814, the movement for independence in Mexico crested and then began to unravel. Under Morelos, the rebels came to control an enormous swath of territory, mostly in southern Mexico; they finally got around to declaring independence from Spain; and they produced a viable constitution. But during that same period, the movement entered into a rapid and devastating decline from which it never recovered. Events in Spain played a small role in the movement's demise—Ferdinand VII returned to his throne in 1814 and did his best to stamp out every vestige of liberalism in Spain and its colonies, permitting the viceroy to crush the rebellion without being bound by legal constraints. But ultimately the movement was undone by its own incoherence. The independence army reflected the rural Mexican society from which most of its fighters hailed, and that worked decidedly to its disadvantage. The rebellion's ethnic makeup (roughly 60 percent Indian, 20 percent black and caste, and 20 percent white) was the same as in Mexican society at large, and one could hardly expect it to be free of the racial and class antagonisms that characterized the larger society. It also sprang from very local, rural roots, and people's reasons for fighting often had little to do with any stated aim of the movement. In reality, the "movement" for independence was a collection of local revolts that were sparked by the same set of political crises, but had little else in common.

Morelos Vanquished

As the Spanish Cortes conducted its bold experiments in republican government and Mexico held its first popular elections, the rebels too were working to forge new institutions and ideologies of government. Already, in early 1812, Ignacio Rayón had written a draft constitution featuring many progressive ideas, including press freedom, the right of habeas corpus, a liberal immigration policy, and abolition of caste distinctions, slavery, and torture. Rayón's constitution also put forth a puzzling formula regarding the location of sovereignty: sovereignty, said his constitution, originated with the people, resided in the person of Ferdinand VII, and was to be exercised by the Supreme National Junta of Mexico. The provinces would elect the junta, and it would share power with a congress elected by property owners. Rayón solicited comments from Morelos, who took several months to respond and then objected to several points, including the recognition of Ferdinand VII and the liberal immigration policy, which he feared would tend to corrupt the Catholic religion.

Rayón's influence had been waning at least since his initial seat of government, Zitácuaro in Michoacán, had been seized and razed by the royalists in January 1812. Rayón remained president of the Supreme National Junta, while Morelos held the title of captain general of the American armies and member of the supreme junta. But relations between Morelos and Rayón had been steadily deteriorating, mostly due to intense rivalries and chronic bickering among Rayón and his colleagues. Morelos denounced the factionalism as a "cancer." "Should all of us become involved in it," he wrote, "our perdition will be assured."[1] In a letter of June 28, 1813, while still engaged in the siege of Acapulco, Morelos called for the governing junta to meet on September 8 in the hot-land town of Chilpancingo. Morelos's choice of location was itself an indication of the poisonous rancor that had crept into the rebel movement. He wrote that he settled on Chilpancingo simply "so that no one can say he rules over anyone else," and because it was roughly equidistant from the current headquarters of the various rebel chieftains.

Morelos made it clear that he envisioned a thorough overhaul of the structure of the rebel government. He proposed the formation of a new congress composed of representatives elected by the provinces, and the writing of a new constitution for an independent Mexican republic. That, of course, meant that Rayón and the other four acting members of the supreme junta would have to stand for election or relinquish power. Rayón charged insistently that Morelos was trying to usurp power over the rebellion and that he had no authority to call a meeting of the supreme junta. Morelos, for his part, swore he had no ambitions: "I do not aspire to the Presidency; my functions shall cease once the Junta is established and I shall be very honored merely with the humble title *Servant of the Nation*."[2] He maintained that a congress was vital, since it would give a patina of legitimacy to the insurgent cause and make it more likely that European powers and the United States would grant the rebels recognition and aid.

In response to Morelos's convocation, a small group of insurgents gathered—some reluctantly—at Chilpancingo on September 8, 1813, to begin their deliberations, styling themselves "the Congress of Anáhuac" ("Anáhuac" was the Aztec name for central Mexico, the center of the Aztec empire). Morelos opened the congress on September 14, less than a month after his victory at Acapulco. At the congress he premiered what would be his most famous statement of principles, the "Sentiments of the Nation," which he intended to serve as a blueprint for the rebel constitution. The first article declared that America was "free and independent

of Spain and of all other Nations, Governments, or Monarchies."
Subsequent articles provided for popular sovereignty, free elections, and separation of powers into legislative, executive, and judicial branches; denied foreigners the right to hold public office
and limited their right to immigrate to Mexico; decreed an end to
inherited privilege, caste distinctions, torture, and slavery; and
eliminated all taxes except for a very moderate tax on income.
Morelos's document insisted that Roman Catholicism should be
the only legal religion in the republic, and it required all citizens to
pay monthly devotions to the Virgin of Guadalupe, with December 12 being set aside as a holiday in the Virgin's honor. It also
decreed another, patriotic holiday: "That the sixteenth of September shall be celebrated each year as the anniversary of the cry of
independence and the day our sacred liberty began, for on that
day the lips of the Nation parted and the people proclaimed their
rights and they grasped the sword so that they would be heard, re-
membering always the merits of the great hero, *señor* don Miguel
Hidalgo y Costilla and his *compañero*, don Ignacio Allende."[3] So began the apotheosis of Father Hidalgo.

While waiting for the representatives to arrive, the congress
endowed Morelos with the title of generalíssimo of the insurgent
armies, which, in the words of the resolution, "includes the dignity
of Supreme Executive Power of the National Sovereignty." Morelos's political power thus reached its apogee, and his rival Rayón
was accordingly more disgruntled than ever. In late October, with
all of the elected representatives present, the congress finally began its discussions. It was decided that the first order of business
should be to formally declare Mexico's independence from Spain,
and Carlos María de Bustamante was detailed to draw up the declaration. Although Rayón continued to object to so radical a measure, insisting that King Ferdinand VII was still adored by the
Indians and that declaring independence would be tantamount to
insulting a sacred institution, the congress approved the declaration, which was issued formally on November 6, 1813.

Bustamante's declaration, in stark contrast to the correspond-

ing documents of the American and French Revolutions, was
curiously lacking in ideology. Apart from declaring that Mexico's
dependence on the Spanish throne was "forever broken and dissolved," the declaration seemed most intent on announcing religious intolerance and threatening dissenters. The Congress of
Anáhuac, read the declaration,

> does not profess or recognize any religion other than the
> Catholic, nor will it permit or tolerate the public or secret
> use of any other; it will use all its power to guard and pro-
> tect the purity of the faith and its dogmas, and the mainte-
> nance of the regular orders. It declares that anyone who
> opposes its independence directly or indirectly, whether by
> protecting the European oppressors . . . or refusing to con-
> tribute to the expenses, subsidies and pensions to continue
> the war till independence be achieved and recognized by
> foreign nations, is guilty of high treason.[4]

The sterility of the declaration of independence issued by the
Congress of Anáhuac is indicative of the movement's fatal weak-
ness. In restricting itself to only those points that had broad support from the fractious rebel leadership, the document contained
glaring omissions, which spoke eloquently of the movement's lack
of vision. It declared Mexico to be independent, but beyond that
it gave little hint as to what the new nation would be like, except
that it would not tolerate dissent. Its real-world impact was virtually nil, and Mexican and Spanish authorities paid it little heed.

Rayón signed the declaration, though he continued to complain, and within days he was pleading with the congress to suspend the document on the grounds that it was overly hasty and
would cause soldiers to desert. The Congress of Anáhuac also
adopted decrees abolishing slavery and restoring the Jesuits to education in Mexico, but beyond that it accomplished little, and the
squabbling did not abate.

Morelos hoped that military victories might help to bring greater harmony to the insurgent ranks, and he set his sights on what would have been a formidable prize: his old hometown of Valladolid. He believed the city to be lightly defended, and he hoped to make it the seat of his new government. He was supremely confident, with ample supplies, thirty cannons, and some six thousand men, the largest army of his career. Valladolid, for its part, was garrisoned by only about eight hundred royalists. The recapture of Valladolid, Morelos reasoned, would surely lend greater credibility and legitimacy to the insurgent cause, as well as providing a well-situated base for military operations throughout central Mexico.

Morelos was surely aware of the demoralized condition of the royalists. In October 1813, while Morelos and his congress deliberated, Calleja was telling the Spanish minister of war that the struggle, at least as it was currently being fought, was practically hopeless. He complained that the vast majority of the inhabitants of Mexico sympathized with the cause of independence, and that the rebels gained enthusiastic adherents wherever they went. The troops being sent from Spain usually had to spend long periods of time in the unhealthy port of Veracruz, where roughly half of them died or were immobilized by disease. Royalist forces in Mexico, meanwhile, were steadily diminished by desertion, "seduction" to the rebellion, exhaustion, or death, and they had to be replaced by vagabonds and prisoners who made for poor soldiers. Calleja asked the Ministry of War to send a new superior political chief who, "combining robust talents and the necessary authority, can fulfill the nation's hopes, permitting me, as I now beg you, to move with my family to the Peninsula."[5] It seemed that the time was indeed ripe for a strong rebel offensive, and that victory was at hand.

Morelos and his army stationed themselves on Santa María Hill overlooking Valladolid on December 22, and demanded that the city surrender within three hours or face harsh consequences.

Unfortunately for them, Calleja had used the time while Morelos and his forces were preoccupied with the siege of Acapulco to reorganize his military operations, and he was now able to muster and dispatch forces rapidly to nearly anywhere in central Mexico. With good intelligence regarding Morelos's intentions, he was able quickly to move a three-thousand-man army under the command of General Ciriaco de Llano to Valladolid, where they arrived on December 23. The royalist forces launched a cannonade at the rebel army, then attacked in force, throwing the rebels into a panic and forcing them to break ranks. The royalists then entered the city amid noisy demonstrations of approval from the townsfolk. The rebels tried to secure their position on Santa María Hill by stretching a line of cavalry and infantry before their encampment. At dusk on Christmas day, Llano ordered his second-in-command, Colonel Agustín de Iturbide, to reconnoiter the rebel ranks. Seeing an opportunity, Iturbide recklessly exceeded his orders, launching a bold attack on the hill itself and taking the rebels entirely by surprise. Iturbide's men very nearly captured Morelos as frightened rebels scattered in all directions.

Understandably, the insurgents were stunned by this turn of events, and the royalists were elated. Iturbide reasoned that the most crucial factor in the victory was simply that it proved Morelos was not invincible. And indeed, that fact became increasingly obvious in the coming weeks and months. On January 5, 1814, Morelos's forces were attacked at the Hacienda of Puruarán, sixty miles southwest of Valladolid, where they had sought refuge after the catastrophe at Valladolid. Although the rebels put up brave resistance, they were badly outgunned and easily defeated, suffering staggering losses. Worse, Morelos's valued second-in-command, General Mariano Matamoros—like Morelos, a priest of great military talent—was captured and executed, despite Morelos's desperate offer to free two hundred Spanish prisoners in exchange for Matamoros's life. Three weeks later the royalist General Gabriel de Armijo approached Chilpancingo, forcing the congress to flee.

The string of royalist victories opened the gateway to southern Mexico, and the rebel cause there was virtually lost.

Disaster followed upon disaster for the insurgency. The internal squabbling that had paralyzed the Congress of Anáhuac grew steadily worse, occasionally turning lethal. The congress was dispersed and constantly hounded by royalist forces. Morelos's prestige declined precipitously after the catastrophe at Valladolid, and his enemies rushed to take their revenge. Led by Morelos's archrival Rayón, the congress stripped Morelos of supreme executive power, assigning that authority instead to a five-member junta. The congress allowed him to retain the title of generalísimo, but the designation had little meaning. Morelos lost command over the insurgent armies, commanding only a small escort of about 150 men. Military authority was now divided among three generals—Ignacio Rayón, José María Cos, and Juan Nepomuceno Rosáins—though effective cooperation among those men was rare. On February 24, while a portion of the congress was camped at Tlacotepec in the mountains of Puebla, royalist forces attacked and scattered them, seizing their archives, including correspondence with the Guadalupes, the insurgents' vital allies in Mexico City. The damage to the insurgent cause was severe, perhaps irreparable.

In March, Morelos went to Acapulco to oversee its evacuation before the unstoppable royalist onslaught. Morelos ordered the port burned to the ground, which may have denied the royalists their prize, but it was also a stark and bitter reminder of the time and resources Morelos had squandered in capturing it. In April, the rebels were driven out of Oaxaca, and soon the royalists had regained control of all southern Mexico. And in June, one of Morelos's oldest and closest collaborators, Hermenegildo Galeana, was killed in battle. His head was severed and proudly displayed in the town of Coyuca.

The Restoration

While the Mexican rebel forces suffered a dizzying spate of setbacks, momentous events were taking place in Europe. Napoleon
invaded Russia in 1812, where he suffered one of history's epic
military disasters. Spanish and British armies fighting the French
in Spain benefited when Napoleon, hoping to recoup his position,
summoned his best troops to central Europe, leaving his brother
Joseph virtually defenseless. In June 1813, combined British, Spanish, and Portuguese forces handed the French a catastrophic defeat
at the Battle of Vitoria in northern Spain, effectively ending Napoleonic rule in Spain. Napoleon sent the captive King Ferdinand VII back to Spain in March 1814, having first obliged him to
sign a treaty of alliance against Britain.

Ferdinand VII, still a thoroughly unknown quantity among his
countrymen, had come to be known as "El Deseado" (the Desired
One), during this captivity. Most of the people of Spain soon
learned to be careful what they wished for. Ferdinand VII set to
work earning the many scornful epithets that historians have
heaped upon him ever since, laying the groundwork for decades of
civil strife in Spain. Ferdinand was vain, vindictive, petty, paranoid, and woefully shortsighted. He succumbed to the flattery of
hidebound conservatives, who urged him to restore the country to
the status quo ante, abolishing every vestige of liberalism. In May,
he declared that the Cortes was illegal and that all of its legislation—including, of course, the Constitution of 1812—was null
and void. Many liberal deputies, including the Mexican delegates
to the Cortes Miguel Ramos Arizpe, Joaquín Maniau, and José
María Gutiérrez de Terán, were thrown in prison, while many
others fled for their lives. Ferdinand imagined that he was truly
restoring a system where aristocrats and clergymen enjoyed tremendous privilege and the king's power was absolute.

Unfortunately for him, Spain and its progeny had already traveled too far from the old regime to ever turn back: the dignity of
the monarchy had been damaged by Charles IV and Godoy, and
now Ferdinand VII had begun to do his bit to shatter it entirely be-

yond repair. The people had tasted the forbidden fruit of liberty, equality, popular sovereignty, and the impersonal rule of law, and no decree, no matter how draconian, could erase the changes of 1808–1814 from memory. Rather than restoring the absolutist monarchy, Ferdinand VII, in the words of historian Richard Herr, "was only giving the crown a partisan role in the new political life, hardly different from other interest groups."[6]

Calleja received the news of Ferdinand's return on August 5, 1814. His reaction, in his own words, was one of "unspeakable joy," something that the pro-Spanish elements in Mexico were soon celebrating with Te Deums, bullfights, and fiestas. The impact of the change was somewhat contradictory. On the one hand, most Mexicans already reviled the government in Mexico City and sympathized with the notion of either autonomy or independence. The restoration of absolutism was a potential boon to the rebel cause, insofar as it brought the Mexico City government into still greater disrepute. On the other hand, Calleja was elated that he need no longer be restrained by having even to appear to be abiding by the niceties of constitutional government. He quickly dismissed all elected officials and nullified all of their projects, decrees, and reforms. He restored those who had held office prior to the Napoleonic usurpation of 1808 to their positions. He reestablished the Inquisition and put it to work tracking down the writings of liberals. In 1815, Calleja had four ex–city councilmen arrested and held incommunicado. One of those four died; the survivors were shipped off to a penal colony in the Mariana Islands. Many other alleged rebel sympathizers were arrested and tried, and by the middle of 1815 royal officials in Mexico City were confident that the threat of internal subversion had been eliminated.

The Constitution of Apatzingán

Some liberals, faced with the prospect of arrest and imprisonment, did flee to join the rebellion. Calleja sought to prevent any boon to the rebellion by issuing stern warnings that all who took up arms would be shot, while all who surrendered them would be pardoned, and the policy was fairly effective. The rebels, seeing their military fortunes in steady decline, were desperate to shore up their legitimacy. In June 1814, they issued a call for a constitutional convention to convene in the town of Apatzingán in the province of Michoacán. Four months later the convention promulgated the product of their labors, the Constitution of Apatzingán. The rebel constitution was hardly a model of concision: it consisted of twenty-two chapters and 242 articles. Like Morelos's proposed reforms, it decreed Roman Catholicism to be the only legal religion, and it included many liberal features. Sovereignty, it said, originated with the people, who would elect representatives according to a complicated, indirect system. Powers were separated into executive, legislative, and judicial branches. The executive branch would consist of a president and vice president whose powers were relatively weak, limited by a strong legislature—a hedge against rule by a single strongman, something the delegates greatly feared.

Modeled fairly closely after the Spanish Constitution of 1812, the Constitution of Apatzingán broke no new ground. It did, however, prompt a reaction. The Inquisition took it seriously enough to threaten with excommunication anyone caught with a copy. The government ordered that all copies be collected and burned, even going so far as to demand that local officials disavow the constitution and congress in writing. Priests were enjoined to rail against the document from their pulpits. The constitution likely helped to lift the movement's sagging morale. The rebels also hoped it might give their efforts greater credibility and legitimacy, aiding them in their ongoing efforts to attract the sympathetic attention of the United States, something that seemed all the more crucial as the rebellion's military fortunes waned.

Already, by 1814, the rebels had made several attempts to secure aid from the United States, all of them ill-fated. Back in the early summer of 1811, Morelos had dispatched two agents, the

Anglo-American David Faro and the Mexican Mariano Tabares, with an offer to cede the province of Texas to the United States in exchange for aid to the rebellion, an indication of just how desperate he was for U.S. support. That expedition was derailed by Ignacio Rayón, who intercepted the two emissaries and sent them back south. Another early emissary was more successful: Bernardo Gutiérrez de Lara managed to secure a meeting in late 1811 with the U.S. secretaries of state and war, who made no firm commitments but led Gutiérrez to believe they would do nothing to stop him should he organize an expedition against Texas. Gutiérrez, with some official U.S. support, recruited volunteers in New Orleans for what he called the Republican Army of the North, which included some 150 Anglo-American adventurers under the command of Augustus Magee, a former lieutenant in the U.S. Army. The expedition invaded Texas in August 1812, seizing several towns and eventually the capital of the province, San Antonio de Béxar, in April 1813. They thereupon declared Texas an independent state. The Anglo-American volunteers had little zeal for the independence cause and scant admiration for Gutiérrez. Most returned to Louisiana, while the remaining invaders took to quarreling among themselves. They became fairly easy prey for a royalist force under the skilled leadership of Joaquín de Arredondo in August 1813, who executed several hundred men in a singularly brutal pacification.

In fact, the rebels' timing was terrible, for they were trying to win U.S. support at the very moment when that nation was fighting Britain in the War of 1812. Although there was much popular sympathy for the rebellion among North Americans, the United States had few resources to spare to help the rebels, and it was loath to antagonize Spain, which might seize upon U.S. support for the rebellion as a pretext to enter the war on the side of Britain. And even after the War of 1812 ended, the United States had powerful disincentives to aiding the Mexican rebels. The Americans were understandably reluctant to commit immediately to another conflict, and they still wished to remain in Spain's good graces, hoping Spain might be persuaded to part with its colony of East Florida, a territory that the United States was determined to annex.

Such considerations did little to dampen the ardor and optimism of the rebels, who continued to hatch schemes to attract U.S. sympathies. After 1814, they could point to their constitution and incipient government as proof that they were a force to be reckoned with. Morelos's next agent, Juan Pablo y Anaya, reached New Orleans in early 1815, just in time for the climactic battle of the War of 1812. In those circumstances, he was unable to find a ship to take him to Washington and had to content himself with sending a letter to President James Madison in which he made the curious case that "between [Mexico] and these States there is no other difference than that of language, but the interest, rights, etc., are all alike." In July 1814, the rebel congress named José Manuel Herrera as its minister plenipotentiary to the United States. Herrera carried a letter from Morelos to President Madison which boasted of the new constitution and boldly overstated its impact: "We flatter ourselves," it read, "that the sanction and promulgation of our constitutional law and the effective organization of our government have driven consternation into the poisoned hearts of our enemies, dealing a deadly blow to their hopes while it has filled with joy the hearts of our people whom it has inspired again with special ardor to carry on our grand enterprise."[7] Herrera set out from the rebel camp in July 1815. He had a difficult overland journey to Veracruz, where the ship he was supposed to sail on was destroyed by fire. He managed to catch a ride on a schooner to New Orleans, arriving in October, where he spent all of the money he had been furnished on outrageously overpriced munitions and supplies. After spending four months in New Orleans, he reluctantly abandoned his mission.

This is not to say that the United States was irrelevant to the insurgency. Insurgent bands operating in northern Veracruz province had long enjoyed trading contacts with New Orleans, which allowed them to purchase surplus weapons from the United States in the wake of the War of 1812. New Orleans, in fact, became a center for conspiracies aimed at aiding the rebellion. A group of U.S. citizens formed the New Orleans Associates, an organization dedicated to supporting the Mexican insurgency. They, in league with a variety of merchants, rogues, and rascals, supplied arms and munitions to the rebellion, and aided and abetted pirates who preyed on Spanish shipping in the Gulf of Mexico. In 1816, a French pirate named Louis-Michel Aury established a base on Galveston Island from which to plunder Spanish shipping and attack Spanish possessions. Even so, from 1815 onward the United States adopted an official posture of "impartial neutrality," albeit one that tended to work more in favor of the insurgents than of Spain, since ships flying flags of the rebellion were given free use of U.S. ports, making it easy for Spanish American insurgents to purchase war materials in the United States. But this was far from the sort of full-bore commitment that men like José María Morelos hoped for.

The End of Morelos

Unfortunately, the Constitution of Apatzingán did nothing at all to soothe the bitter feelings that had arisen among the various revolutionary chieftains. The feuding built continuously throughout 1814, mostly involving jurisdictional disputes among the triumvirate of leaders, Rayón, Rosáins, and Cos. Rayón and Rosáins, both of whom were headstrong, impetuous, ambitious, and stubborn, soon began a mortal feud that severely damaged the cause. The two men took to issuing statements filled with harsh accusations and defamations, and, most damning to the military efforts, instead of cooperating they rejoiced in one another's ill fortune. In this dispute Rosáins made himself notorious, executing an emissary sent by the congress to investigate his conduct and subsequently perpetrating, in the words of Lucas Alamán, "such atrocities more fitting to the tyrannies of Romagnese cities in the time of Cesare Borgia than to the history of our own days." By the summer of 1815, those atrocities had caused the insurgent leaders in Veracruz to declare themselves independent of Rosáins's authority.[8] Rosáins led his forces out in an attempt to subjugate the rebellious chieftains, but found himself on the losing side. He was detained by the Veracruz chiefs and sent eastward, where the congress was supposed to decide his fate, but he escaped en route and fled to the royalists, who pardoned him in exchange for much useful intelligence about the rebellion and advice on how to stamp it out. In October, the third member of the triumvirate, José María Cos, disavowed the authority of the congress and was subsequently arrested and imprisoned. The rebellion had surely reached its nadir, for the insurgents were now fighting one another as determinedly and deliberately as they had battled the royalists.

The discord among the various rebel chieftains was in some ways advantageous to Morelos, who had been biding his time in the hope of recovering his prestige and authority. By the autumn of 1815, leadership of the rebellion was practically up for grabs, and when the congress decided to move its headquarters from the town of Uruapan, Michoacán, in the west, to the city of Tehuacán, Puebla, in the east, Morelos was tapped to head up the congressional escort, even though his military and political power was still circumscribed. The congress had many good reasons for relocating. The zone of greatest rebel activity lay to the east, in the provinces of Veracruz and Puebla. Tehuacán was closer to the coast of the Gulf of Mexico, with relatively good access to the port of Veracruz. Since there was still reason to hope that Herrera's mission to the United States might bear fruit, access to the coast was a must. Tehuacán was surrounded by hills, which provided greater protection and stability, and the surrounding region was relatively prosperous, affording greater resources than could be had in the west. Further, the town was securely under the control of one of the rebellion's more talented and reliable officers, Colonel Manuel de Mier y Terán. The congress also hoped that the new location might help it to assert its authority more effectively over the troublesome lesser chieftains of Puebla and Veracruz. With a stable and secure base of operations, it was hoped, perhaps the internecine feuding might at last be brought under control.

It would not be an easy trip: the party had to pass through roughly 450 miles of territory swarming with royalists who believed the rebellion was broken beyond repair and saw their current mission as less a military campaign than a vindictive manhunt. At times the party would have to pass practically within sight of royalist outposts and fortifications. They set out from Uruapan on September 29, a day before Morelos's fiftieth birthday. Morelos had about one thousand men, half of them with rifles, and two cannons.

It was a formidable group that set out that day. Heavily weighted with supplies, archives, and munitions, and including many women and children, they resembled, according to one witness, "more the migration of a vast body of people, than the march of an army. The road, for several leagues, was covered with baggage wagons and mules; no order was observed in the march; and the military forces were so scattered, that, in the case of attack, it would have been impractical to form a junction with promptitude."[9] Morelos did not expect an attack, for he traveled a route he knew well. The party set out early each morning and camped wherever they found themselves at dusk.

Calleja and his officers were well aware that the congress was on the move, but Morelos, with feints and false clues, managed to frustrate them for the entire month of October. He led the party along the banks of the Balsas River, eventually turning northward and moving along a Balsas tributary known as the Mescala. On November 2, at the town of Atenango, the party forded the river. It was there they were spotted by Mariano Ortíz de la Peña, royalist captain at Iguala, who in turn notified Lieutenant Colonel Manuel de la Concha, who was operating in the environs of Iguala with some six hundred well-armed men. Concha, soon joined by an

infantry force under the command of Lieutenant Colonel Euge-
nio Villasana, hurried toward Atenango. On the night of November 3, as a ferocious storm pelted the region, Lieutenant Colonel
Concha and his troops rested at an hacienda called Tecuacuilco,
leaving there at four in the morning for the village of Tulimán,
where he learned that Morelos had been seen the previous day
in a village called Temalac (often referred to as Tesmalaca or
Temalaca). The village was situated in a small hollow in the midst
of palm-covered hills and near a small freshwater spring, and it
had been regarded since pre-Columbian times as a sacred place.
Concha hurried there, arriving at around nine o'clock on the
morning of November 5. He did not expect to find Morelos still
there, and stopped at Temalac only so his troops could quench
their considerable thirst at the spring. As they drew near they spotted Morelos's rear guard as they were disappearing over a nearby
ridge. Realizing he had been seen, Morelos mustered his troops
and sent the congress and other noncombatants onward, hoping
to battle the royalist forces long enough to allow them to escape.

At eleven that morning Concha ordered a charge, and the fire-
fight was fierce. Morelos divided his forces into three sections, defending the center himself. The rebels' right flank and part of the
center, badly outgunned, soon collapsed. Morelos ordered everyone to run for their lives. Many rebels were killed, and the fleeing
congress was obliged to abandon their supplies, which—except
for five silver bars, which were surrendered to the government—
were pillaged by the royalist troops. Morelos, who remained calm
throughout the action, was captured by Matías Carranco, who
had once fought in Morelos's forces in southern Mexico but had
defected to the royalists. Upon learning that the notorious rebel
leader had at last been captured, the royalists gave themselves over
to such lively celebration— beating on drums, shouting *vivas* to the
king and Lieutenant Colonel Concha—that they failed to pursue
the main body of the congress. Most of the representatives arrived
safe and sound at Tehuacán on November 16.

Concha brought his two prize prisoners—Morelos and José María Morales, the chaplain of the congress—first to Atenango, where they were forced to witness the execution of twenty-seven other rebel prisoners. Lieutenant Colonel Villasana took the opportunity to ask Morelos how he and Concha would have been treated had they fallen into the hands of the rebels. Morelos replied frankly: "I give you two hours for confession and have you shot." The royalists were stunned into a momentary silence by the rebel's candor, after which Villasana opined, rather disingenuously, that "the king's troops are not as cruel, we give quarter."

The prisoners were heavily shackled and loaded on muleback, traveling by night to avoid any "accident." They reached Mexico City very early on November 22 and were taken to the secret prisons of the newly restored Inquisition. The trial of Morelos began at midmorning of that same day, and the matter would likely have reached a speedy conclusion had it not been for a complex jurisdictional dispute among the military, ecclesiastical, Inquisition, and government powers over who had the right to try and pass sentence upon the prisoner.

Morelos was charged by a joint military-ecclesiastical court with treason, disloyalty to the king, and promoting the independence of Mexico. Morelos responded calmly to the charges, arguing that he could not possibly have been disloyal to the king, for at the time he opted to pursue independence Spain had no king, and therefore no one against whom to commit treason. He maintained that he had not expected Ferdinand VII ever to return to the Spanish throne, and that even if he did so, he would be compromised forever by his treasonous surrender to Bonaparte. When the court charged Morelos with causing death and destruction, the ruin of families and fortunes, and the general desolation of the country, Morelos responded that those were the "necessary effects of all revolutions," but that when he began his revolutionary activity he had not expected so much destruction.

Morelos's fate, of course, was a foregone conclusion, and his trial ended twenty-five hours after it began with the unsurprising decision to turn the prisoner over to church authorities so he could be formally degraded from his priestly vocation in preparation for his execution. The church authorities recommended, however, that Morelos's life be spared; they then handed him over to the Inquisition, which was still struggling to recover some of its lost prestige. The Inquisition brought a colorful list of charges against Morelos. He was, they claimed, a "heretic, apostate, atheist, materialist, deist, libertine, implacable enemy of Christianity and the state, a vile seducer, hypocrite, and traitor." Oddly, the charges of immorality were founded not so much on the priest's having fathered illegitimate children, but that he had sent one of those children—Juan Nepomuceno Almonte—to the United States, a Protestant country, for his education. The Inquisition ordered that Morelos be subjected to an elaborate and humiliating public auto-da-fé, wherein, dressed in a ridiculous penitential robe and holding a green candle symbolizing heresy, he was forced to kneel at the altar while being gently whipped with strokes of "purification" as the formal sentence of degradation was read by the bishop of Oaxaca. All of Morelos's property was confiscated, his children and their children were declared infamous, and a plaque with his name and list of crimes was placed on display in the cathedral.

Morelos was then heavily shackled and returned to the custody of the government. The sentence was harsh, as expected: Morelos was to be executed and his corpse dismembered; his head was to be placed in an iron cage and exhibited in Mexico City, while his right hand was to be severed and sent to Oaxaca for public display. The viceroy relented on the matter of dismemberment, but the death sentence remained in force. On December 22, Morelos was placed in heavy shackles and taken by coach to the village of San Cristóbal Ecatepec, all the while muttering the penitential prayers Miserere and De Profundis. He recited still more prayers with the town priest of Ecatepec, downed a bowl of soup, and then was taken to the yard of the town hall. His eyes were covered with a white handkerchief and his arms were bound behind him with gun slings. He was forced to kneel, and then he was shot four times in the back. His body was buried in the yard of that obscure parish church to await the apotheosis that would come with Mexico's independence. Thus the inglorious end of a man whom the conservative statesman and historian Lucas Alamán—an admirer neither of the revolution nor of Morelos—called "the most extraordinary man that the revolution of New Spain had produced."[10]

Eventful Interlude

The capture and execution of José María Morelos certainly did not end the rebellion, but it did help put an end to the sense that the rebellion constituted a real threat to the regime in Mexico City. The perennially troubled insurgent congress arrived safely at Tehuacán, but discord quickly arose once again, this time between the congress members, who expected deference, and the military commander at Tehuacán, Manuel de Mier y Terán, who had no intention of providing such deference. Terán, moreover, was appalled that the representatives expected to be defended and cared for, along with their many hangers-on. The congress took financial administration out of Terán's hands and began working to turn his own troops against him. On December 15, only a month after the representatives had completed their harrowing journey, Terán arrested the leaders and dissolved the congress, charging that it had never been legitimately elected. The rebellion was now completely adrift.

Most of the credit for containing the rebellion belongs to Félix María Calleja, but that did little to endear him to the powerful folks of Mexico City. They resented his war taxes as excessive and arbitrary; they decried his dictatorial methods and penchant for cruelty; and some even charged that his harsh methods were responsible for perpetuating the rebellion. Ferdinand VII gave a sympathetic ear to those complaints—after all, Calleja's initial appointment had been made by the liberal Cádiz government during his captivity in France, and he was keen to undo as many of their acts as possible. He recalled Calleja to Spain, granting him the title of Count of Calderón in honor of his memorable defeat of Hidalgo's army at the battle of that name. His replacement was Juan Ruiz de Apodaca, a man known for his patient and even temperament, open-mindedness, and unquestioning devotion to the Spanish monarchy. Apodaca assumed the office of viceroy on September 16, 1816, after surviving an attack by a rebel band while en route to the capital from Veracruz. He immediately adopted a conciliatory policy in place of Calleja's policies of terror. He eased up considerably on war taxes, ordered an end to the summary executions of captured rebels, and was remarkably generous with amnesties for rebels who surrendered. These policies bore some fruit: some seventeen thousand rebels received amnesty during his five years in office, including several of the rebellion's most important leaders; mail and supplies now flowed far more freely, relieving the desperate hunger and shortages that had plagued central Mexico for years; some silver mines reopened, and the silver convoys resumed; and even the crime rate dropped as Apodaca instituted new policies for conscripting vagrants and criminals into the army.

Historians often depict the years from 1816 to 1820 as a lull, a time when the country gradually recovered its equanimity. Recently this picture has been muddied by historian Christon I. Archer, who points out that it is based largely on Viceroy Apodaca's own reports, which were intended to convey precisely this sunny impression. In fact, however, the rebellion merely became dispersed and disorganized, the domain not of prominent commanders like Hidalgo, Allende, or Morelos, but rather of freelancers leading small bands of raiders. Certain areas—such as the province of Veracruz, the mountains of Guanajuato, and large portions of Michoacán and Jalisco—were largely controlled by guerrilla bands except on rare occasions when the army would sweep through with large divisions. Throughout 1818, bands of two hundred to three hundred rebels were reported to be conducting almost daily assaults on haciendas around Querétaro. Such raiders were likely motivated more by lust for booty or vengeance than by the desire to free Mexico from foreign domination and create a more just society, but that did not make them any less troublesome to the viceregal regime. Moreover, throughout the years after 1816 the royalist army was perpetually on the brink of collapse. After 1816, Spain stopped sending expeditionary battalions to Mexico, leaving the Mexican army perilously shorthanded. The crisis of the treasury meant that soldiers went unpaid for long periods of time; their clothing and equipment deteriorated and could not be repaired or replaced; discipline and morale declined; and desertion became alarmingly commonplace. In short, the struggle entered into a prolonged, violent, and desultory stalemate.

For the rebels, there was at least one flurry of hope in 1816 and 1817. It came from an unlikely quarter. A dashing twenty-seven-year-old Spanish liberal named Francisco Xavier Mina, who had distinguished himself as a guerrilla fighter in the Peninsular War against the French, was outraged by the restoration of royal absolutism under Ferdinand VII. After a failed attempt to overthrow the reactionary king, Mina fled to England, where he made the acquaintance of General Winfield Scott of the United States (the same General Scott who, thirty years later, would capture Mexico City in the U.S.-Mexican War, and who in 1816 was taking a leave of absence in Europe to study military matters on the Continent and to recover from wounds received in the War of 1812) and Father Servando Teresa de Mier, a prominent Mexican liberal. Scott and Mier persuaded Mina that the best way to fight Ferdinand VII would be to invade Mexico. Mier helped Mina arrange loans from London merchants and bankers, while Scott assured him that the U.S. government would do nothing to impede him from raising an invasion force in the United States. Mina then traveled to the United States, where merchants at Baltimore supplied him with a ship and ample arms and munitions. In November, Mina reached

Galveston Island, where he joined forces with the French pirate Louis-Michel Aury. Mina and Aury cordially disliked one another, but they shared an interest in invading Mexico. The expedition set out in March 1817, reaching the mouth of the Soto la Marina River in what is now the state of Tamaulipas in April.

Some forty-five miles inland lay the village of Soto la Marina, where Mina ordered the construction of a fort. His force consisted of 235 men, most of them claiming officer rank and including Mexicans, Anglo-Americans, at least one Italian, and fifteen blacks who had joined the expedition in Haiti. The tiny force was well supplied, carrying two thousand muskets, a thousand swords, and much ammunition and clothing. Mina was confident that his ranks would soon be swelled by Mexican independence fighters.

General Joaquín de Arredondo, the same man who had crushed the Gutiérrez-Magee expedition in Texas back in 1813, was now military governor of the province of Nuevo Santander, as Tamaulipas was then called. Arredondo's troops, like most of the royalist forces, were demoralized and undersupplied, "tired of enduring misery and privations." A serious drought had caused the deaths of so much livestock that there were few beasts available to transport men and artillery. With much difficulty, however, Arredondo made his way to Soto la Marina with over a thousand troops, and commenced a bombardment. By that time, Mina had already left Soto la Marina and headed inland to evade Arredondo's attack. The invaders at Soto la Marina suffered terrible losses, and soon surrendered. Now separated from much of his original invasion force, Mina sought to join the rebel forces operating around Guanajuato. He won enough minor victories over royalist forces to cause considerable excitement, particularly after his men killed a much-hated royalist officer named Castañón. In the words of one enthusiastic chronicler, "The churches resounded with Te Deum. From town to town the praises of Mina were echoed. The blessings of heaven were implored upon his head, by the widows and orphans of the victims of Castañón. Old and young, from Sombrero to the environs of the city of Mexico, and from San Luis Potosí to Zacatula, were chaunting hymns in honour of their deliverer."[11]

Mina's successes were fleeting. Soon he lost the respect of the Anglo-Americans among his forces, and his efforts were weakened by the bickering and desertions that had plagued so much of the rebellion. On October 27, 1817, he was defeated decisively at a ranch near Guanajuato called Venadito. He was taken to Mexico City, tried, and executed along with twenty-five of his officers on November 11. The Mina invasion may have briefly raised the morale of the rebellion, and the presence of Anglo-Americans among the invading party raised Mexican suspicions regarding the expansionist proclivities of the United States. But in the end, the episode had virtually no impact on the course of the rebellion.

EIGHT

INDEPENDENCE

By early 1820, the royalist government in Mexico City appeared to have the situation well in hand, and Viceroy Apodaca indulged in much self-congratulation. The major rebel nuclei had been dispersed, and Apodaca had divided the royal army into small garrisons to track down and crush those groups—often indistinguishable from bands of brigands—that remained in the field. Apodaca's generous amnesty program had persuaded thousands of rebels to switch sides. People all over Mexico, from all walks of life, endured a heavy burden of taxes to support the royalist effort, but although they grumbled unceasingly, they did not resort to overt disobedience. In Spain, King Ferdinand VII was approaching a sixth year of unrestrained power.

But the apparent tranquillity was a chimera, for the royal regime rested on a brittle foundation indeed. It had practically no popular support from any class of Mexicans, most of whom—as the viceroys themselves acknowledged—favored autonomy or independence, and were only awaiting an opportunity to unburden themselves of the hated war taxes. The violence in the countryside was far more intense than the viceroy's reports indicated, and harsh royalist measures aimed at snuffing out the remaining rebels tended instead to alienate an ever-growing number of Mexicans. The viceroy's amnesty program looked successful in the ledger books, but recently amnestied rebels, who were coming to form an increasingly large portion of royalist militias, were notoriously unreliable. They were often quick to desert the royalist ranks; some rebels accepted five or six amnesties, sloppy record keeping enabling them to switch sides easily. Despite the heavy tax burden, the royalist army was severely underfunded. Even the mildest tremor, it seemed, might bring the edifice of royal control crashing to the ground. Just as in 1808, when Napoleon's invasion had set in motion the chain of events that led to Mexico's independence war, the tremor was felt first in Spain.

Revolution in Spain

In Spain, liberals had been conspiring for six grueling years to undo Ferdinand VII's restoration of royal absolutism and to bring the liberal Constitution of 1812 back into force. Much of their conspiring took place in Masonic lodges, which met in secret, and thus had managed to elude Ferdinand's vicious crackdowns. Their cue to act came on January 1, 1820. On that date, as several battalions of soldiers under the command of Mexico's ex-viceroy, Félix Calleja, waited to set sail to fight in the Americas, the commander of one of those battalions, Major Rafael Riego, declared a rebellion demanding the restoration of the 1812 Constitution. Resentment of the autocratic Ferdinand was widespread, and the movement quickly gained momentum. In March, mutinous soldiers surrounded the royal palace in Madrid and Ferdinand VII had no choice but to accede to their demands. He reluctantly accepted his status as a constitutional monarch.

Later that same month, Ferdinand VII sent instructions to the American colonies for the election of deputies, which were nearly identical to the procedures that had been followed back in 1813.

The king also issued a proclamation to the Americans apologizing for his abrogation of the constitution in 1814 and begging them to forgive his errors in judgment. He urged them to cease their rebellions, inasmuch as the constitution gave them virtually everything they had been clamoring for. Ferdinand's actions, however, were not heartfelt. In fact, he was already conspiring with the most reactionary powers in Europe, begging them to invade Spain and restore his absolute power.

Most Mexicans were delighted by the news of the sweeping changes in Spain. Villages quickly set up popular councils, and elections were planned and carried out with remarkable speed. By the time the Cortes reassembled in 1821, it included forty-nine deputies from Mexico. Viceroy Apodaca agreed to republish the Constitution of 1812, although zealous conservatives had destroyed so many copies of that document that few could now be found. Once again, Mexico enjoyed a free press, Indian tribute was canceled, and the Inquisition was abolished. Any officeholder who refused to swear allegiance to the constitution was dismissed from his post. The clergy were instructed to preach the glories of the constitution from their pulpits, even though that document abolished their traditional immunity from civil prosecution, suppressed monasteries, and banished the Jesuit order. Some conservative clergymen, joined by military officers, who also saw their privileges evaporate, urged a disavowal of the constitution and the constitutional regime.

Iturbide

The change of regime in Spain delivered a profound shock to the imperial system, but it was not inevitable that it would lead to the independence of Mexico. That dramatic development came about in an unexpected manner, and was sparked by an unexpected protagonist.

Colonel Agustín de Iturbide was thirty-seven years old in 1820, the son of an immigrant from the Basque regions of northern Spain and a creole woman of Basque descent. He had been born in Valladolid—the same city where José María Morelos had been born and where Miguel Hidalgo had reached the apogee of his priestly and scholarly career. But Iturbide's life had taken a very different course from those of Hidalgo and Morelos. His family claimed an aristocratic lineage and a fair degree of wealth, with two homes in Valladolid and an hacienda in the countryside nearby. Not much attracted to the life of the mind, Iturbide only briefly attended a theological seminary in Valladolid before beginning his military career at the tender age of fourteen. In 1805, when he was twenty-two years old, Iturbide increased his fortune by marrying Ana María Huarte, a rich man's daughter with a substantial dowry. When the rebellion erupted in 1810, Father Hidalgo offered Iturbide a commission in his rebel army. But Iturbide, "animated by a mistaken zeal,"[1] as one of his admirers later put it, embraced the royalist cause.

In his several portraits, Iturbide appears as a powerfully built man with dark, piercing eyes, a kindly expression, a prominent nose, and emphatic sideburns. By most accounts, he had an appealing personality. Even Carlos María de Bustamante, one of Iturbide's bitterest enemies, left a fairly flattering description: "He pleases everyone; and his arguments seldom fail to convince . . . Although mild in time of peace, Iturbide is relentless during a campaign. He marches twenty leagues in one night . . . He lassos a bull like a vaquero. He eats ravenously. He is patient, valiant, and constant in his endeavors, even though they may be rash."[2]

Later in his life, Iturbide's enemies would retail lurid tales of the young Agustín cutting the toes off chickens for the ghoulish pleasure of watching them hobble along on stumps. Though the stories are surely apocryphal, many historians, impressed by Iturbide's penchant for cruelty in war, have found them plausible enough. A week after the rebels issued their Constitution of Apatzingán in October 1814, Iturbide announced an intemperate scorched earth policy: in order to deprive the rebellion of its support, he declared that all supporters and female relatives of insurgents were to be imprisoned. Later he threatened to execute one of every ten of the insurgents' wives, and to execute them all at once should a royalist soldier or messenger be killed. Although apparently he ordered the execution of only one insurgent's wife, he followed through to a greater degree on his proposal to raze all towns that harbored insurgents. At one point he boasted of killing more than nine hundred rebels in the space of two months, clearly taking great pride in this savagery. Such measures at times proved too much even for the infamously cruel Viceroy Calleja, who suppressed some of Iturbide's more merciless decrees.

Brutal though he may have been, Iturbide was undeniably an effective military leader. His reckless bravery in December 1814 at the city of Valladolid had denied the rebels what might have been a signal victory. He later boasted that he had lost only one battle—the Battle of Cóporo Hill in March 1815—and he saw that loss as a stain less on his own record than upon that of higher-ups who ordered him to do battle even though he had deemed the attack unwise. Cóporo Hill was Iturbide's only defeat, and it was a costly one.

Not long after the Battle of Cóporo Hill, Iturbide became the object of complaints. By the spring of 1816, the volume of charges had become torrential, and the viceroy ordered him to Mexico City to defend his conduct. Iturbide relinquished his command and went to the capital, where he heard a range of damning charges. He had, said his critics, acted with needless cruelty, meting out unjust punishments and abusing the wives and children of insurgents; he had destroyed agriculture and commerce by allowing his men to raze farms and seize livestock, failed to maintain proper military discipline and organization among his own troops, and even behaved as a "bad Christian." Iturbide's chief accuser— a priest named Antonio de Labarrieta—claimed that Iturbide had used his command to create monopolies in products such as oil, tallow, wood, tobacco, sugar, and oil. His illicit self-enrichment,

according to Labarrieta, had enabled him to buy homes in Irapuato and Querétaro, and to lay by a tidy sum for his own use. It is
true that his chief accuser, despite early support for the government, was known to have shifted his sympathies to the rebellion; it
is also true that charges and countercharges of cruelty and corruption were standard fare in the political and military life of Mexico,
and very few prominent people escaped being the object of such
charges at some point in their careers. Even so, the volume and
specificity of the charges against Iturbide suggest that they were
not altogether fanciful. The first military judge to study the case
declared the charges to be baseless, but that was not enough to
ward off damage to Iturbide's career. Though no final judgment
was ever made public, the viceroy ordered that Iturbide be relieved of his command of the armies of the Bajío.

Iturbide thus began a period of estrangement from military affairs, living for a time in Mexico City and later trying his hand at
farming. If his enemies are to be believed, he also passed the time
by indulging in a scandalous extramarital affair, meanwhile squan-
dering his illicit fortune lavishly on the "dissipations of the capital
city."[3] By 1820, he was apparently in severe financial straits.

Iturbide had grown more favorable to the idea of Mexican independence, though the reasons for his conversion are a bit murky.
Some of his grounds might well have been cynical and self-serving.
Given his straitened circumstances, he no doubt appreciated that
leading a successful movement for independence could bring new
financial prospects. And he had long felt that his service to the
Spanish crown had been insufficiently appreciated. Back in February 1814, he had immodestly nominated himself for membership
in a newly created National Order of San Fernando, an honor
recognizing meritorious military service that included a pension, a
salute, and special insignia. The petition was denied. In 1817, after facing charges that he regarded as calumnious, he asked the
king to award him the cross of the Order of Isabella the Catholic,
and to issue a royal statement acknowledging his services and find-

ing him innocent of all the charges lodged against him. Apparently, the king never responded. It must surely have occurred to Iturbide that the government he defended was unworthy of his support.

Iturbide's own stated reason for leading the rebellion was simply a fear that irresponsible individuals might seize upon the changes in Spain to reinvigorate the moribund revolution. "I saw new revolutions on the eve of breaking out," he wrote later, "my country was about to be drenched in blood; I was led to believe that I had the power to save her, and I did not hesitate to undertake so sacred a duty."[4]

Actually, Iturbide had been toying with the notion of independence for some time, and he had an idea of how to bring it about. In March 1815, after suffering heavy losses during his attack on Cóporo Hill, Iturbide spoke frankly to one of his subaltern commanders, Captain Vicente Filisola, expressing great dismay at so much pointless bloodshed, and opining that if the Mexican soldiers then fighting on behalf of Spain were somehow persuaded to join with the insurgents, independence could be easily achieved. In fact, Iturbide could count on a broad base of support for his project, though that support would come from vastly different quarters and would have profoundly different motivations. The threat to abolish their traditional privileges angered the conservative clergy and military men, ensuring that they—previously staunch defenders of the imperial compact—would sympathize with a movement to separate from the newly liberalized mother country. Iturbide was not above exploiting the paranoia of the reactionaries in order to garner support for his movement. Other Mexicans—a substantial majority—had little quarrel with the Constitution of 1812, but they were not sanguine about the shape of things in Spain. The constitution did nothing to placate the desires of the autonomists, for the Spanish delegates to the Cortes made it clear that they had no intention of granting the colonies autonomy, let alone independence. That much would be proved conclusively in June

1821, when Mexican deputies to the Spanish Cortes, led by Miguel Ramos Arizpe, José Mariano Michelena, and Lucas Alamán, proposed remaking the Spanish empire into a "confederative commonwealth" modeled on Britain's arrangement with Canada, where the former colonies would become self-governing, coequal "kingdoms," each with its own Cortes, supreme court, ministries, council of state, and regent executive appointed by the king. The Spanish delegates flatly rejected the plan.

The Cortes was not the only impediment to Mexican liberties. The constitution had theoretically been in effect in Mexico during 1813 and most of 1814, but both of the viceroys of that period—Venegas and Calleja—had felt free to enforce its provisions selectively, suppressing anything they deemed inconvenient. There was no reason to suppose this would cease to be the pattern. In short, arch-reactionaries, moderates, and liberals now could agree that independence was desirable. The trick would be to ensure the collaboration of a sufficient portion of the royalist army, and to win over or somehow neutralize those stubborn rebels who were still in the field.

There were not many of the latter. Isolated rebel bands claimed a few strongholds in the remote mountains of Veracruz and other peripheral regions, but the only real rebel nucleus remaining was a small force under the command of Vicente Guerrero, in the hot lands around Acapulco. Guerrero, who was of mixed Indian, black, and white descent, had fought alongside José María Morelos and subsequently emerged as one of the rebellion's most important chieftains. His key supporters included Pedro Ascencio, an Indian known for his odd personality, and John Davis Bradburn of Kentucky, one of the few survivors of the disastrous Mina expedition. Guerrero and his band were still able to harass royalists in the region to the southwest of Mexico City. Since one of Viceroy Apodaca's fondest hopes was to be able to tell the king that his viceroyalty was thoroughly pacified, eliminating the Guerrero band was a priority.

The man given that task was Colonel Agustín de Iturbide, who marched into the hot country in November 1820 with a force of 2,479 men. At the town of Teloloapan, John Davis Bradburn approached him, soliciting a pardon for himself and twelve other men. Iturbide not only granted that pardon, but he made Bradburn his aide. Bradburn furnished Iturbide with a good deal of information about Vicente Guerrero that soon proved useful.

In its beginning, Iturbide's war on the rebels was no charade. He apparently believed that if he could eradicate the last remaining rebel nucleus, all else would fall into place. He allowed that there would likely be some who would complain of his cruelty, but he dismissed such carping: "We all know that the father who punishes a bad child is not cruel, nor is the physician cruel who operates upon gangrene with fire and steel."[5] But as it happened, the rebels proved annoyingly resilient. Pedro Ascencio's forces hit Iturbide's rear guard at a place called Atlatlaya on December 28, killing 108 royalists. On January 2, 1821, Guerrero, with three or four hundred men, launched a devastating surprise attack at Zapotepec on a party that Iturbide had sent out to find and destroy his forces.

As 1821 got under way, Colonel Iturbide was suffering from a fever and, according to his own account, serious inquietude. He was well aware, he confessed to several correspondents, that Mexicans desired independence, and the consummation of that goal only awaited a leader of wide appeal. He feared that, should such a leader arise and stir up the ignorant masses, a fresh outbreak of ruinous violence was assured. He, on the other hand, had been for some time pondering an ingenious plan for pacification of the country, one that "cannot fail to bring about peace in a short time and without any bloodshed in the entire region under my charge."[6] He had begun confiding some details of his thinking to influential military men and priests, but now it seemed that he would have to recruit support from another quarter. The military setbacks he had suffered in his efforts to exterminate the rebellion once and for all convinced him that he had no choice but to let the surviving rebels in on his plan.

On January 10, he sent a flattering letter to Vicente Guerrero, assuring the rebel chief that John Davis Bradburn had spoken highly of him, and inviting him to place his troops at the disposition of the government. He offered to recognize Guerrero's command of his forces and to provide him means of subsistence. He pointed out that deputies had been elected to the Spanish Cortes, and surely they would soon be able to attend to all of the complaints of the Mexican people, seeing to it that the people of Mexico would have the same rights and privileges as the Europeans. He asked Guerrero to send a trusted representative to the town of Chilpancingo, maintaining that such a representative would be guaranteed absolute security. Iturbide added menacingly that soon his troops would be reinforced, and the campaign against the rebels would be renewed with vigor should Guerrero spurn his generosity.

Guerrero did not take the bait. Iturbide's offer did not differ substantively from the general offer of pardon that had been on the table for years. Viceroy Apodaca had recently offered Guerrero a pardon, employing the good offices of Guerrero's own father and a prominent priest to convey that offer, but Guerrero had refused. The rebel chief replied scornfully on January 20, explaining in detail the rebels' motives and assuring the colonel that he would never suffer the indignity of accepting a "pardon." He urged Iturbide to turn his forces against the government and fight for independence. Iturbide was undeterred. He sent a second letter on February 4 in which he again flattered the rebel leader, calling him friend and inviting him to Chilpancingo. There, the colonel slyly hinted, he would reveal his true intentions. While this dalliance continued, a pair of small skirmishes were fought by forces ignorant of the slowly developing alliance. These desultory actions may be regarded as the final armed clashes of what had been a bitter and bloody ten-year civil war that, amid violence, famine, and disease, had likely cost the lives of 600,000 people, one of every ten Mexicans.

Guerrero, suspecting treachery, refused to meet Iturbide in

person, instead sending his aide and treasurer, José de Figueroa, to
hammer out the terms to which Guerrero could agree. Iturbide
promised the rebels that, in independent Mexico, racial discrimination would no longer exist. On February 10, in the so-called
Abrazo de Acatempan, Guerrero formally united his forces with
those of Iturbide. Having assured himself of Guerrero's adherence to his plan for independence, Iturbide carried on a ruse,
telling Apodaca that he had at long last persuaded the last serious
rebel band to submit.

The Plan of Iguala

The plan that Iturbide proposed to free Mexico once and for all
from Spanish domination was written at the city of Iguala, in the
modern state of Guerrero, and is hence known to history as the
Plan of Iguala (though it is sometimes referred to as the Plan of
the Three Guarantees). Iturbide issued the plan on February 24,
1821. It was ingenious, albeit highly imperfect; neither liberal nor
reactionary, revolutionary nor counterrevolutionary; and in the
end it said much about the condition of Mexico's fractured society.
It was a compromise, though it has been less charitably described
as a panacea. Iturbide's plan offered every major constituency in
Mexico something they could endorse with enthusiasm. The first
three of the plan's twenty-three articles—soon to be known as the
Three Guarantees—amply demonstrated its conciliatory intent.
The first article promised the clergy and their flock of faithful that
the Roman Catholic religion would be the only one tolerated in
Mexico, and a subsequent article assured the clergy that their
properties and privileges would be protected; the second article
promised that Mexico would be fully independent; and the third
mollified liberals and monarchists alike by promising that Mexico
would be a constitutional monarchy, preferably one with Ferdinand VII or one of his brothers as king. A curious preamble to the
plan sought the support of Spaniards and their allies by including

effusive praise for Spain, calling it "the most Catholic and pious, heroic and magnanimous of Nations" and crediting the former mother country with making Mexico an opulent, beautiful, and prosperous place. But Mexico was not to be the exclusive province of Europeans and their progeny. The preamble was addressed to the *Americanos*, which explicitly included Spaniards, creoles, Indians, Africans, and castes, and Article 12 of the plan promised that "all of the inhabitants of the Empire, with no consideration except those of merit and virtue, are citizens qualified to accept any employment." This clause seemed to consummate the visionary dreams of Hidalgo, Morelos, and their heirs, that Mexico might one day overcome its paralyzing racial divisions.

The plan's great strength, of course, was that in the short term it made possible a broad consensus that proved powerful and popular enough to attract a broad cross section of the Mexican population. Its weaknesses were, in the longer term, extremely damaging. Nearly every constituency found something in it they could endorse and something to which they objected. Not everyone, for example, was pleased that the plan prescribed a constitutional monarchy for the new country. Among the independence fighters and their liberal backers were many who favored creating Mexico as a republic. Even some who backed a monarchy were unenthusiastic about seeking a king from among the Spanish Bourbon line, which in the eyes of many had fallen into disrepute. The plan addressed the problem of what should be done if none of the Spanish Bourbons took the job, but only in the vaguest terms (a regency would govern "until the matter of who shall be crowned king is resolved"), which promised major disputes in the offing.

On a more abstract level, unlike the fundamental statements of the American and French Revolutions, the Plan of Iguala did not propose an ideology that would represent a real break from the colonial past. It allowed all current officeholders to remain in office so long as they did not oppose the plan; it maintained religious intolerance, allowing the clergy to retain all of their properties and

privileges; it clung to the institution of monarchy; and it declared
the Spanish Constitution of 1812 to be Mexico's fundamental law
until a new constitution could be written. And even while the Plan
of Iguala gave a nod to racial equality, its commitment was more
rhetorical than real, a matter of winning the support of nonwhites
and Spaniards over to the cause with toothless promises. Poisonous
divisions of race, class, region, culture, and ideology were part of
the warp and woof of Mexican society, and a mere statement that
such divisions were no longer acceptable was unlikely to bring
about the needed transformations. Iturbide's plan offered each
segment of Mexican society—peasants, landlords, merchants,
priests, monarchists, republicans, Indians, Spaniards, creoles, and
castes—just enough to get them to sign on, but there was a glaring
emptiness at the plan's core.

The Final Fight for Independence

Of course, the Plan of Iguala did not automatically free Mexico
from Spanish domination. Iturbide was disappointed when Viceroy
Apodaca, whose cooperation he urgently hoped for, declined to
participate in the independence project and instead made it clear
that he would fight to defend Spain's prerogatives. Apodaca issued
a broadside instructing the population to stay faithful to the current government, admonishing priests to deliver that message from
their pulpits. The Plan of Iguala was declared a seditious document, and all copies were to be rounded up and destroyed. Apodaca divided the royal army into three units, ordering one to
defend Acapulco, another to defend important points in Veracruz,
and a third to defend the capital.

But Iturbide's revolution moved too fast for the royalists to contain. In fact, the royal army had been deteriorating for some time.
In order to fight the increasingly decentralized insurgency, the
viceroy had dispersed the army into tiny garrisons, which were unable to coalesce to fight a movement that became suddenly both

large and potent. Funding for the military was in short supply. Many well-heeled creoles had reluctantly supported the royal government since 1810 only because the alternatives—the violent and unruly rebellions of Hidalgo and Morelos—were unthinkable; they had paid the onerous war taxes grudgingly, waiting eagerly for the conflict to end. When the Iturbide movement offered them a new alternative, they happily took it, refusing to pay the taxes. Brigadier General Manuel de la Concha, who headed the royalists' counterinsurgency efforts in the critical Apam region east of the capital, reported that his provincial treasury was entirely bankrupt, his soldiers unpaid, badly armed, demoralized, and practically naked. The increasing reliance on amnestied rebels meant that desertion was rife (tellingly, the large number of amnesties granted did not perceptibly reduce the number of rebels under arms). "With such a small force," Concha complained to the viceroy, "how can you ask that I should resist an enemy in a country in which for my misfortune, I do not encounter a friend of the King!"[7]

Meanwhile, the royalist militias, which the government had relied on to do the bulk of the fighting, evaporated almost overnight. In early 1821, many towns took to insisting that the Spanish Constitution of 1812 forbade local taxation to support militias. When Ciriaco de Llano, the intendant of Puebla, tried to collect taxes to support the militias, delegations appeared from the towns of the region telling him bluntly that they had no intention of paying, and that he would be unwise to press the matter. It was a spontaneous tax revolt, and it spelled doom for the royalist cause.

For his part, Iturbide sought to provide his rebellion with needed resources by seizing a convoy of silver that left the capital for Acapulco, destined to pay for the cargo of a Manila galleon at that port. He also commissioned a young officer named Antonio López de Santa Anna—soon to become a hero of the independence movement and the key player in Mexico's early national politics—to take over Orizaba and Córdoba, which were depots for the government's lucrative tobacco monopoly. The battles for those towns left perhaps fifty or sixty casualties on each side. Iturbide styled his army "the Trigarantine Army," or the Army of the Three Guarantees, and he promised two oxen and a piece of farmland to any who joined it within six months.

Iturbide decided to focus his attention on the Bajío, that rich and fertile land to the north of the capital that had played such a key role in the struggle since its inception. He ordered his forces to engage only in defensive actions, avoiding bloodshed as much as possible—an indication that perhaps he was sincere in his frequent insistence that cruelty was merely a tactic that was periodically necessary, not something he reveled in for its own sake. One by one, important royalist commanders adhered to the Plan of Iguala, and the fighting was minimal. By early April, the intendancies of New Galicia, Zacatecas, and San Luis Potosí had joined the rebellion. Iturbide set his sights on his hometown of Valladolid, which had changed hands several times during the past decade and had consequently suffered horrendous destruction, its population declining by 80 percent. For all its suffering, Valladolid was now, apart from the capital, the best-defended city in Mexico. Iturbide played on the sentiments of the city's residents, reminding them that it was he who had driven the bloodthirsty hordes of Morelos out of their town in December 1813, sparing them a horrible fate. The royalist commander in charge of the city, Colonel Luis Quintanar, at first planned to make a stand, but so many of his troops deserted to the rebellion that he had no choice but to capitulate. His army now swelled with old insurgents and royalist deserters, Iturbide soon took the key cities of Querétaro, San Luis Potosí, and Guanajuato.

The defenders of the old regime were now in truly desperate straits, their tenuous control reduced to only Puebla and Mexico City. The royal army's general staff in Mexico City was scandalized by what it saw as Viceroy Apodaca's excessive respect for the liberal constitution—he even respected the provisions regarding freedom of the press—and by his apparent dilatoriness in combating the Iturbide movement. Rumors ran that Apodaca was secretly in league with the revolutionists. Apodaca was in an untenable position, unable to appease one group without alienating another. He capitulated to the army officers' demand that he suspend freedom of speech and the press on June 5, 1821, whereupon Mexico City's city council, which was dominated by creoles, announced that it would cease cooperating with his regime. Apodaca further inflamed resentment when, two days after instituting censorship, he ordered that all men between the ages of sixteen and fifty, with no exemptions, enlist in the army.

The city council howled its protests, but even these measures were not enough to placate the hard-line officers. On the evening of July 5, 1821, a force of about eight hundred men from various regiments of the city entered the viceregal palace and demanded that Apodaca resign. Apodaca, demanding only safe conduct out of Mexico for himself and his family, stepped down in favor of Field Marshal Francisco Novella, the army's second-highest-ranking officer (the highest-ranking, General Pascual de Liñán, refused to cooperate in the coup).

Novella was sworn in as Mexico's new viceroy on July 8. In some ways, this was a replay of the overthrow, thirteen years earlier, of Viceroy Iturrigaray, the act that had set the stage for the calamitous wars for independence. This coup featured some important differences from that earlier episode, however. For one, this was a decidedly military affair, while civilians had engineered the 1808 coup; the Novella coup thus qualifies as Mexico's first— though, lamentably, not last—military coup. And in contrast to that earlier episode, the Novella coup was a pathetic and delusional act of desperation: rather than preparing the stage for a decade of brutal war, this was the war's last, whimpering gasp.

Novella tried vainly to shore up the city's defenses. He issued a torrent of decrees and pronouncements demanding the loyalty and cooperation of the city's people, prohibiting "suspicious meetings,"

forbidding political discussions, demanding special monetary contributions, and prescribing severe penalties for any soldiers who
deserted or induced others to desert. He ordered all men between
the ages of sixteen and sixty to appear for military service within
forty-eight hours, threatening all who failed to do so with six years
of forced service on the front lines and quite possibly eternal
perdition. Like earlier regimes, Novella's did not neglect to seek divine intervention, ordering a week's worth of novenas in honor of
the royal army's protectress, the Virgin of Los Remedios.

It was all futile. The people of Mexico City simply ignored
these imperious decrees. When Novella demanded that all citizens
surrender their horses to the royal army for use in defending the
city against the expected attack, not a single horse appeared. The
city council, ordered to raise funds for defense, simply refused.
When the city council made plain that it had no intention of supporting the Novella regime, that regime lost its last tenuous claim
to political legitimacy. It became a true military dictatorship.

Meanwhile, Iturbide's rebels continued their irresistible campaign. Veracruz, Puebla, and Mexico City were now the only
major cities not controlled by the rebels. Puebla, Mexico's second-
largest city, lay astride the route from Veracruz to the capital. It
was heavily garrisoned and armored under the command of the
highly competent intendant, General Ciriaco de Llano. Iturbide
surrounded the city with about eighteen thousand soldiers, and
Llano wisely decided that resistance would be futile: he surrendered, and Iturbide's army made its triumphal entry on August 2.
With the fall of Puebla, there was no serious impediment to the
seizure of the capital other than the absurd obstinacy of Novella
and his dwindling group of supporters, who had taken to sporting
slogans on their hats reading *Vivir y morir fieles y útiles* (Live and die
faithful and useful). Despite his reputation for cruelty, Iturbide sincerely hoped to avoid bloodshed, but no amount of cajoling could
lessen Novella's resolve. Iturbide plotted his assault on the capital.

It was at this point, as Iturbide was advancing toward the capital from the north, that he received a fateful letter that seemed to point the way toward a peaceful resolution. That letter came from Lieutenant General Juan O'Donojú, who had just arrived at Veracruz from Spain. It informed Iturbide that King Ferdinand VII had appointed him, O'Donojú, captain general and superior political chief of Mexico. O'Donojú was named to the position at the insistent urging of the liberal Mexican deputies to the Cortes, chiefly Miguel Ramos Arizpe and José Mariano Michelena. O'Donojú was an old friend of Ramos Arizpe, a Freemason, and a man of well-known liberal sentiments. He had served as war minister for the liberal regime in Spain from 1810 to 1814, and had been among the many imprisoned by Ferdinand VII. He also, unlike Novella, had a sober and clear-eyed appreciation of reality. Upon his arrival at Veracruz, he was able to size up the situation quickly. It was abundantly obvious that, Novella's stubbornness notwithstanding, Mexico was lost to Spain. Most of the royal army, of which O'Donojú was technically commander in chief, had deserted to Iturbide. Nearly all of Mexico's towns had fallen to the rebels. It only remained to persuade the hard-liners in Mexico City of the bitter reality that Spain's three centuries of colonial rule in Mexico had come to an end.

O'Donojú's letter to Iturbide said nearly everything the rebel leader most wished to hear. O'Donojú wrote that he had come to America at the urging of his Mexican friends, and that his goal was to establish peace and to win the love and esteem of the Mexican people. He suggested a meeting and hinted at the possibility that a treaty could be signed based on the Plan of Iguala. Wisely anxious to put some distance between himself and the notoriously unhealthy city of Veracruz, O'Donojú met Iturbide at Córdoba, a beautiful town located at roughly three thousand feet above sea level, in the shadow of the majestic, perpetually snow-covered Orizaba volcano. It was there that, on August 24, 1821, Iturbide and O'Donojú signed the Treaty of Córdoba, which incorporated the provisions of the Plan of Iguala, and which also granted

Spain's formal recognition of Mexico's independence, albeit without the knowledge or approval of the Spanish government or king.

Article 17 of that treaty acknowledged that there was still an obstinate regime in Mexico City that would have to be dealt with before independence could finally be assured. Field Marshal Novella dismissed notes from both Iturbide and O'Donojú as trickery, and he taunted the rebels to attack—a foolish strategy indeed, considering that Mexico City's defense forces numbered only about 2,500, while Iturbide now headed an army of some 30,000. Skirmishes took place on the outskirts of the capital, including a particularly bloody one at Atzcapozalco. Rebels took control of the villages of Guadalupe, Tacuba, and Tacubaya, all at the city gates. On August 29, a representative of O'Donojú appeared in Mexico City bearing copies of the Treaty of Córdoba and demanding that Novella submit. Novella held frantic meetings with his supporters, and issued dire proclamations warning citizens of an imminent attack. Still suspecting a trick, Novella sent agents to Puebla to meet with O'Donojú and verify his identity. It was not until September 13 that Novella agreed to meet with Iturbide and O'Donojú at an hacienda near the basilica of Guadalupe. There, finally satisfied that O'Donojú was exactly who he claimed to be and that military resistance would be suicidal, Novella submitted to O'Donojú's authority. By September 23, all of the troops still loyal to Spain had evacuated the city, and Mexico's independence was, at long last, complete. On September 27—his thirty-eighth birthday—Iturbide made his triumphant entry into Mexico City at the head of an army of sixteen thousand men.

It was a moment of euphoria the likes of which Mexico has seldom experienced, either before or since. On that clear, bright day, before wildly cheering crowds, the triumphant armies filed through the streets, some with fine uniforms and healthy mounts, most—including the former insurgents from the south—dark-skinned, hungry, and half-naked. A soldier of Guerrero's forces later recalled how he felt as his bedraggled legion filed through the streets.

"Ah! the enthusiasm became delirious, they threw flowers at us, they uttered many tender expressions, and we, full of gratitude, felt ourselves becoming proud of our poor appearance, of our ragged clothing, of our obsolete weapons, and of our dark skin— blackened by the rays of the sun of the south and by the powder of many battles."[8] People had decorated their homes with floral arches and tapestries in red, green, and white, colors representing the Three Guarantees, while women sported hair ribbons and sashes in those same newly patriotic colors. Lucas Alamán, writing some thirty years after the events, his nostalgia colored by the tumultuous early history of the Mexican nation, described the scene wistfully:

> The joy was universal. It may be said that this was, in the long course of forty years of revolution, the only day Mexicans experienced when pure enthusiasm and enjoyment were not mixed with sad memories or word of some new misfortune. To this day, those who witnessed it keep fresh the memory of that day when the satisfaction of having obtained something long desired, and the enduring hope of boundless grandeur and prosperity, cheered spirits and caused hearts to beat with pleasure.[9]

The consummation of Mexico's independence was a joyous and cathartic moment, to be sure, but the delirium would soon be dampened by harsh realities. The death and destruction wrought by ten years of war was immense, greater than the country's liberators seem to have appreciated at their moment of triumph. Of equal concern, the questions left unanswered by the Plan of Iguala were also immense. The plan had resolved that Mexico was to have a king, but who would that king be? It had resolved that Mexico would have a congress, but who would form that congress, and how much power would it have? It had resolved that Mexico would have a constitution, but what sort of government would that constitution create? It had decreed social equality, but how would that equality be guaranteed? A head-on confrontation with those questions could not be long postponed, and that virtually guaranteed tumultuous times in the offing. On that glorious day in September 1821, almost no one quite anticipated just how tumultuous those times would be.

NINE

THE TRAGIC EMPIRE

The essential ingredients of the Plan of Iguala—independence, Roman Catholicism, and constitutional monarchy—seemed agreeable to most Mexicans in 1821. But the insistence on monarchy, which the plan's authors imagined would be a barrier against ambition, raised a host of thorny issues. Many Mexicans considered the institution of monarchy to be antiquated, and they would have preferred to follow the hemispheric trend toward republicanism (Brazil was the only other Latin American country to buck that trend); others liked the idea of constitutional monarchy, but could not agree whether the emphasis should be on the constitution or the monarch; and the issue of precisely who was to occupy the throne could not be long delayed. The euphoria that attended the triumph of Iturbide's revolution was genuine, but it was fleeting. The reckoning was at hand.

The State of the Nation, circa 1821

After more than a decade of war, Mexico was in a deplorable condition. Roughly half a million people had died from violence, hunger or disease, and the destruction that the rebellion had wrought was nearly incalculable. Bandit gangs terrorized the rural roads, and the once elegant capital was nearing collapse. Terrible flooding had hit the city in 1819, bringing on yet another wave of wild dog attacks, to which the authorities responded with ferocious slaughter, killing 1,326 dogs during one week in August. In 1820, the fevers returned with a vengeance, and all the while the crime rate soared. The city's streets, embankments, bridges, and aqueducts were decaying, and there was no money in the city's coffers to attend to their upkeep.

Even so, many Mexicans clung to the optimistic notion that their country's wealth was practically boundless, its resources having scarcely been tapped owing to the imprudence of the Spanish regime. But rebels and royalists alike had spent the past ten years demolishing or misappropriating that wealth, and in the short term, at least, the situation could only deteriorate. Spain's overzealous tax policies had been one of the chief causes of the rebellion in the first place, and any leader who hoped to garner support in the rebellion's aftermath would perforce have to decree sharp tax reductions. In the last three months of 1821, therefore, Iturbide's government decreed a reduction in the despised sales tax (*alcabala*) from 16 percent to 6 percent, with a tax of 8 percent on imported goods. It likewise abolished the tax on cane liquor, all special war taxes, Indian tribute payments, taxes on the value and rent of homes, and taxes on henequen fiber.

The problem, of course, was that even with all its taxes and exactions, the royalist government had been virtually bankrupt even before the war began, and had barely survived the decade with a series of desperate measures. Virtually all of the principal sources of revenue had dried up. The tobacco monopoly, which had provided some funding for the royalist war effort, was a shadow of its former self. The rebels had commandeered many tobacco storehouses and intercepted shipments; tobacco farmers, dismayed at the low prices the government offered, had taken to selling their product to smugglers. Iturbide hoped to secure a loan to revitalize the industry, offering future sales as collateral. But the loan was complicated by the fact that no one seemed to be able to agree whether the tobacco monopoly should be reestablished or disbanded, a disagreement that would continue for many years.

Maritime commerce seemed a promising source of income, for with independence the Spanish commercial monopoly had been broken and Mexico was now ready to do business with all comers. But Mexico's only legal trading partner for the past three hundred years had been Spain, and the stepped-up tensions between Spain and Mexico brought that trade to a screeching halt. No other countries yet had offices or warehouses in Mexican ports, and those that sent ships found themselves waylaid by the Spaniards, who still held the fortress of San Juan de Ulúa at the entrance to Veracruz harbor. The Spaniards collected their own duties from those ships, meanwhile helping them to unload their cargoes and smuggling that merchandise into the port, avoiding all Mexican duties. Revenues from customs were disappointing, to say the least.

Before the war, silver mining had been the economic engine of the colony, yet no sector of the Mexican economy had been quite as badly damaged as mining. Mines had been neglected, machinery destroyed, and the ore-processing mills were in need of repair. The insurgents had looted the funds that the Spanish government had used to purchase bullion, and they had intercepted many silver shipments, selling the ore at drastically discounted prices. Production for 1818 was less than a quarter what it had been in 1810, with only the mines of Zacatecas showing continued profitability. In the hope of reviving the mining sector, Iturbide decided that his only recourse was to cut taxes on the industry, which only added further to the government's fiscal woes.

Making matters worse still, the drastic decline in revenues coincided with a dramatic increase in expenses. Iturbide's primary base of support was his own Army of the Three Guarantees, and he was keenly aware that its happiness must be his top priority.

Every officer, it seemed, aspired to be a general, and Iturbide came close to granting every officer's wish. Anyone who joined the army after August 31, 1821—that is, shortly after the signing of the Treaty of Córdoba—was automatically granted a promotion of one rank, whether he had done anything to deserve it or not. Those officers deemed truly worthy were given promotions of four or more grades, with, of course, a corresponding increase in pay. Spectators at a military parade through Mexico City in December 1821 were amazed to see an army with about one officer or musician for every two rank-and-file soldiers. Adding further to the drain on the beleaguered treasury were the costs of new civil service positions created to reward supporters, and the Iturbide government's decision to provide for the six thousand or so Spanish soldiers who remained on Mexican soil, unable to afford their passage back to Spain. The government tried to persuade the wealthy folk of the capital to make voluntary contributions, without much luck. After all, wealthy merchants and landowners had signed on to Iturbide's plan because they had been given to understand that their wealth and privileges would be protected in the new scheme of things.

Creating a Government

Although Mexico's problems were hard to ignore, the country's new leaders made a valiant effort to do just that. They became fairly consumed, in the short term at least, with the ceremonial side of politics. At the time of his glorious entrance into Mexico City, Iturbide was the object of spontaneous and heartfelt popular adoration. A flood of pamphlets and broadsheets called Iturbide the Immortal Liberator, the New Moses, the Honor and Glory of America, America's Alexander, the Luminous Torch of Anáhuac, and the Redeemer of the Fatherland. Even a few foreigners joined in the eulogizing. James Smith Wilcocks, the first consul of the United States to Mexico, wrote to his home government that Amer-

ica "has produced two of the greatest heroes that ever existed—
Washington and *Iturbide.*"[1]

To prepare the way for a new government, Iturbide named a
Sovereign Provisional Governing Junta, made up of thirty-eight
clergymen, military officers, high-level bureaucrats, landowners,
and titled nobles. All were cronies of Iturbide's, and not one of
them had fought for or sympathized with the independence movement that had begun in 1810. The president of the junta was Antonio Joaquín Pérez, the bishop of Puebla, who, as a Mexican
deputy to the Spanish Cortes in 1814, had signed a manifesto
calling on King Ferdinand VII to overthrow that same Cortes
and declare himself absolute monarch. The junta chose five of its
members, including Iturbide and Juan O'Donojú, to form a regency. Tragically, O'Donojú, who might well have played a major
role in the ensuing events, died of a respiratory ailment on October
8, only two weeks after Iturbide's triumphal march into the capital.
Iturbide and his junta made clear their sentiments by denouncing
Miguel Hidalgo and minimizing the influence of men like Vicente
Guerrero, Nicolás Bravo, and Guadalupe Victoria. Those former
rebels were now styled "old patriots," perhaps in an effort to consign
them to respectful irrelevance. Their opinions were not solicited.

The Sovereign Provisional Governing Junta laid the groundwork for much of the strife that soon followed. Rather than deal
with the many pressing questions of the day, it occupied itself
largely with such trivial matters as distributing promotions, prizes,
and appointments, and designing a new national flag and seal.
The junta was determined to reward the Liberator handsomely in
both power and wealth: it bestowed upon Iturbide the titles of
generalíssimo and admiral, giving him supreme authority over the
military; it also set aside for him a million pesos taken from the
properties of the abolished Inquisition, along with twenty square
leagues of land in the province of Texas and a budget-busting
salary of 120,000 pesos, more than twice what the Spanish viceroys had received.

To the junta also fell the task of creating a constituent congress to write a constitution for Mexico. The mechanism for electing such a congress sparked some controversy. Iturbide favored representation by class and occupation, with bureaucrats and clerics taking the lion's share of seats. Others felt that representation should be proportional to the population, even though reliable population data were lacking, the most recent census dating from 1792. For reasons that are unclear, the junta joined those two approaches into a strange amalgam. It decided that each intendancy or province should have representation equal to two-thirds of the number of its *partidos*, or districts. Unfortunately, the *partidos* had been drawn up during colonial times with territorial extent and defense in mind, not numbers of people. Every intendancy or province whose representation included more than three deputies was required to send the congress a priest, a soldier, and a lawyer. This arrangement, of course, ensured that the congress, which was elected in December 1821 and January 1822, was in no sense representative of the Mexican population. Iturbide was soon railing against the "monstrous inequality" of the congress, where, he complained, "one deputy was appointed for a province containing a hundred thousand inhabitants, and four for a province scarcely peopled by half that number."[2] Iturbide, who made no secret of his elitist proclivities, also complained that there was no mechanism for weeding out people who lacked sufficient education, wealth, and preparation for the task they confronted.

Signs of serious dissension were appearing at the very same time that the junta was setting up its rules for electing the congress. In November 1821, Iturbide's government claimed that it had evidence that several prominent "old patriots" had conspired to kidnap Iturbide and hold him prisoner during the elections to ensure that he would not be able to meddle. Seventeen individuals were arrested, including prominent rebel leaders Nicolás Bravo, Miguel Barragán, and Guadalupe Victoria. Although the alleged conspirators were released after only one night in jail, Iturbide's critics never forgave the outrage.

Adding to the Liberator's woes, by late 1821 three clear political factions had emerged, and two of those factions had no great love for Iturbide. One faction, the Bourbonists, was intent on calling a member of the Spanish Bourbon family to the throne of Mexico, despite the fact that all of the possible candidates—Ferdinand and his two brothers—would likely refuse the invitation or be too unpopular to gain it in the first place. A second faction, which joined forces with the Bourbonists out of a shared antipathy for Iturbide, consisted of those who wished to jettison the institution of monarchy entirely, and instead establish Mexico as a republic. But they would be hamstrung from the outset, because the form of Mexico's government had already been settled. The Plan of Iguala and the Treaty of Córdoba meant that they simply were not allowed to opt for anything but a constitutional monarchy. The third faction in Mexico's increasingly turbulent political firmament was the "Iturbidists," who hoped to enthrone the hero of independence.

It was amid this nascent wrangling that the congress opened on February 24, 1822. Its first act was to uphold the Three Guarantees, namely, independence, religious intolerance, and constitutional monarchy with a preference for the Spanish Bourbon family. The congress duly affirmed the legal equality of all citizens, which was arguably the only feature of the new regime that might result in a significant social transformation. The real promise of this innovation was dubious, however. Iturbide clearly saw legal equality more as a means of protecting the rights of European Spaniards than of elevating the dark-skinned masses. That much had been made evident in December 1821, when a man named Francisco Lagranda published a pamphlet in which he denounced European Spaniards, suggesting that they should be forced to sell their properties and leave Mexico. Several Spanish-born officers protested the publication to Iturbide, charging it aimed to "destroy the union of Americans and Europeans, to disturb the tranquility, and to plunge the Empire into an abyss."[3] Iturbide obliged them: he had the offending pamphlet seized and destroyed, and its author was sentenced to six years' imprisonment. This was yet another harbinger of coming disharmony. Hatred of European Spaniards had fueled the Hidalgo rebellion and much of the popular violence of the revolutionary decade; the superficial paean to fellowship in the Plan of Iguala did nothing at all to diminish that hatred, which was in fact a key element in Mexico's incipient nationalism. Attacks on Spaniards would be a staple of Mexican political life for decades.

Popular resentment of Spaniards got a fresh boost in March 1822, when Mexico received momentous news: the Spanish king and Cortes had declared that General O'Donojú had acted without authority when he signed the Treaty of Córdoba recognizing Mexico's independence. They declared that treaty null and void. That left the Bourbonist faction bereft, for it ensured that no Spanish Bourbon would be assuming the Mexican throne. It also forced the Mexicans to confront the daunting reality that all links to the Spanish empire were irrevocably severed.

Iturbide sent a questionnaire to local authorities asking them whether they favored a monarchy or a republic. With the significant exception of the northern provinces of Coahuila and Texas, all favored monarchy. There was a widespread presumption that monarchy, apart from its virtue of familiarity, was the only reliable barrier against unbridled ambition. Of course, monarchist theory made the most sense when the kings in question were born and bred to rule, but presumably any king who is put in place for life would be above the political fray, not swayed by political passions or fleeting trends. "Monarchy has in its favor reason, experience, and authority," declared one Puebla newspaper, and apparently a large majority of Mexicans, at least for the time being, agreed.[4]

But the Bourbons' snubbing forced the Mexicans to look outside of the established European royal houses to fill the position of emperor. The matter was given a curious twist as a result of a dispute between Iturbide and the congress. Iturbide still presided over the regency, which wielded executive power while the search for a suitable king was under way. Always keenly aware of where his power lay, Iturbide pleaded with the congress, in May 1822, to fund an army of seventy thousand men, half regular and half militia forces. He conjured the fear that Russia, Prussia, and Austria, whose Holy Alliance threatened to smother the flames of revolution wherever they should flare up, might seek to help Spain reconquer its lost colony. When the congress balked at the expense of such a military buildup, Iturbide threatened to resign. On May 18, the congress gave in and authorized the expenditure, but the standoff with the congress had irritated certain members of the military, who now determined to force the issue.

On that same evening, soldiers marched through the streets of the capital, approaching Iturbide's home and demanding that he accept the title of Emperor Agustín I. The soldiers were joined in their march by a mob of the city's impoverished denizens. In the small hours of the morning of May 19, sixty-two of the army's highest-ranking officers signed a memorandum to the congress asking it to consider elevating Iturbide to the dignity of emperor.

From there, events moved quickly. In the congress's session of May 19, a deputy from Guadalajara named Valentín Gómez Farías—later renowned as Mexico's most intransigent liberal—made a motion to proclaim Iturbide emperor, with the proviso that he agree to support the yet-to-be-written constitution and the laws, orders, and decrees of the congress. Forty-six deputies seconded the motion, and in the ensuing vote, a solid majority of the deputies voted to proclaim Iturbide emperor immediately. Fifteen deputies voted to refer the matter to the provinces for a decision, but not a single deputy present voted against the motion. On May 21, the congress issued a manifesto declaring Iturbide's election.

Iturbide seems clearly to have enjoyed the acclamation he received, but at the same time he protested strenuously—and probably not altogether disingenuously—that he had no desire to become emperor. According to his own account, when the crowds gathered in front of his residence demanding he be named emperor, he had to be forcefully dissuaded from going out to "declare my determination not to yield to the wishes of the people." A friend warned him that "the people" would consider this an insult, "and the people know no restraint when they are irritated. You must make this fresh sacrifice to the public good; the country is in danger; remain a moment longer undecided, and you will hear their acclamations turned into death shouts."[5] Though surely there was a strong element of self-service in Iturbide's protestations, to the end of his days he insisted that he accepted the crown only under duress and in order to save his life and to save his country from anarchy.

Iturbide's enemies later claimed that the congress had likewise acted under duress, fearful that the rabble would rebel if their hero were not crowned. Iturbide's critics also complained later that the congress that elected Iturbide lacked a quorum, and hence the election was illegitimate. Thanks to such critics, who had an inordinate influence on the subsequent writing of history, Iturbide's elevation to the throne is most often presented as something akin to a coup d'état, the result of a megalomaniac's devious machinations. Historian Timothy Anna, who studied Iturbide's elevation to the throne closely, concluded that in fact the election was perfectly legal in accordance with the Spanish Constitution of 1812, which was recognized as Mexico's supreme law at the time. More importantly, Anna insisted that Iturbide's election had widespread, enthusiastic popular support. The liberal Lorenzo de Zavala impugned Iturbide by declaring scornfully that he was elected emperor only because he enjoyed the support of "the clergy, the miserable nobility of the country, the army in its greater part, and the common people who saw in that chief nothing more than the liberator of their country." In other words, quipped a later writer, Iturbide's support came from "the immense majority of the nation."[6]

The congress made sure that Iturbide clearly understood the limited nature of his monarchy. The oath that they had him swear was severe: Iturbide was made to promise that if he failed to observe the yet-to-be-written constitution and abide by its laws, did anything leading to the dismemberment of the empire, took away anyone's property, or failed to respect the liberty of all citizens, then he should not be obeyed and his oath would be rendered null and void. The congress even denied the emperor veto power, something that the Constitution of 1812 granted to the Spanish king. Iturbide acknowledged that his power was inferior to that of the congress, and claimed he found the arrangement unobjectionable. For many in the congress, the emperorship was only justified as a symbol of tradition and continuity. The emperor should have little real power, of course, and it made no sense to make the position elective, as that would negate the system's principal virtue. The deputies were also aware that politicizing the position could threaten some bitter and tumultuous elections in the future. Accordingly, in June the congress decreed the monarchy to be hereditary. The succession was to pass first to Iturbide's eldest son—styled "the Prince Imperial"—while royal titles were bestowed on all of Iturbide's nearest relatives.

The coronation of Agustín I, which took place on Sunday, July 21, 1822, was supposed to be as splendid and majestic as any similar event in the Old World, but even despite the irresponsibly lavish funding from Mexico's anemic treasury, the affair struck many as but a ridiculous imitation of true imperial grandeur. In advance of the big day, the city authorities ordered that all balconies and windows were to be adorned with curtains, and the facades of public buildings and church towers were to be festooned with banners, streamers, and tapestries. Prior to his coronation, Iturbide, fearing he might suffer by comparison with real royalty, ordered that the equestrian statue of King Charles IV in the capital's main square be covered with a blue globe—a covering the monument wore until 1824.

The festivities began early, with the royal party departing from the Moncada Palace, where the Iturbides had taken up residence, at around ten in the morning. The emperor and his wife rode in a coach, he dressed in his military finery, she in a glamorous gown made in imitation of the couture used during the coronation of Napoleon Bonaparte. The party made its way to the metropolitan cathedral, attended by artillery salvos and the music of military bands. Upon arrival at the cathedral, the monarchs were sprinkled with holy water, supplied with new imperial vestments, and seated on thrones made especially for the occasion. A crown, fashioned in Mexico, was placed on the emperor's head, and he in turn placed a tiara on the head of the empress. After that, the bishop of Puebla delivered a sermon explaining how Iturbide's selection as emperor had been divinely inspired. Many other speakers followed, and the ceremony dragged on for a grueling five hours. The elderly U.S. general James Wilkinson, a Revolutionary War veteran who was in Mexico hoping to secure a land grant in Texas, reportedly found time for "two good naps." Some saw in all this pomp little but vanity, an ersatz coronation of an ersatz emperor.

Whatever else it may have been, Iturbide's empire was indisputably vast. Simultaneous with Iturbide's coronation, all of the provinces of Central America voted to join the empire, prodded by Iturbide's threat to send Mexican troops should they decide otherwise (he did in fact send troops to subdue El Salvador when it tried to break away in early 1823). The Mexican empire stretched from the forty-second parallel in the north—roughly the modern-day border between the U.S. states of Oregon and California—down to Panama, an area approaching two million square miles. It was the seventeenth-largest contiguous empire in world history.

The Empire

Iturbide's empire was unpromising from the start. Two powerful trends were already at work to undermine his tenuous authority. One was the desire of a number of highly influential Mexicans for a republic. This demand had been temporarily muted by the enthusiasm generated by independence and the adulation of Iturbide, but the partisans of the republic were actively conspiring against the empire from its inception. The conspirators worked through the Scottish Rite Masonic lodge, which ironically had been instrumental in bringing Iturbide to power in the first place. Further undermining Iturbide's position was the presence in Mexico in late 1822 of Joel Roberts Poinsett of South Carolina, who authored an influential report on conditions in Mexico that was decidedly unflattering to Iturbide, damaging the emperor's reputation with Mexico's powerful neighbor to the north.

The other trend working to undermine Iturbide's authority was a growing spirit of regionalism, which was already an unstoppable force by the time of his coronation. Back in 1811, at the urging of Mexican deputies, the Spanish Cortes had allowed for the creation of provincial deputations, or popularly elected regional governing bodies. Since that time, regionalism had been given a boost by the independence war, during which local chieftains had gained much power that they would not now relinquish without a fight. During the session of 1820–1821, the American deputies to the Cortes revived the demand for provincial deputations, and the Cortes formally ordered their creation on May 9, 1821. By late 1821, Mexico had eighteen provincial deputations; that number increased to twenty-three during the following year. The makeup of the constituent congress further increased the decentralization of power. Because of the flawed system for choosing deputies, the country's most densely populated region—Mexico City and its environs—was badly underrepresented, while the peripheral regions dominated. In sum, regional elites acquired a strong taste for home rule, and their pretensions would soon cause a wholesale unraveling of the country.

Meanwhile, Iturbide's relations with the congress were rapidly turning sour. The emperor had cause for complaint. The body that began its meetings in February 1822 was a constituent congress, its primary duty to write a constitution for Mexico. It was never intended to act as a legislative body. And yet for the first several months of its existence the congress ignored the writing of a constitution entirely, instead devoting its time and energies to what Iturbide characterized as "schoolboy disputations," such as "what honors should be paid to the chiefs of the insurrection, who had fallen?"[7] The congress actually dealt with weightier matters than that, but it did little to resolve the most pressing problems of the day, in particular the critical condition of the imperial treasury.

Iturbide had little grounds to criticize the congress in the area of finance, however, for in fact his own family represented one of the greatest drains on the treasury. The family had three grandiose homes to choose from while the viceregal palace was undergoing an extensive and expensive remodeling. They also had a formidable entourage: tutors for the Iturbides' many children (the prolific empress was even then pregnant with a ninth child, and would deliver a tenth in 1824); servants; gentlemen of the chamber; military aides and adjutants; majordomos; horse pages; a doctor and a surgeon; ladies-in-waiting, maids of honor, and a wardrobe mistress to the empress; multiple chaplains, preachers, and confessors; and an official printer. The household's expenses included such indulgences as costly clothing, a bearskin saddle studded with gold, and 448 pesos' worth of chocolate for the empress. The household's monthly expenses came to a whopping 23,000 pesos. The Spanish viceroys of old—never known for their frugality—had had to make do with a fifth that amount. During 1823, expenses for the imperial household came to nearly half of the amount allocated for the payment of all civil servants' salaries combined. Pampering the Iturbides was the government's largest single expense after the army, a questionable use of resources indeed, considering that the projected deficit for the year was six million pesos. Iturbide's extravagance was undoubtedly a factor in his eventual undoing, for even his old comrades-in-arms could not help but remark on the sumptuous pretensions of a man who not so long ago had been their equal or subordinate.

The principal disputes with the congress, however, had to do less with funding than with pure power rivalries. Iturbide deeply resented that the congress denied him the power of the veto and the right to appoint members of the Supreme Tribunal of Justice, both of which powers were accorded to the king of Spain under the Spanish Constitution of 1812, which supposedly was serving as Mexico's interim constitution. There is little doubt that he sought ways to enhance his power at the congress's expense.

By the end of July 1822—only a little over two months into the reign of Agustín I—conditions in Mexico had descended into crisis. The country was rife with conspiracies either to topple the emperor and proclaim a republic or to dissolve the congress and proclaim royal absolutism. Street demonstrations in Mexico City made both of those demands. The emperor's council of state in early August urged that military tribunals be established in all of the provincial capitals to punish acts of sedition. At the same time, Iturbide reacted strenuously to rumors of an antigovernment conspiracy involving members of the congress, ordering the arrest of sixty-six individuals, including some fourteen to nineteen deputies to the congress (the major sources disagree on the precise number), who were supposed to be shielded from such indignities by congressional immunity. Many of the detainees were entirely innocent of the charges made against them, and though some were released in December, five deputies remained in prison. These arrests marked a crucial turning point, for they caused some key individuals to lose faith in the emperor, including Valentín Gómez Farías, the man who had proposed Iturbide's election in the congress.

Although Iturbide's support was weakening, the congress was no more popular. That much was demonstrated by a stillborn rebellion that began on September 26, 1822. Felipe de la Garza, military commandant and political chief of the province of Nuevo Santander in northeastern Mexico (the modern state of Tamaulipas), together with the provincial deputation and an assortment of other prominent citizens, sent Iturbide a letter demanding that the imprisoned deputies be set free at once, that the congress be moved to a safe location where it could deliberate freely, that the emperor's cabinet members be deposed and submitted to trial, that all military tribunals be suppressed, and that all other political prisoners throughout the country be released. But few Mexicans were willing to rise up in defense of the congress. Iturbide was able to squelch the rebellion with only a small detachment. The emperor was magnanimous in the abortive rebellion's aftermath, pardoning Garza and even restoring him to his command of the province.

Meanwhile, Deputy Lorenzo de Zavala of Yucatán, who would later emerge as one of Mexico's most renowned liberals, undertook to study the relations between Iturbide and the congress. To the chagrin of many of his fellow deputies, Zavala acknowledged that the emperor had some valid points. Zavala determined that there was indeed a lack of checks and balances in relations between the executive and legislative branches. He also conceded that the methods used to elect deputies had been badly flawed, resulting in a congress that was not truly representative of the country's population. He suggested that the emperor be given veto power and that the present congress be dissolved and a new one elected.

On October 16 and 17, Iturbide met with several deputies in his home to discuss these issues. He scolded the congress for failing to write a constitution or to confront the empire's dire fiscal crisis, and he again denounced the "monstrous inequality" in representation. He suggested that the congress be reduced by seventy members, and sent that demand to the congress, which quickly rejected it. The congress did agree to give the emperor veto power, but Iturbide then chose to up the ante by demanding that he be granted veto power over the still-to-be-written constitution and that he be authorized to create a special police force to bring rampant crime under control. Once again, the congress refused.

On October 31, 1822, Iturbide took a truly fateful step, one that would cost him his empire and, ultimately, his life. He sent Brigadier General Luis Cortazar to the legislative chambers to inform the assembled deputies that they had ten minutes to dissolve or be dissolved by force. The congress had no option but to obey.

Iturbide then established a sort of rump congress he called the National Instituent Junta, which consisted of two representatives for each heavily populated province and one for each sparsely populated province. Iturbide chose the representatives from among the currently serving deputies. Iturbide's enemies charged that the assembly he thus created was little more than a club of his closest cronies, but that was not in fact the case—the junta included some of Iturbide's harshest critics. The new junta, with forty-five members, was formally installed—with, in the words of a critic, "Asiatic pomp"—on November 2. In striking contrast to his own election as emperor, during which he had sworn to obey the laws and to respect the liberty of all citizens, Iturbide now insisted that the junta members vow loyalty to the emperor and work for the good of the empire.

The National Instituent Junta's first act was to confront the fiscal crisis by decreeing a forced loan of 2.8 million pesos. Nearly half of that amount was seized from Spanish merchants in Veracruz, another unwise act since it antagonized one of the reliable bastions of Iturbide's support. The junta also instituted new head taxes and property taxes, provoking immediate protests throughout the country. In desperation, the government authorized the printing of paper money, and was soon reduced to begging citizens to accept the nearly worthless currency.

The junta did do some constructive work. Addressing the long-held concern for Mexico's northern provinces, which were sparsely populated and effectively outside the control of the central government, it drew up a plan to populate (or "colonize") these provinces. The plan, which was passed on January 4, 1823, promised generous rewards for "empresarios" who could guarantee to settle at least two hundred people on those underpopulated lands. Settlers would receive land concessions and exemption from taxes for six years. All settlers would be required to profess the Roman Catholic faith and to respect the government and laws of Mexico, and preference was accorded to native-born Mexicans. With great misgivings, the law allowed for the settlement of foreigners in those territories, of whom Anglo-Americans were the most eager—and the most mistrusted—petitioners. Stephen F. Austin, soon to be the most successful empresario by far, was in Mexico City when the law was written. Iturbide himself issued a decree authorizing Austin to start a colony in Texas. These actions seemed necessary and justifiable at the time, but they were a first step leading to the loss of Texas and, eventually, all of northern Mexico.

The National Instituent Junta also set itself to writing a temporary constitution to take the place of the Spanish Constitution of 1812. Iturbide insisted that the Spanish constitution was poorly suited to Mexico's realities. The provisional constitution that the junta produced was notable for the enhanced power it gave to the emperor, although, oddly, it denied the emperor veto power and expressly prohibited him from interfering with the legislature under normal circumstances. Significantly, during times of "internal convulsions," the emperor's power was to be practically absolute. Opposition to the provisional constitution arose at once. Critics questioned whether the junta had the authority to suspend the Spanish constitution, and they charged that the mere existence of a provisional charter might somehow preclude the drafting of a permanent one. Although the junta voted in favor of the provisional constitution on January 14, debates continued on the issue and the provisional constitution was never actually enacted. By that time, Iturbide's government was facing far more serious problems than criticism of its proposed interim laws. A month earlier, a new and worrisome rebellion had erupted in the province of Veracruz.

The Fall of the Empire

Veracruz was a volatile place, for while Mexicans had control of the city proper, a group of royalists remained in the castle of San Juan de Ulúa, an imposing fortress guarding the northeastern entrance to the harbor. With six hundred men, heavy artillery, and ample food and munitions, it appeared as though the royalists could hold the fort indefinitely. Since October 1822, Brigadier General Francisco Lemaur, who was destined to play a major role in the toppling of the empire, commanded the Spanish garrison of Ulúa. The commander of Mexico's troops in the city of Veracruz was Antonio López de Santa Anna. The headstrong, ambitious twenty-nine-year-old, who had been promoted to general largely owing to his professed loyalty to Iturbide, had been the subject of many complaints from military and civilian leaders as well as ordinary citizens. The complaints against him were not dissimilar to those leveled against Iturbide himself back in 1816: he was accused of taking arbitrary and unjust actions, insubordination, failing to maintain discipline among his troops, and embezzling regimental funds to pay off gambling debts. One of the most serious complaints came from General José Antonio Echávarri, a Spaniard whom Iturbide counted among his closest friends and most loyal officers. Santa Anna apparently resented Echávarri for refusing to name him captain general of Veracruz province. Echávarri suspected that Santa Anna was plotting to avenge this snub by handing him over to General Lemaur. Santa Anna's game, according to Echávarri, was nothing short of treason, for he was risking Spanish recapture of Veracruz in order to accomplish his perfidious and vengeful ends.

With the volume of complaints against Santa Anna reaching torrential proportions, Iturbide determined to personally undertake the delicate task of removing the troublesome officer. For the first and only time during his stint as emperor, he left the capital city for the provinces. Traveling at the head of a large entourage that included several members of the imperial household, among them the very pregnant empress, he called Santa Anna to confer with him at the city of Jalapa, in the tropical highlands northwest of the port. When Santa Anna arrived, Iturbide informed him that he was to join the imperial party on its return to Mexico City.

Santa Anna demurred, claiming he could not afford to make the journey, whereupon Iturbide offered him five hundred pesos from his own pocket. Santa Anna asked the emperor to allow him several days to get his personal affairs in order at Veracruz. That permission granted, Santa Anna hurried to the port, stung by what he knew was the emperor's determination to remove him from his command. On the afternoon of December 2, 1822, Santa Anna raised the cry of revolt against the empire.

This was Santa Anna's debut as a major figure on the national stage, and it gave an early hint of the mercurial disposition for which he would soon be famous. His initial cry of revolt demanded the establishment of a republic, even though only a few months earlier Santa Anna had been as enthusiastic a champion of monarchy in general, and of Iturbide in particular, as anyone in Mexico. On December 6, Santa Anna signed his name to a detailed, confusing plan. Oddly, the plan plagiarized most of its clauses from the Plan of Iguala while at the same time declaring all of Iturbide's acts null and void, insisting the emperor be made to stand trial for his misdeeds, demanding the restoration of the congress that Iturbide had dissolved in October, upholding the Three Guarantees, and calling for free trade and an armistice with Spain. Unlike Santa Anna's original demand, this so-called Plan of Veracruz said nothing about establishing a republic, though it did say that, once restored, the congress would be expected to write a permanent constitution and decide which form of government Mexico was to have.

Santa Anna's rebellion was an annoyance to Iturbide's government, but at the outset it seemed it would be easy enough to contain. The government made a concerted effort to impugn Santa Anna's reputation and question his motives, something that was not especially difficult. Iturbide even claimed to welcome the rebellion as a chance to "clean the land of many weeds and leave it prepared to bring forth good fruit."[8] Militarily, Iturbide had the better hand, and in the first battle of the rebellion—Santa Anna's attempt to take the city of Jalapa on December 21—the emperor's forces won convincingly, killing or capturing nearly all of Santa Anna's infantrymen.

But despite that early success, the prospects for preserving the empire were dim, for Iturbide's government had become steadily more unpopular, and few could now be found who were willing to rise up in its defense. The paper money the government had printed was causing serious economic hardship; Iturbide's dissolution of the congress, while applauded in some quarters, provided his enemies with fodder for damning propaganda; and in the face of Santa Anna's rebellion, Iturbide went ahead with a plan to create military tribunals to punish dissenters, leading inevitably to rumors that the emperor planned to seize dictatorial powers.

In early January, two of the leading lights of the independence movement, the "old patriots" Vicente Guerrero and Nicolás Bravo, raised their own rebellion in the south of Mexico, seconding the Plan of Veracruz. On January 5, Guerrero was nearly killed in battle, and Iturbide congratulated himself on having stifled the rebellion.

Meanwhile, strange things were happening back in Veracruz. The man Iturbide was relying on to crush Santa Anna's rebellion, his old friend, the Spanish-born General Echávarri—whose denunciations of Santa Anna had helped to provoke the rebellion in the first place—found that, despite a nearly constant siege, dislodging the rebels from the city of Veracruz would be no easy task. The rebels had better artillery, and they were receiving supplies and reinforcements from the Spaniards holding the fort of Ulúa— an arrangement that was, by any reckoning, treasonous. Rather than squander resources battling the rebellion, Echávarri decided to issue a dissident plan of his own. That plan was actually the work of men like Miguel Ramos Arizpe and José Mariano Michelena, liberals who, working mostly through Masonic lodges, had long been planning an uprising in favor of republicanism. It was promulgated on February 1, 1823, from Echávarri's headquarters, the small town of Casa Mata just south of Veracruz. The Plan of Casa Mata, as it was called, did not call for the restoration of the dissolved congress—that congress had contained too many men of dubious convictions to please the die-hard liberals—but rather for the election of a new congress using the same rules as had been used to elect the dissolved congress. That newly elected congress would, in turn, make all of the crucial decisions.

The Plan of Casa Mata was as brilliant, stealthy, and fundamentally flawed as Iturbide's own Plan of Iguala had been, designed, as it was, to please many and offend few. It was perhaps most remarkable for what it did not do: unlike the Plan of Veracruz, it did not call for the simple restoration of the dissolved congress; nor did it call for a republic, demand the removal or punishment of the emperor, criticize the methods of deciding representation, or, in fact, state any clear political preference at all. There was nothing, then, to alienate either the emperor's supporters or those who were up in arms against him. Those who had criticized the old congress could take comfort in the thought that the new elections would yield a more agreeable result, while those who had admired the old congress were heartened by the fact that reelection of the old representatives was a possibility. It was an ingenious act of subterfuge that tricked even its most prominent sponsor, Echávarri, and the emperor Iturbide himself.

Just as the devious liberals had hoped, Iturbide appointed a commission to confer with Echávarri and his confederates to see if there was some way to resolve the dispute peacefully. The emperor let it be known that he did not object to the creation of a new congress, and for the most part the discussion revolved around whether to hold elections using the old rules, to establish new, more equitable rules, or to simply reseat the dissolved congress.

While these parleys were going on, liberals had time to pursue their real aim, which was to rouse republican and federalist sentiments in what they knew to be its natural venue, the Mexican provinces, where an aspiration to autonomy from, and resentment of, Mexico City had long simmered. The plan itself contained a provision for sending copies to the country's provincial deputations. Those provincial deputations did not hesitate to adopt the plan enthusiastically, each declaring that it would assume full political control until the new government could be formed. The provinces took it upon themselves to reverse some of the emperor's more unpopular measures, including hated taxes and the use of paper money. By mid-March 1823, the provinces of Mexico had effectively declared themselves autonomous. Iturbide's power barely extended beyond Mexico City. In a remarkably short span of time, Mexico had unraveled. The problem would long outlast the hapless emperor.

On March 4, Iturbide decreed that those members of the dissolved congress who were then present in Mexico City should reassemble as quickly as possible and that, once reassembled, he would ensure they would have complete freedom to deliberate and act. Not surprisingly, there were many who questioned the legitimacy of the newly reassembled congress—the Plan of Casa Mata had called for new elections, not the restoration of the old congress—so the moment would have been one of great confusion in any event. Iturbide added to the confusion when, on March 19, he sent a handwritten statement to the congress declaring that he was abdicating his throne. He allowed that he had accepted the throne in the first place with "great repugnance," and only because he believed he was acceding to the people's wishes. Now, he said, he had determined that his presence in Mexico had become the cause of discord. He asked for a couple of weeks to settle his affairs, after which he and his family would leave Mexico and take up permanent residence in some unspecified foreign country.

Contemporaries and historians have interpreted Iturbide's abdication variously. Some maintain that he offered his resignation only because he believed the congress would reject it, though such a belief would have been delusional. Others find his stated reasons perfectly convincing, and this position has much to recommend it.

In fact, the evidence is persuasive that Iturbide, despite his notorious cruelty as a military leader, had a genuine horror of disorder
and a sincere aversion to the needless shedding of blood. He could
accept harsh methods when demanded on the field of combat, but
he could not abide violence and disorder knowing that his presence in power was the cause.

The Army of Liberation (as Echávarri's force had styled itself)
marched into Mexico City on March 27, 1823, and two days later
it announced the creation of an executive triumvirate to exercise
power until a more permanent solution could be arranged. On
April 8, the triumvirate issued a series of vindictive decrees: it decreed that the ex-emperor's election had been an act of violence,
and hence was legally null; it sent notices to the provinces that anyone who acclaimed Iturbide as emperor was to be considered a
traitor; and it ordered that the eagle depicted on the national flag
be stripped of its crown. The congress stopped short of nullifying
all legislation related to the empire, for presumably such a decree
would have included the Plan of Iguala and the Treaty of Córdoba—some sticklers for detail pointed out that those documents
had created the congress in the first place, and if they were nullified then the congress itself would have no legal existence. While
some, notably the liberal clergyman Servando Teresa de Mier,
insisted that Iturbide should be hanged, the congress instead decided he should be sent to Italy, and that so long as he stayed there
and caused no trouble he would receive an annual pension of
twenty-five thousand pesos. Carlos María de Bustamante wrote that
April 8, 1823—the date the empire was formally abolished—
should be considered Mexico's true independence day. It was now
the third candidate for that distinction.

On March 30, Iturbide and his family, accompanied by an escort of fifty armed men led by General Nicolás Bravo, departed
Mexico City for the coast along a route designed to avoid cities—
especially Puebla, long a bastion of conservative Catholicism—
where popular demonstrations in favor of Iturbide could be ex-

pected. There was some tension, for Iturbide seems to have be-lieved that he was on his way into an entirely voluntary exile, while his escort, General Bravo, accorded him the indignity of treat-ment as a state prisoner. Another disappointment awaited, for Iturbide's elderly father and frail sister both appeared unable to endure the hardships of the journey, and they begged the congress to allow them to remain in Mexico, which the congress reluctantly conceded. At the time of the Iturbide party's arrival, the port of Veracruz was being ravaged by yellow fever—not an uncommon problem, but one that made swift departure essential. Iturbide im-plored a Mexican customs official to inspect his baggage to put to rest rumors that he was absconding with state treasure; the official declined to do so, and the rumors continued.

On May 11, Iturbide, his large family, and several retainers and friends set sail on the British merchant ship *Rawlins*. Even be-fore the ship had arrived at the port of Livorno in northwest Italy, the Mexican government had arranged a fairly elaborate system of espionage to ensure that Iturbide be prevented from returning to Mexico.

Despite his constant complaints of penury, Iturbide lived well enough in Livorno, residing in a luxurious palace decorated with paintings by the old masters. But he was also plagued by serious in-quietudes. No doubt he was aware that the Mexican government had launched an unsubtle campaign to demonize him, revising history in ways that have jaundiced historians ever since: it charged that he bribed the ignorant rabble with money and liquor to demonstrate in his behalf, suborned soldiers and nobles to sustain his election as emperor, and seized the crown in what amounted to a coup d'état. The congress was recast as an innocent victim of the emperor's absolutist tyranny. The partisans of the failed revo-lutions of Hidalgo and Morelos were lionized as the true authors of independence, thus depriving Iturbide of even his greatest achievement, securing Mexico's independence from Spain. The man who had only a few months before been hailed as his country's savior was now denounced as an "iniquitous traitor" and "the new Caligula." In an attempt to counter the propaganda, Iturbide penned his own brief account of events, which was self-serving but not as inaccurate as many have assumed.

The End of Iturbide

Iturbide was surely concerned about his own reputation, but to his credit he seems to have been more profoundly troubled by the dangers facing Mexico, where conditions deteriorated steadily. "May God grant that I am mistaken," he wrote, "and that they are happy!" The perils were very real and growing. The United States, France, and Spain all posed threats to the nation's sovereignty. Although the United States had signed a treaty with Spain in 1819 recognizing Spain's possession of the northern province of Texas, there were some on both sides of the border who questioned the legitimacy of that treaty; regardless, there was nothing particularly subtle about the United States' desire to extend its borders. More frightening—albeit grossly exaggerated—was the potential threat posed to Mexico's independence by Europe's Holy Alliance. Formed after the defeat of Napoleon's empire, the Holy Alliance began as an informal gathering of European states, which vowed to conduct themselves in accordance with Christian principles. By 1820, the views of the alliance's most powerful statesman, Tsar Alexander I of Russia, had shifted decidedly rightward, and he, along with the leaders of Austria and Prussia, signed the Protocol of Troppau, wherein the powers vowed to use force if necessary to restore "order and stability" to states that had been disrupted by revolutions. In 1822, the Holy Alliance turned its attention to Spain, where King Ferdinand VII had been chafing under the dominance of the liberal Cortes. Ferdinand entered into secret negotiations with the Holy Allies, which obliged him by encouraging the French king Louis XVIII to send his armies across the Pyrenees to reestablish royal absolutism in Spain. The invasion began in April

1823 and achieved a definitive victory on August 31. His absolute power restored, Ferdinand lost little time in once again indulging his love of merciless vengeance against his liberal foes. The restoration of absolutism in Spain gave rise to the fear that the Holy Allies intended to interfere with the recently liberated nations of the Americas, restoring them to Spanish control. In December, President James Monroe announced the Monroe Doctrine, expressing U.S. displeasure at that prospect. In Mexico, some feared that perhaps Iturbide would make common cause with the Holy Allies, serving as their agent in a bid to reconquer Mexico.

Iturbide found himself in a curious position indeed. Some Mexicans suspected him of conniving with the Holy Alliance. But inasmuch as he had accomplished the separation of Mexico from Spain, conservative Spaniards detested him, and he was a potential *target* of the Holy Alliance. In November 1823, the Spanish consul at Livorno, who was a liberal, advised Iturbide that he was not safe in the region of Tuscany, for reactionary supporters of the Holy Alliance were stationed in Florence and they took an unforgiving attitude toward all those stigmatized as rebels: there was a possibility they might deliver him to Spain, where he would likely become a victim of Ferdinand VII's purges.

Accordingly, on November 28, Iturbide left Livorno on a British ship bound for London. Agents of both Mexico and the Holy Alliance kept close track of Iturbide's whereabouts. Weather impeded his passage to London by sea, so he took an overland route through northern Italy, Switzerland, Germany, and the Low Countries.

Since the Mexican congress had decreed that Iturbide's pension was dependent on his remaining in Italy, the departure at the very least portended some financial hardship for the ex-emperor. But in the overheated atmosphere of the time, Iturbide's peregrinations gave rise to furious speculation. Few doubted that his ultimate aim was to make his way back to Mexico, but opinions differed as to his true purpose in doing so. Some reckoned he would return as an agent of the absolutist Spanish Bourbons or of the Holy Alliance; others feared that he was conspiring with elements in Mexico to restore himself to the imperial throne, a fear given some credence by the many monarchist and Iturbidist plots that had become a staple of Mexican life, both in fact and in rumor. His own stated purpose was to return so he could do whatever he could to restore stability to Mexico and to defend it against invasion, allowing that he was especially fearful of the designs of the Holy Alliance. He sent a letter to the Mexican congress on February 13, 1824, offering his services and declaring that he could supply Mexico's defenses with money, arms, and munitions.

The real prospect of intervention by the Holy Alliance waned considerably when both Britain and the United States made clear that they would strenuously resist such a move, but that did little to stem the paranoia in Mexico. In May, the congress voted to suspend all payments on Iturbide's pension until he satisfactorily explained his reasons for leaving Italy; a month later, on April 28, as reports from England continued to raise concerns about Iturbide's intentions, the congress passed a harsh law declaring that, should he return to Mexico, Iturbide would be considered "outside the pale of the law, an enemy of the State, and a traitor to his country." That meant that if he returned to Mexico and was caught, he would face immediate execution.

Only two weeks later—before he could possibly have been apprised of the draconian declaration—Iturbide left Southampton on the British ship *Spring*, bound for his native land. He brought along his wife (now pregnant with the couple's tenth child) and two youngest children (the rest were left in school in England).

On July 17, 1824, the *Spring* anchored near the town of Soto la Marina, having been unable to make it to the port of Tampico owing to contrary winds. Stationed at Padilla, a dusty little town of some three thousand inhabitants, was the commandant of the Eastern Interior Provinces, a region that included the newly created states of Tamaulipas, Coahuila y Texas, and Nuevo León. By an odd twist of fate, that commandant was none other than General Felipe de la Garza, who less than two years earlier, as political chief of Tamaulipas, had headed an abortive rebellion against the emperor Iturbide. Garza had reason to consider Iturbide fondly, for the emperor had pardoned his treasonous act and even reinstated him in his post.

Iturbide went ashore along with Colonel Charles Beneski, a Polish officer who had been his faithful aide both in Mexico and during his European sojourn. Garza arrested the pair, informing them of the draconian law that the congress had passed against him in April. Garza—with grave misgivings—decided to leave Iturbide's fate in the hands of the state legislature of Tamaulipas, which was then in session at Padilla. Iturbide tried to explain his purpose in traveling to Mexico, and attempted to submit documents attesting to his sincerity, but the legislators refused to consider clemency. On July 18, by a nearly unanimous vote, the state legislators chose to strictly enforce the national law of April 28. The next day the president of the legislature ordered Garza to carry out the death sentence at once.

Iturbide had time to write his protest, defending his actions as emperor and insisting that his only crime was his determination to defend Mexico's independence against foreign foes. He also wrote a final farewell to his wife and children. On July 19, Iturbide confessed his sins three times and handed his confessor the letter to his wife along with a rosary for his eldest son and a handful of coins for his executioners.

His last words before the firing squad launched the fatal volley were "No! I am not a traitor! No!"

EPILOGUE

Only two years after he had been crowned emperor in a lavish ceremony in Mexico City's enormous and elegant cathedral, Agustín de Iturbide lay dead in a barren room, shrouded in a Franciscan habit and flanked by four candles. On the morning of July 20, 1824, his corpse was taken to the decrepit, roofless chapel of the forlorn village of Padilla and buried in a spare ceremony attended only by some members of the local legislature and a few soldiers and local people. Iturbide did not live to see the birth of his tenth child, a son.

The collapse of Iturbide's empire left a political void, and there was no shortage of ambitious men who rushed to fill it. Mexico was at last free to create whatever kind of government it wished. The problem was that there was no agreement among the various claimants to power as to what sort of government that should be. Almost immediately, a vigorous and ultimately poisonous debate began as to what exactly independence meant, and who should receive the blame or the credit.

Posthumous Careers

Iturbide's historical legacy was defined by his most bitter adversaries, who blamed him for many, if not most, of the ills that Mexico suffered in the decades after his death. His demise brought to power a group of men dedicated to republicanism and federalism. Those men pressed hard to see Miguel Hidalgo, Ignacio Allende, and José María Morelos enshrined as the true fathers of Mexican independence. In September 1823, the headless remains of Hidalgo, Allende, and several of their confederates were disinterred from the resting place in the parched deserts of the north, reunited with the severed heads that had spent the last decade decorating the corners of the granary in Guanajuato, and reburied with lavish ceremonies beneath the Altar of the Kings in the Cathedral of Mexico. The remains of Morelos received the same honor. In 1824, a federalist constitution was adopted, and the following year began the ritual celebration of September 16—the date of Father Hidalgo's Grito de Dolores—as Mexico's independence day. The celebrations became more elaborate with each passing year, the penurious government straining its meager budget to provide for full-dress parades, garlands of flowers, orchestras, and fireworks. Monuments were erected to the heroes in various parts of the republic; Hidalgo and Morelos each had states named in their honor; Valladolid, where Iturbide had handed Morelos a crushing defeat in 1815, was renamed "Morelia" in homage to the rebel priest.

Iturbide was not forgotten, merely overshadowed. September 27, the date of his triumphal entry into Mexico City at the head of the Army of the Three Guarantees, was routinely celebrated with ringing church bells, volleys of rifle fire, and bullfights. Iturbide's legacy was burnished whenever conservatives attained power, as they frequently did prior to the 1850s. In 1833, President Antonio López de Santa Anna—the same man who had begun the pro-republican rebellion against Iturbide in 1822—renounced liberalism and ordered that Iturbide's remains be exhumed from the little church at Padilla and brought to Mexico City for a hero's burial. Due to budget shortfalls and political turmoil, the order was not carried out until 1838, during the presidency of Anastasio Bustamante, a man who so idolized Iturbide that he put a clause in his will providing that, upon his death, his heart should be cut out and buried alongside the Liberator. Iturbide's bones were buried in the Cathedral of San Felipe de Jesús, northeast of the capital. In 1865, when Mexico was once again an empire—this time presided over by Maximilian of Hapsburg, a puppet of the French—Iturbide's remains were placed in a bronze sarcophagus in the Cathedral of Mexico, alongside the remains of Hidalgo and others. The childless Maximilian and his hapless empress Carlota adopted two of Iturbide's grandsons to ensure a species of royal continuity.

Once the French imperialists were ejected from Mexico in 1867, the triumph of the old patriots in the official pantheon of heroes was definitive. The most extravagant commemoration came in 1910, when the dictator Porfirio Díaz—who celebrated his eightieth birthday on September 15, the eve of independence day—ordered a month of celebrations for the centennial of Hidalgo's Grito. Díaz had the bell taken from the church at Dolores—the same bell Father Hidalgo had ordered rung in 1810 to gather the people to begin his insurrection—and brought to Mexico City, where it was installed in the National Palace. The dictator invited the world's nations to send representatives to join the festivities, and most of them obliged. Those emissaries were feted with sumptuous banquets and fine wines, and treated to guided tours designed to showcase the impressive modernization Mexico had achieved during the thirty years of Díaz's dictatorship. To ensure that the dignitaries saw nothing embarrassing or offensive, city officials warned the legions of beggars and impoverished Indians to stay off the streets, and five thousand tons of grain were imported from Argentina to provide temporary relief for the hungry masses in the hope they would not create a spectacle. There were grand balls and banquets, bullfights, and parades chronicling key episodes in the nation's history—or at least those episodes that could be made to aggrandize the Díaz regime. Camilo Polavieja, ambassador extraordinary from the Spanish court of King Alfonso XIII, staged a dramatic ceremony of reconciliation, presenting Porfirio Díaz with a dress uniform, a sword, and other artifacts that had been seized by Spanish troops from José María Morelos upon his capture in 1815—items that for decades had languished at the Artillery Museum in Madrid.

Most spectacularly, Díaz had years earlier commissioned the creation of a great monument to independence on the city's elegant Paseo de la Reforma, and that monument was inaugurated during the centennial festivities. Around the base of the monument were bronze figures, cast in Florence and Paris, representing Law, Justice, War, and Peace; another bronze sculpture depicted an enormous lion being led by a child, symbolizing, according to the sculptor, docility in peace and ferocity in war. Further up the monument's base were marble sculptures of the now official heroes of independence—Hidalgo, Morelos, Vicente Guerrero, Francisco Xavier Mina, and Nicolás Bravo. Above the heroes rose a 118-foot marble column, which was topped by a seven-ton bronze angel representing Winged Victory. The angel held a laurel wreath in one hand, in the other a broken chain.

The Angel of Independence was supposed to represent the coming of age of the Mexican nation, the realization of brotherhood and progress. But the problems that had helped to make Mexico's wars for independence so prolonged, bloody, and chaotic still simmered: whites continued to monopolize wealth and political power; Indians and mestizos remained illiterate, and they still lived, for the most part, in grinding poverty; the poor continued to comprise the vast majority of Mexico's population; sprawling haciendas still covered the countryside, exploiting labor in the most ruthless fashion; the specter of famine still reared its head on occasion, as it did in that centennial year of 1910, when lean harvests forced massive importation of grain, though still failing to keep pace with demand. Moreover, the people of Mexico—with the exception, of course, of a handful of the politically well connected—continued to have no voice in how the country was run.

The centennial year turned out to be pivotal in that regard. A couple of years earlier, Porfirio Díaz had given an interview in which he promised to relinquish power and allow free and fair elections to take place in 1910, when his current term was due to end. Almost spontaneously, it seemed, a vigorous political opposition appeared, celebrating mass rallies in every corner of the republic. But in July, when the presidential election was held, most of the prominent opposition figures were in jail or in hiding, and the opposition press had been shut down. Porfirio Díaz claimed to have won the election by a wildly implausible margin, a result that was duly confirmed by the congress, after careful "scrutiny," in September, even as the gaudy centennial celebrations were under way. A dissident group gathered at the recently inaugurated monument of independence to pay their own homage to the patriot heroes and to protest the election results: they were violently dispersed by mounted police, and two dozen of them were thrown in prison. Other dissidents pelted Porfirio Díaz's home with rocks and fruit. More ominously, in October, the leading opposition candidate, Francisco I. Madero, jumped bail and made his way to Texas, where he plotted a violent revolution to rid Mexico of the dictator and institute needed reforms. It was the start of the most ferocious bloodletting in Mexican history, the decade-long Mexican Revolution.

But even that bloodletting was not enough to fix the profound problems that continued to divide Mexicans. That point was made poignantly clear during yet another independence day ceremony in September 1925, when the mortal remains of many heroes—Hidalgo, Allende, Morelos, Bravo, Mina, Guerrero, Juan Aldama, José Mariano Jiménez (a top lieutenant to Hidalgo), Mariano Matamoros (a top lieutenant to Morelos), Andrés Quintana Roo

and his wife, María Leona Vicario (active supporters of the Morelos rebellion), and Guadalupe Victoria, rebel chieftain and first
president of republican Mexico—were removed from the cathedral and reburied in a mausoleum under the independence
monument. Iturbide—the man who in fact achieved Mexico's
independence—remained behind in the cathedral. The president
at that time, Plutarco Elías Calles, who considered himself a radical reformer, explained his reasoning to Ernest Gruening, an
American journalist: "I left Iturbide there among his kind, where
he belongs." Gruening was savvy enough to understand that
Calles's opinions were not universally shared. "To the Mexican
conservatives and clergy to-day," Gruening wrote, "Iturbide is *the*
liberator, the others a shabby lot, and the issue is thoroughly alive.
It has been presented to me with as much heat as if it dealt with
contemporary figures. Deep is the cleft which divides Mexico."[1]

What It All Meant

Mexico's political independence from Spain did nothing at all to
bridge that deep cleft. The divisions of Mexican society had been
artfully concealed during the three centuries of colonial rule by a
mystifying veil of tradition, custom, and culture. For the people at
society's lowest depths, the tender mercies promised by religion—
as ubiquitously represented by the Roman Catholic Church, its
saints, and its clergy—made the dreadful realities of everyday life
somewhat more bearable; comfort could also be had in the
thought that the king, a remote and benevolent father, might take
pity on his suffering subjects. The colony was rife with injustice, but
it also featured institutions—inalienable landholdings for villages,
for example, and special courts to hear Indians' complaints—that
meted out just enough justice to keep the resentments of the poor
more or less in check. For those at the top of society, tradition and
culture had the obvious advantage of undergirding a system that
maintained them in their power and privileges.

During the independence era, that veil of tradition, custom, and culture was lifted. The first shocks to the system arrived courtesy of the Bourbon kings, who tampered, at times quite clumsily, with the traditional arrangements. Next came Bonaparte, who removed the Spanish king and replaced him with a usurper. Enlightenment ideas—which captivated many of Mexico's educated creoles—played their part, with their bold questioning of monarchical and aristocratic privilege and their heretical notions that perhaps God was not puppet master of the universe, that the people might be able to divine what was best for themselves. Intransigent Spaniards moved the story along by overthrowing the viceroy, which crushed the creole bid for autonomy and began a process of polarization that led inexorably to crisis. The liberal Spaniards of the Cortes of Cádiz complicated things by apparently opening political channels to the advocates of autonomy for the colonies, but then refusing to take the matter to its logical conclusion for fear the empire would disintegrate.

Then, of course, came Father Hidalgo, who made Mexico's rural poor major players in the unfolding drama. The movement's creole leaders hoped to enlist the disinterested help of the masses to advance their project, which would have brought autonomy or independence to Mexico, with prominent creoles at the helm. The movement was undone by several factors. The poor, it soon became evident, had their own agenda, which did not resemble that of the creole leadership in the least. Their objectives were mostly defined by long-standing local conflicts and grievances, and their tactics looked like mindless savagery to most creoles, who reluctantly threw their support to the Spanish regime as the lesser of two evils. The split among Mexico's creoles was mirrored in the leadership of the movement itself, for not even the heroic efforts of the brilliant and diplomatic Morelos could stanch the feuding among rebel chieftains. The demise of the insurgent movement was further ensured by several monumental military blunders, such that by 1816 the violence had become aimless and scattered, much sound and fury, signifying little.

The surprising denouement that was ushered in by Iturbide

owed much to political changes in Spain—the mutiny that revived
the liberal Constitution of 1812, which alienated conservatives
and convinced moderates that Spain was beyond hope. But in
theory, at least, independence could have been achieved at almost
any time during the revolutionary decade. Had viceroys Venegas,
Calleja, and Apodaca been more realistic about the royal regime's
long-term prospects, and had they been open to negotiation, a political settlement similar to the one effected by Iturbide might possibly have been reached—a settlement representing a superficial
consensus among Mexico's key powerbrokers. Ignacio Rayón, in
fact, suggested such a project to General Calleja in the spring of
1811, only to have it rejected out of hand. Such a settlement might
well have spared the nation much bloodshed, but it would have
had the same defects as Iturbide's project.

Generations of historians, enthralled by the noble aims of Hidalgo and Morelos, have demonized Iturbide, even though it was
he who finally secured Mexico's independence. Ernest Gruening
typifies this view fairly well: "Viewed in terms of progress the political revolution of 1821 was a defeat. Its champions intended to
change nothing. For the moment it was a step backward. Its consummation embodied the quintessence of the colonial vices. It
was achieved by duplicity, perjury, treason, and robbery. Its instrument and dominating figure was a militarist wholly devoid of prin-
ciple whose hands had for ten years been steeped in the blood of
his countrymen."[2]

In this view, Iturbide carried out a counterrevolution, one that
renounced the goals of the insurgency and the liberalism of the
revived Constitution of 1812. In fact, however, Iturbide's Plan of
Iguala adopted the Constitution of 1812 as Mexico's interim constitution, with an apparent understanding that eventually a similar
charter would be produced for Mexico. The Constitution of 1812
aimed to bring sweeping changes to the old order: it ended royal
absolutism; abolished seignorial privilege; guaranteed basic civil
rights, including freedom of speech and the press; provided for an
elected legislature; allowed for local autonomy through provincial

deputations; mandated government support for public education; and declared all Spanish citizens legally equal, although excepting persons of African descent. The Plan of Iguala took these reforms further, explicitly abolishing all distinctions of caste and declaring that all Mexicans regardless of race were to be accorded the same rights. It would be hard to defend the proposition, then, that Iturbide's project, at least given its stated intentions, "embodied the quintessence of the colonial vices." The insurgency, in fact, rested upon a very similar legal foundation, for the rebels' Constitution of Apatzingán was itself modeled closely on the Spanish Constitution of 1812.

For all his many errors and defects, Iturbide cannot reasonably be held responsible for the many problems that Mexico encountered as it began its career as an independent nation. In the end, his project failed for the same reason the insurgency failed. Both were capsized by the potent legacy of three centuries of Spanish colonialism. In the colony, social inequality was regarded not as a necessary evil, but as a positive good, for hierarchies were created and sustained by God; conflict was not an aberration, but rather an integral feature of the empire's divide-and-rule ethos. The Spanish system did not anticipate the modern nation-state, wherein a collectivity of citizens overcomes their differences and coalesces into a single "imagined community."[3] The system was set up precisely to perpetuate separateness: it was a jumble of localities, jurisdictions, and ethnicities, all united principally by their membership in the community of Roman Catholic believers and their allegiance to a distant, powerful king. The people of Mexico could not make common cause during their wars for independence; and although Iturbide did bring some temporary respite to a war-weary country, the crucible of ten years' war had not forged Mexico into a nation but in fact had deepened the already existing divisions of race, ethnicity, class, and region. For Mexico, becoming a nation would have required a thoroughgoing social revolution of the sort that takes generations, not a few years.

The founders of the new republic made a valiant effort to forge unity: they promoted the patriotic cult of the heroes of independence, even though they could not all agree who those heroes were; they created a plethora of national holidays, and promoted symbols such as the Virgin of Guadalupe in the hope of instilling in Mexicans a sense of national community. Anti-Spanish xenophobia also served as a superficial substitute for genuine national sentiment in the early decades of the republic. And yet, even after another century of war and revolution had passed, the historian Frank Tannenbaum could still state flatly that "Mexico is not a nation. It is becoming one, but the process is painful and harsh. Mexico can never have peace unless it achieves internal unity and harmony. It cannot do that unless it destroys the enormous disequilibrium that lies at its roots."[4]

The early decades after Mexico's independence were tumultuous and traumatizing. In 1824, the republic adopted a federalist constitution that gave considerable autonomy to the various states. Having tasted such autonomy, the regions of Mexico became loath to follow the dictates of the central regime, creating a formidable impediment to coherent government. Those who advocated greater regional autonomy also tended to advocate greater social equality, and they at times attacked the wealth and power of the Catholic Church. Their adversaries railed against the principles of liberalism and federalism, arguing instead that power in Mexico should be concentrated in Mexico City and should be exercised by conservative, educated white men—the *hombres de bien* (men of goodness), as they eventually styled themselves. Conservatives also maintained that the Hispanic heritage, with its emphasis on orthodox religion and deep-rooted tradition, could provide a viable model for the nation. The two sides—which took the labels liberal/federalist and conservative/centralist—agreed on little. During the 1820s, they divided into rival Masonic lodges, political societies that met and plotted in secret; and even after those lodges were abolished, opposing partisans continued to attack one another with stubborn ferocity. While the partisans fought, effective power fell into the hands of men like Antonio López de Santa Anna, Mexico's great nineteenth-century caudillo, who espoused no particular ideology but who knew how to attract a dedicated following.

The result was persistent penury and political paralysis. Decades of Mexican history are commonly told as a depressing litany of coups and countercoups too numerous to mention, civil wars (1832–1833 and 1857–1861), and foreign invasions (1829, 1838, 1846–1849, and 1862–1867). Civil strife led to territorial dismemberment: the provinces of Central America separated from Mexico upon the downfall of the empire, and in 1848 Mexico lost its vast northern territories to the United States in a devastating and humiliating war. It was not until the 1880s that Mexico finally achieved a measure of stability and economic progress, but even then the nature of stability and progress was perverted by the persistent inequities of Mexican society, such that in 1910 the republic exploded in an epic "fiesta of bullets."

For conservatives like Lucas Alamán, the achievement of independence brought little apart from bitter disappointment:

Seeing in so few years the immense loss of territory; the ruin of the treasury, leaving behind an enormous debt; the annihilation of a once flourishing and valiant army, leaving us without means of defense; and above all, the complete extinction of public spirit, which has erased all notion of national character: one does not find Mexicans in Mexico, and we contemplate a nation that has gone from infancy to decrepitude, without ever having enjoyed more than a glimmer of the exuberance of youth, or any signs of life apart from violent convulsions . . .[5]

For conservatives, the most baneful consequence of independence was the rise to power of a generation of liberals intent on demolishing all of the good and venerable features of the Spanish colonial period. Liberals, for their part, while not denying the obvious hardships of the early national era, were able to put a more positive spin on the matter. Historian and statesman Lorenzo de Zavala saw the gains of independence outweighing the negatives, for independence freed Mexico from the overbearing tyranny and stagnation of the colonial regime: "Since the time prior to the events of 1808 is a period of silence, of sleep, and of monotony . . . the interesting history of Mexico begins only in that memorable year."[6]

Yet Zavala and his ilk were hardly sanguine about the depth of Mexico's woes. As he wrote on another occasion, "It is very easy to put a country into combustion, when it possesses the elements of discord; but the difficulties of its re-organization are infinite."[7]

NOTES

Preface

1. Humboldt quoted in John J. Johnson, *Simón Bolívar and Spanish American Independence, 1788–1830* (Princeton, NJ: Van Nostrand, 1968), 128.
2. Ibid., 125.
3. See John Womack, Jr., *Zapata and the Mexican Revolution* (New York: Vintage, 1969), 7–8.

1: The Colony

1. Ignacio Allende to Miguel Hidalgo, August 31, 1810, in Luis Castillo Ledón, *Hidalgo: La vida de heroe*, vol. 1 (Mexico City: n.p., 1948), 165.
2. Mendoza quoted in Lewis Hanke, *The Spanish Struggle for Justice in the Conquest of America* (Boston: Little, Brown, 1965), 13.
3. The statement is cited in Lyle N. Mcalister, "Social Structure and Social Change in New Spain," *Hispanic American Historical Review* 43, no. 3 (August 1963): 364.
4. Gage quoted in John Rydjord, *Foreign Interest in the Independence of New Spain: An Introduction to the War for Independence* (New York: Russell and Russell, 1972; reprint of 1935 edition published by Duke University Press), 5.
5. Mcalister, "Social Structure and Social Change," 364.
6. John Leddy Phelan, *The People and the King: The Comunero Revolution in Colombia, 1781* (Madison: University of Wisconsin Press, 1978), xviii.

2: Shocks to the System

1. Charles III quoted in John Lynch, *Bourbon Spain, 1700–1808* (Oxford: Blackwell, 1989), 344.
2. Letter quoted in Salvador de Madariaga, *The Fall of the Spanish American Empire* (New York: Macmillan, 1948), 334.

3. Broadside quoted in Nancy Farriss, *Crown and Clergy in Colonial Mexico, 1759–1821: The Crisis of Ecclesiastical Privilege* (London: Athlone Press, 1968), 3–4.
4. José de Gálvez quoted in David Brading, *The First America: The Spanish Monarchy, Creole Patriots, and the Liberal State, 1492–1867* (Cambridge: Cambridge University Press, 1991), 475.
5. Bernardo de Gálvez quoted in Silvia Marina Arrom, *Containing the Poor: The Mexico City Poor House, 1774–1874* (Durham, NC: Duke University Press, 2000), 25.

3: Crisis
1. Charles III quoted in John Rydjord, *Foreign Interest in the Independence of New Spain: An Introduction to the War for Independence* (New York: Russell and Russell, 1972), 75.
2. Salvador de Madariaga, *Spain* (New York: Creative Age Press, 1943), 57.
3. Abad y Queipo quoted in Doris M. Ladd, *The Mexican Nobility at Independence, 1780–1826,* Institute of Latin American Studies Monograph 40 (Austin: University of Texas Press, 1976), 104.
4. Calleja quoted in Christon I. Archer, "The Army of New Spain and the Wars of Independence, 1790–1821," *Hispanic American Historical Review* 61, no. 4 (November 1981): 710.
5. Bustamante quoted in Lucas Alamán, *Historia de México*, vol. 1 (Mexico City: Editorial Jus, 1972), 194.

4: The Querétaro Conspiracy
1. Lucas Alamán, *Historia de México*, vol. 1 (Mexico City: Editorial Jus, 1972), 227.
2. Miguel Domínguez, "Relación sobre la economía de Querétaro, 1807–1811," *Boletín del Archivo General de la Nación* 11, 2d ser. (1970): 288.
3. Hugh Hamill, *The Hidalgo Revolt: Prelude to Mexican Independence* (Gainesville: University of Florida Press, 1966), 123.
4. Alamán, *Historia de México*, 1:244.

5: The Hidalgo Rebellion
1. Flon quoted in Christon I. Archer, "The Army of New Spain and the Wars of Independence, 1790–1821," *Hispanic American Historical Review* 61, no. 4 (November 1981): 705.
2. Lucas Alamán, *Historia de México*, vol. 1 (Mexico City: Editorial Jus, 1972), 281.
3. Ibid.
4. Ibid., 1:287 n. 52.

5. Calleja to Flon, October 2, 1810, quoted in Christon I. Archer, "The Royalist Army in New Spain: Civil-Military Relationships, 1810–1821," *Journal of Latin American Studies* 13, no. 1 (May 1981): 62.

6. Alamán, *Historia de México*, 1:292.

7. Calleja quoted in Archer, "The Royalist Army," 65.

8. Alamán, *Historia de México*, 1:309.

9. "Primer edicto contra la revolución iniciada en Dolores por el Sr. Hidalgo, fulminado por D. Manuel Abad y Queipo, canónigo penitenciario, electo Obispo de Michoacán, September 24, 1810," in Juan E. Hernández y Dávalos, *Colección de documentos para la historia de la Guerra de independencia de México de 1808–1821* (Mexico City, 1877–1882; reprint edition, 1968), 2:105.

10. Allende to Hidalgo, November 19, 1810, in Hernández y Dávalos, *Colección de documentos*, 2:232.

11. Hidalgo quoted in Hugh Hamill, *The Hidalgo Revolt: Prelude to Mexican Independence* (Gainesville: University of Florida Press, 1966), 182.

12. Hidalgo quoted in Enrique Krauze, *Mexico: Biography of Power* (New York: HarperCollins, 1997), 100.

13. "Manifiesto del Sr. Hidalgo," in Hernández y Dávalos, *Colección de documentos*, 1:59.

14. Hubert Howe Bancroft, *History of Mexico*, vol. 4, 1804–1824 (San Francisco: Bancroft, 1885), 286.

15. Timothy E. Anna, *The Fall of the Royal Government in Mexico City* (Lincoln: University of Nebraska Press, 1978), 76.

16. Alamán, *Historia de México*, 2:139–147.

17. Hamill, *The Hidalgo Revolt*, 219–220.

6: War, the Cortes, and the Constitution

1. Hidalgo quoted in Wilbert Timmons, *Morelos: Priest, Soldier, Statesman of Mexico* (El Paso: Texas Western College Press, 1963), 40.

2. Morelos to D. Manuel Ignacio del Campillo, Bishop of Puebla, November 24, 1811, in Ernesto Lemoine Villicaña, *Morelos: su vida revolucionaria a través de sus escritos y de otros testimonios de la época* (Mexico City: Universidad Nacional Autónoma de México, 1965), 184.

3. "Bando de Morelos suprimiendo las castas y aboliendo la esclavitud," November 17, 1810, in Villicaña, *Morelos*, 162.

4. Guridi y Alcocer quoted in W. Woodrow Anderson, "Reform as a Means to Quell Revolution," in Nettie Lee Benson, ed., *Mexico and the Spanish Cortes, 1810–1822* (Austin: University of Texas Press, 1966), 189.

5. Lequérica and Arizpe quoted in James F. King, "The Colored Castes and American Representation in the Cortes of Cádiz," *Hispanic American Historical Review* 33, no. 1 (February 1953): 41 and 59.

6. Memorial of the merchants' guild quoted in Jaime E. Rodríguez O., *The Independence of Spanish America* (Cambridge: Cambridge University Press, 1998), 85.

7. Arizpe quoted in John H. Hann, "The Role of the Mexican Deputies in the Proposal and Enactment of Measures of Economic Reform Applicable to Mexico," in Benson, *Mexico and the Spanish Cortes*, 177.

8. Venegas quoted in Wilbert Timmons, *Morelos*, 67.

9. "1812, 1 de enero. Informe de un espía realista que desribe la entrada de Morelos y su trops en Cuautla," in Villicaña, *Morelos*, 187.

10. Morelos to Calleja, April 4, 1812, in Villicaña, *Morelos*, 200–201.

11. Calleja quoted in Lucas Alamán, *Historia de México*, vol. 2 (Mexico City: Editorial Jus, 1972), 328.

12. Henry George Ward, *Mexico*, 2nd ed., vol. 1 (London: Henry Colburn, 1829), 149.

13. Calleja quoted in Wilbert H. Timmons, "Los Guadalupes: A Secret Society in the Mexican Revolution for Independence," *Hispanic American Historical Review* 30, no. 4 (November 1950), 465.

14. Morelos quoted in Timmons, "Los Guadalupes," 466.

15. *Audiencia* quoted in Timothy E. Anna, *The Fall of the Royal Government in Mexico City* (Lincoln: University of Nebraska Press, 1978), 115.

16. The discussion of the crisis of 1813 is greatly indebted to Anna, *The Fall of the Royal Government*, especially ch. 6.

7: The Unraveling Revolution

1. Wilbert H. Timmons, *Morelos: Priest, Soldier, Statesman of Mexico* (El Paso: Texas Western College Press, 1963), 99.

2. Morelos to Rayón, August 3, 1813, in Ernesto Lemoine Villicaña, *Moreles: su vida revolucionaria a través de sus escritos y de otros testimonios de la época* (Mexico City: Universidad Nacional Autónoma de México, 1965), 346.

3. Ibid., 372–373.

4. "Acta Solemne de la Declaración de la Independencia de la América Septentrional," ibid., 424–425.

5. Calleja to Minister of War, October 5, 1813, ibid., 385–390.

6. Richard Herr, *Spain* (Englewood Cliffs, NJ: Prentice-Hall, 1971), 76.

7. Juan Pablo y Anaya to President James Madison, March 18, 1815; José María Morelos, José María Linaga, and Remigio de Yarza to James Madison, July 14, 1815, both in William R. Manning, *Diplomatic Correspondence of the United States concerning the Independence of the Latin-American Nations*, vol. 3 (New York: Oxford University Press, 1925), 1594–1595, 1596–1598.

8. Lucas Alamán, *Historia de México*, vol. 4 (Mexico City: Editorial Jus, 1972), 153.

9. William Davis Robinson, *Memoirs of the Mexican Revolution: Including a Narrative of the Expedition of General Javier Mina*, 2 vols. (London: Lackington, Hughes, Harding, Mavor and Lepard, 1821), 1:68.
10. Alamán, *Historia de México*, 4:220.
11. Robinson, *Memoirs of the Mexican Revolution*, 1:259–260.

8: Independence
1. James Smith Wilcocks to John Quincy Adams, October 25, 1821, in William R. Manning, *Diplomatic Correspondence of the United States concerning the Independence of the Latin-American Nations*, vol. 3 (New York: Oxford University Press, 1925), 1601.
2. Carlos María Bustamante, *Diario histórico*, vol. 1, 166–167, quoted in William Spence Robertson, *Iturbide of Mexico* (Durham, NC: Duke University Press, 1952), 235.
3. Lucas Alamán, *Historia de México*, vol. 5 (Mexico City: Editorial Jus, 1972), 49.
4. Augustín de Iturbide, *Memoirs of Agustín de Iturbide* (Washington, DC: Documentary Publications, 1971), 15.
5. Iturbide quoted in Robertson, *Iturbide of Mexico*, 56.
6. Ibid., 60.
7. Concha to Venadito (Apodaca), April 20 and April 25, 1821, cited in Christon I. Archer, "Insurrection—Reaction—Revolution—Fragmentation: Reconstructing the Choreography of Meltdown in New Spain during the Independence Era," *Mexican Studies/Estudios Mexicanos* 10, no. 1 (winter 1994): 94.
8. J. de Dios Peza, "Entrada del ejército trigarante a México," in Agueros, ed., *Episodios históricos*, 2:445–454, quoted in William Forrest Sprague, *Vicente Guerrero, Mexican Liberator: A Study in Patriotism* (Chicago: n.p., 1939), 141 n. 23.
9. Alamán, *Historia de México*, 5:218.

9: The Tragic Empire
1. Wilcocks to Adams, October 25, 1821, in William R. Manning, *Diplomatic Correspondence of the United States concerning the Independence of the Latin-American Nations*, vol. 3 (New York: Oxford University Press, 1925), 1613.
2. Augustín de Iturbide, *Memoirs of Agustín de Iturbide* (Washington, DC: Documentary Publications, 1971), 28.
3. Officers quoted in William Spence Robertson, *Iturbide of Mexico* (Durham, NC: Duke University Press, 1952), 154.
4. *El Farol de Puebla*, November 4, 1821, quoted in Timothy E. Anna, *The Mexican Empire of Iturbide* (Lincoln: University of Nebraska Press, 1990), 58.
5. Iturbide, *Memoirs*, 39.

6. Anna, *The Mexican Empire*, 75.
7. Iturbide, *Memoirs*, 35–36.
8. Anna, *The Mexican Empire*, 163.

Epilogue

1. Ernest Gruening, *Mexico and Its Heritage* (New York: Century, 1928), 80.
2. Ibid., 38.
3. The phrase "imagined communities" was coined by Benedict Anderson, *Imagined Communities: Reflections on the Origin and Spread of Nationalism*, 2nd ed. (New York: Verso, 1991).
4. Frank Tannenbaum, *Peace by Revolution: Mexico After 1910* (New York: Columbia University Press, 1933), 111.
5. Lucas Alamán, *Historia de México*, vol. 5 (Mexico City: Editorial Jus, 1972), 566.
6. Zavala quoted in Charles A. Hale, *Mexican Liberalism in the Age of Mora, 1821–1853* (New Haven: Yale University Press, 1968), 25.
7. Zavala quoted in Frances Calderón de la Barca, *Life in Mexico* (Berkeley: University of California Press, 1982), 270.

SUGGESTIONS FOR FURTHER READING

Two accounts penned by participants in the events of the independence era have become standard sources for the period. Lucas Alamán's masterful *Historia de México, desde los primeros movimientos que prepararon su independencia en el año de 1808, hasta la época presente*, published in five weighty tomes between 1849 and 1852, presents a conservative view of the epoch, praising Spain and denouncing the rebellion. Alamán's history was written largely to refute the work of the lawyer Carlos María de Bustamante, whose *Cuadro histórico de la revolución mexicana* (2 vols., 1843–1844) presents the views of a collaborator in the rebellion. Other important works include José María Luis Mora, *Mexico y sus revoluciones* (3 vols., 1836); and Lorenzo de Zavala, *Ensayo histórico de las revoluciones de México, desde 1808 hasta 1830* (2 vols., 1831–1832). A still-useful, highly detailed narrative of the events of the period can be found in Hubert Howe Bancroft, *History of Mexico*, vol. 9 (1885), which covers the period from 1804 to 1824. A massive collection of primary documents relating to the independence era is Juan E. Hernández y Dávalos, ed., *Colección de documentos para la historia de la Guerra de independencia de México de 1808–1821* (6 vols., Mexico City, 1877–1882).

For more recent overviews of the era, see Jaime E. Rodríguez O., *The Independence of Spanish America* (Cambridge: Cambridge University Press, 1998), as well as his edited volumes *The Evolution of the Mexican Political System* (Wilmington, DE: SR Books, 1992), *The Independence of Mexico and the Creation of the New Nation* (Los Angeles: UCLA Latin American Center Publications, 1989), *Interpretaciones sobre la independencia de México* (Mexico: Nueva Imagen, 1997), *Patterns of Contention in Mexican History* (Wilmington, DE: SR Books, 1992), and *The Origins of Mexican National Politics* (Wilmington, DE: SR Books, 1997). A brief but useful overview is Timothy Anna, "The Independence of Mexico and Central America," in Leslie Bethell, ed., *The Independence of Latin America* (Cambridge University Press, 1987), 49–95. Also see John Lynch's essay in the same volume, titled "The Origins of Spanish American Independence," 1–48. The story of the independence era from the perspective of Mexico City is told in Timothy E. Anna, *The Fall of the Royal Government in Mexico City* (Lincoln: University of Nebraska Press, 1978).

For useful general histories of the colonial period, see Ida Altman, Sarah Cline, and Juan Javier Pescador, *The Early History of Greater Mexico* (Englewood Cliffs, NJ: Prentice Hall, 2003); Colin M. MacLachlan and Jaime E. Rodríguez O., *The Forging of the Cosmic Race: A Reinterpretation of Colonial Mexico* (Berkeley: University of California Press, 1980); D. A. Brading, *The First America: The Spanish Monarchy, Creole Patriots, and the Liberal State, 1492–1867* (New York: Cambridge University Press, 1991). For an intriguing argument regarding the meaning of race in colonial Mexico, see R. Douglas Cope, *The Limits of Racial Domination: Plebeian Society in Colonial Mexico City, 1660–1720* (Madison: University of Wisconsin Press, 1994). For wonderfully engaging tales of the "customary arrangements" of the middle colonial period, see Irving A. Leonard, *Baroque Times in Old Mexico* (Ann Arbor: University of Michigan Press, 1959).

There are many excellent studies that focus on the late colonial period and the Bourbon reforms. For changes in Spain, see John Lynch, *Bourbon Spain, 1700–1808* (Oxford: Blackwell, 1989). Various aspects of the social and economic history of the period in Mexico are discussed in D. A. Brading, *Miners and Merchants in Bourbon Mexico, 1763–1810* (Cambridge: Cambridge University Press, 1971); John Tutino, *From Insurrection to Revolution in Mexico: Social Bases of Agrarian Violence, 1750–1940* (Princeton, NJ: Princeton University Press, 1986); Eric Van Young, *Hacienda and Market in Eighteenth-Century Mexico: The Rural Economy of the Guadalajara Region, 1675–1820* (Berkeley: University of California Press, 1981); Herbert Ingram Priestly, *José de Gálvez, Visitor-General of New Spain, 1765–1771* (Berkeley: University of California Press, 1916); Doris M. Ladd, *The Mexican Nobility at Independence, 1780–1826* (Institute of Latin American Studies, University of Texas at Austin, 1976); Juan Pedro Viqueira Albán, *Propriety and Permissiveness in Bourbon Mexico*, trans. Sonya Lipsett-Rivera and Sergio Rivera Ayala (Wilmington, DE: SR Books, 1999); Brian R. Hamnett, *Roots of Insurgency: Mexican Regions, 1750–1824* (Cambridge: Cambridge University Press, 1986); and L. N. Mcalister, "Social Structure and Social Change in New Spain," *Hispanic American Historical Review* (hereafter *HAHR*) 43, no. 3 (August 1963): 349–370.

Two indispensable articles on late colonial tensions in Guadalajara and Jalisco are Eric Van Young, "Moving Toward Revolt: Agrarian Origins of the Hidalgo Rebellion in the Guadalajara Region," in Friedrich Katz, ed., *Riot, Rebellion, and Revolution: Rural Social Conflict in Mexico* (Princeton, NJ: Princeton University Press, 1988), 176–204; and William B. Taylor, "Banditry and Insurrection: Rural Unrest in Central Jalisco, 1790–1816," ibid., 205–246.

Church and religious matters are considered in William B. Taylor, *Magistrates of the Sacred: Priests and Parishioners in Eighteenth-Century Mexico* (Stanford, CA: Stanford University Press, 1996); Nancy M. Farriss, *Crown and Clergy in Colonial Mexico, 1759–1821: The Crisis of Ecclesiastical Privilege* (London: Athlone Press, 1968); Michael P. Costeloe, *Church Wealth in Mexico: A Study of the "Juzgado de Capellanías" in the Archbishopric of Mexico, 1800–1856* (Cambridge: Cambridge University

Press, 1967); Pamela Voekel, *Alone Before God: The Religious Origins of Modernity in Mexico* (Durham, NC: Duke University Press, 2002).

The notorious Law of Consolidation is the subject of two articles: Brian R. Hamnett, "The Appropriation of Mexican Church Wealth by the Spanish Bourbon Government: The *"Consolidación de Vales Reales,"* 1805–1809, *Journal of Latin American Studies* 1 (1969): 85–113; and Asunción Lavrin, "The Execution of the Law of *Consolidación* in New Spain: Economic Aims and Results," *HAHR* 53 (1973): 27–49. A very valuable resource on the eve of independence is the study by the traveler Alexander von Humboldt, *Ensayo político sobre el reino de la Nueva-España*, 4 vols., translated into Spanish by Vicente González Arnao (Paris, 1822).

On military matters, see the many works of Christon I. Archer, which include *The Army in Bourbon Mexico, 1760–1810* (Albuquerque: University of New Mexico Press, 1977); "'La Causa Buena': The Counterinsurgency Army of New Spain and the Ten Years' War," in Jaime E. Rodríguez O., ed., *The Independence of Mexico and the Creation of the New Nation* (Berkeley: University of California Press, 1989), 85–108; "Insurrection—Reaction—Revolution—Fragmentation: Reconstructing the Choreography of Meltdown in New Spain during the Independence Era," *Mexican Studies/Estudios Mexicanos* 10, no. 1 (winter 1994), 63–98; "The Royalist Army in New Spain: Civil-Military Relationships, 1810–1821," *Journal of Latin American Studies* 13, no. 1 (May 1981): 57–82; "The Army of New Spain and the Wars of Independence, 1790–1821," *HAHR* 61, no. 4 (November 1981), 705–714; "Pardos, Indians, and the Army of New Spain: Inter-Relationships and Conflicts, 1780–1810," *Journal of Latin American Studies* 6, no. 2 (November 1974): 231–255; "Bourbon Finances and Military Policy in New Spain, 1759–1812," *The Americas* 37, no. 3 (January 1981): 315–350; "To Serve the King: Military Recruitment in Latin Colonial Mexico," *HAHR* 55, no. 2 (May 1975): 226–250; and "The Key to the Kingdom: The Defense of Veracruz, 1780–1818," *The Americas* 27, no. 4 (April 1971): 426–449.

A classic study of the Hidalgo rebellion is Hugh Hamill, *The Hidalgo Revolt: Prelude to Mexican Independence* (Gainesville: University of Florida Press, 1966). See also Luis Castillo Ledón, *Hidalgo: la vida del héroe*, 2 vols. (Mexico City: n.p., 1948–1949); and Christon I. Archer, "Bite of the Hydra: The Rebellion of Cura Miguel Hidalgo, 1810–1811," in Jaime E. Rodríguez O., ed., *Patterns of Contention in Mexican History* (Wilmington, DE: Scholarly Resources, 1992), 69–94. An ambitious interpretive account of rank-and-file participation in the rebellion is Eric Van Young, *The Other Rebellion: Popular Violence, Ideology, and the Mexican Struggle for Independence, 1810–1821* (Stanford, CA: Stanford University Press, 2001).

On Morelos, see Wilbert H. Timmons, *Morelos: Priest, Soldier, Statesman of Mexico* (El Paso: Texas Western College Press, 1963); Timmons, "José María Morelos—Agrarian Reformer?" *HAHR* 45, no. 2 (May 1965): 183–195; Ernesto Lemoine Villicaña, *Morelos: su vida revolucionaria a través de sus escritos y de otros testimonios de la época* (Mexico City: Universidad Autónoma de México, 1965). For in-

formation on Morelos's secret urban support network, see Timmons, "Los
Guadalupes: A Secret Society in the Mexican Revolution for Independence,"
HAHR 30, no. 4 (November 1950): 453–479; Ernesto de la Torre Villar, *Los
"Guadalupes" y la independencia, con una selección de documentos inéditos* (Mexico City:
Editorial Jus, 1966); and Virginia Guedea, "Las sociedades secretas durante el
movimiento de independencia," in Jaime E. Rodríguez O., ed., *The Independence of
Mexico and the Creation of the New Nation* (Los Angeles: UCLA Latin American Cen-
ter Publications, 1989), 45–61.

On Vicente Guerrero see William Forrest Sprague, *Vicente Guerrero, Mexican
Liberator: A Study in Patriotism* (Chicago: n.p., 1939); and Theodore E. Vincent, *The
Legacy of Vicente Guerrero, Mexico's First Black Indian President* (Gainesville: University
of Florida Press, 2001).

On the activities of Mexicans and other Spanish Americans in the Spanish
Cortes, see the essays collected in Nettie Lee Benson, ed., *Mexico and the Spanish
Cortes* (Institute of Latin American Studies, University of Texas at Austin, 1966);
and James F. King, "The Colored Castes and American Representation in the
Cortes of Cádiz," *HAHR* 33, no. 1 (February 1953): 33–64. On political develop-
ments in Mexico, see Benson, "The Contested Mexican Election of 1812,"
HAHR 26, no. 3 (August 1946): 336–350; and Virginia Guedea, "The First Pop-
ular Elections in Mexico City, 1812–1813," in Jaime E. Rodríguez O., ed., *The
Origins of Mexican National Politics, 1808–1847* (Wilmington, DE: SR Books, 1997),
39–63.

Mexico's international relations during the period is the topic of John Rydjord, *Foreign Interest in the Independence of New Spain* (Durham, NC: Duke University
Press, 1935); Arthur P. Whitaker, *The United States and the Independence of Latin Amer-
ica, 1800–1830* (New York: Norton, 1964); and Virginia Guedea and Jaime E.
Rodríguez O., "How Relations between Mexico and the United States Began,"
in Jaime E. Rodríguez O. and Kathryn Vincent, eds., *Myths, Misdeeds, and Misun-
derstandings: The Roots of Conflict in U.S.-Mexican Relations* (Wilmington, DE: SR
Books, 1997). On the Mina expedition, see Harris Gaylord Warren, "Xavier
Mina's Invasion of Mexico," *HAHR* 23, no. 1 (February 1943): 52–76; and
William Davis Robinson, *Memoirs of the Mexican Revolution; including a Narrative of the
Expedition of Xavier Mina*, 2 vols. (London, 1821).

On the final phase of the independence struggle, see William Spence
Robertson, *Iturbide of Mexico* (Durham, NC: Duke University Press, 1952); Timothy E. Anna, *The Mexican Empire of Iturbide* (Lincoln: University of Nebraska
Press, 1990); and Nettie Lee Benson, "The Plan of Casa Mata," *HAHR* 25, no. 1
(February 1945): 45–56. Mexican reactions to the attainment of independence is
the subject of Javier Ocampo, *Las ideas de un día: el pueblo mexicano ante la consumación
de su independencia* (Mexico City: Colegio de México, 1969). On the trend toward
regionalism in the independence and postindependence eras, see Nettie Lee Benson, *The Provincial Deputation in Mexico: Harbinger of Provincial Autonomy, Independence,*

and Federalism (Austin: University of Texas Press, 1992). There are a number of good regional studies, including Peter Guardino, *Peasants, Politics, and the Formation of Mexico's National State: Guerrero, 1800–1857* (Stanford, CA: Stanford University Press, 1996); Guardino, *The Time of Liberty: Popular Political Culture in Oaxaca, 1750–1850* (Durham, NC: Duke University Press, 2005); and Michael Ducey, "Village, Nation, and Constitution: Insurgent Politics in Papantla, Veracruz, 1810–21," *HAHR* 79, no. 3 (1999): 463–493.

On the posthumous careers of the heroes of independence, see Christon I. Archer, "Death's Patriots—Celebration, Denunciation, and Memories of Mexico's Independence Heroes: Miguel Hidalgo, José María Morelos, and Agustín de Iturbide," in Lyman L. Johnson, ed., *Death, Dismemberment, and Memory: Body Politics in Latin America* (Albuquerque: University of New Mexico Press, 2004), 63–104; and William H. Beezley and David E. Lorey, eds., *¡Viva México! ¡Viva la Independencia! Celebrations of September 16* (Wilmington, DE: SR Books, 2001).

ACKNOWLEDGMENTS

The author of a book of this nature—that is, a book that does not claim to break new ground, but that aims instead to synthesize existing knowledge into a relatively brief and readable account for general readers—naturally ends up deeply indebted to those who blazed the trail. I wish especially to thank the late Nettie Lee Benson, with whom I had the honor of taking a graduate research seminar back in 1987. Other scholars whose work has been of immense importance to this book are Timothy E. Anna, Eric Van Young, Jaime E. Rodríguez O., Doris M. Ladd, John Lynch, John Tutino, William Taylor, Virginia Guedea, Hugh Hamill, Brian Hamnett, D. A. Brading, Wilbert Timmons, and Peter Guardino. Chris Archer has not only written invaluable books and articles on the independence period, but was generous with his advice when I sheepishly confessed that I was engaged in this project. I hope it goes without saying that none of these folks bears any responsibility for any errors or wayward interpretations I may have committed.

John Womack kindly helped me to locate the town of Temalac, where José María Morelos was captured. My thanks to many mentors and friends who, in one way or another, have influenced my thinking about Mexico. A list of these must include Jurgen Buchenau, Doug Murphy, Gil Joseph, Alan Knight, Susan Deans-Smith, David Baird, Richard Sinkin, John Mraz, Robert Bell and Marcela Escobedo, David LaFrance, Steve Bachelor, José Luis González

Girón, Alejandra García Quintanilla, and Greg Crider. I am extremely grateful to Wayne and Sally Greenhaw for putting me up in their home in San Miguel de Allende while I retraced the steps of Hidalgo and Allende.

Thanks to John Chasteen for getting me started on this project, and to Karren Pell and Liz Maples for their expert editing and sage advice. Thanks also to Carl Simpson of Auburn University at Montgomery's Information Technology Services for scanning pictures. And a very big thank-you to the folks in the Inter-Library Loan Department of Auburn University at Montgomery, especially Karen Williams. They are true professionals, and we couldn't get much done without them.

INDEX